The Dachau Defendants

The Dachau Defendants

Life Stories from Testimony and Documents of the War Crimes Prosecutions

FERN OVERBEY HILTON

McFarland & Company, Inc., Publishers
Jefferson, North Carolina, and London

Thanks to those who helped: Wesley V. Hilton, Donald Hilton, Robert J. Higgs, Ed Speer, and the exceptionally nice folk of NARA II.

Photographs courtesy of the National Archives and Records Administration, College Park, Maryland.

LIBRARY OF CONGRESS CATALOGUING-IN-PUBLICATION DATA

Hilton, Fern Overbey, 1936–
    The Dachau defendants : life stories from testimony and documents of the war crimes prosecutions / Fern Overbey Hilton.
        p.   cm.
    Includes bibliographical references and index.

    ISBN-13: 978-0-7864-1768-1
    softcover : 50# alkaline paper ∞

    1. World War, 1939–1945 — Atrocities — Germany.
    2. War criminals — Germany — Biography.   I. Title.
    D804.G4H46   2004
    364.1'38'09224336 — dc22   2004010967

British Library cataloguing data are available

Manufactured in the United States of America

On the cover: defendant Peter Goldmann (National Archives and Records Administration, College Park, MD)

McFarland & Company, Inc., Publishers
  Box 611, Jefferson, North Carolina 28640
   www.mcfarlandpub.com

For
Andrew, Ben, Bill, Don, Jack, Quentin, and Wes

Contents

Preface

The trial at Nuremberg was the grand theater of war crimes tribunals; here, the arch criminals of the Third Reich had their appointment with justice. Practitioners like Julius Streicher lost their lives on the gallows. Hermann Göring avoided the gallows by committing suicide via one of the Nazis' favored escape routes—a smuggled cyanide capsule. Albert Speer, Hitler's architect and engineer, escaped a death sentence through a well-executed defense strategy.

Heinrich Himmler escaped capture for a short time but managed to take the Göring route before he could be brought to trial. Adolf Eichmann was captured when he was approaching old age and faced Jewish anger and justice in Israel. The diabolical Dr. Josef Mengele fled Germany to live out his life in South America, thus escaping formal justice altogether.

Fifty years after World War II ended, history was still giving little attention to nearly 1,700 other criminals who had faced American justice in 489 trials at Dachau. Those brought to trial in this series were accused of war crimes in Austria and the American Zone of Occupation in Germany. Several of the defendants were major figures in the Reich, and some were second-order functionaries. Others were doctors, engineers, schoolteachers, and similar professionals. Many were simple folk: housepainters, weavers, farmers, factory workers, students, and even village idiots. Inattention to these trials has allowed many hands-on criminals to escape proper scrutiny. An examination of these trials makes it safe to say that, without the labors of these criminals, the Third Reich could not have grown into the monster it finally became.

Early in the war, observers realized that the aggression carried on by Nazi Germany and its Fascist cousin Italy came with a particular brutality. At the Moscow Conference of October 1943, a Joint Four-Nation Declaration (the fourth nation being China) was issued:

> The United Kingdom, the United States and the Soviet Union have received from many quarters evidence of atrocities, massacres and cold-blooded mass executions which are being perpetrated by Hitlerite forces in many of the countries that they have overrun and from which they are now being steadily expelled.

Additionally, the Declaration warned of consequences and defined the nature of their grievances:

> At the time of granting of any armistice to any government which may be set up in Germany, those German officers and men and members of the Nazi party who have been responsible for or have taken a consenting part in the above atrocities, massacres, and executions will be sent back to the countries in which their abominable deeds were done in order that they may be judged and punished according to the laws of these liberated countries and of free governments which will be erected therein. Lists will be compiled in all possible detail from all these countries having regard especially to invaded parts of the Soviet Union, to Poland and Czechoslovakia, to Yugoslavia and Greece including Crete and other islands, to Norway, Denmark, [the] Netherlands, Belgium, Luxembourg, France and Italy.
>
> Thus, Germans who take part in wholesale shooting of Polish officers or in the execution of French, Dutch, Belgian or Norwegian hostages of Cretan peasants, or who have shared in slaughters inflicted on the people of Poland or in territories of the Soviet Union which are now being swept clear of the enemy, will know they will be brought back to the scene of their crimes and judged on the spot by the people whom they have outraged.
>
> Let those who have hitherto not imbrued their hands with innocent blood beware lest they join the ranks of the guilty, for most assuredly the three Allied powers will pursue them to the uttermost end of the earth and will deliver them to their accusers in order that justice be done.
>
> The above declaration is without prejudice to the case of German criminals whose offenses have no particular geographical localization and who will be punished by joint decision of the government of the Allies.

The document indicated that at least as early as the autumn of 1943, the Allies planned to establish war crimes trials, and Germany must surely have been aware that justice awaited them and those who collaborated with them. An important element of the document was the provision that would return war criminals to the soil upon which they had committed their crimes.

Another document of interest is the London Charter of 1945, which came out of a series of conferences. The Charter established the International Military Tribunal (IMT) that conducted the trial at Nuremberg.

Soon after Germany capitulated, it was divided into four "zones of military occupation." Each zone, in effect, fell under the sovereignty of the nation (or "power") to which it was assigned. The United Kingdom, France, the Soviet Union, and the United States could each conduct their own trials.

Americans had an advantage over the other powers. As far back as the American Civil War, the United States had in place guidelines containing important language concerning the treatment of peoples of occupied lands. The protocol, written by the international philosopher Francis Lieber and titled "Instructions for the Government of Armies of the United States in the Field," was issued by President Abraham Lincoln on April 28, 1863, as *Laws of War: General Orders No. 100.* It not only outlined those abuses against civilians and military personnel that would be considered unlawful, but it additionally protected institutional entities such as art museums, libraries, and medical facilities. Americans, as they prepared for the trials, also had available products of the Hague Convention and the Geneva Convention, each of which pushed forward an understanding of what is fair and what is not fair in international war.

The trials began just weeks before the capitulation in April 1945 and were completed on December 30, 1947. Although a few trials were held elsewhere, most were held in the old administration building of the defunct Dachau concentration camp. The administration building is still standing, but other buildings have been razed because they were so saturated with disease agents it was not safe for later generations to walk through the old barracks. A single replica has been erected for the benefit of scholars and for those who are curious. Because most trials were held at the site, they are often referred to as the Dachau trials.

The trials resembled American courts-martial. Defendants had rights like those guaranteed by the American Constitution and the American justice system save that the Court, consisting of several officers, was both judge and jury. At least one officer was required to have a law degree. The trials were conducted under a bifurcated system with one branch conducting trials and the other conducting reviews. No appellate court sat. A "General Court," as opposed to an "Intermediate Court," conducted trials that could lead to the death penalty; only field grade officers could sit on this Court. Counsel represented the prosecution and the defense, and each could present and challenge evidence. The Court appointed defense counsel, but defendants were allowed to use additional or alternate counsel if they desired it and could afford it. The prosecution was represented by the Judge Advocate General's office (JAG). These details and other particulars concerning the trials are found in summary form in a report issued by Col. C. E. Straight at the end of the proceedings.

Many different offices and organizational entities were created, and
sometimes discontinued, as tasks associated with the trials waxed and
waned. The list of acronyms and designations is mind-boggling, but a
good summary of the broad strokes of the evolution is found in a catalogue of documents at the National Archives and Records Administration
(NARA II) in College Park, Maryland.

On November 1, 1946, the 7708 War Crimes Group, headed by the Deputy
Theater Judge Advocate for War Crimes, United States Forces, European Theater, was organized to supervise the development and trial of war crimes
cases involving American nationals as victims and mass atrocity cases committed in American zones of occupation in Germany and Austria. Located
in Munich, the group consolidated existing war crimes prosecutorial activities of the various Army Judge Advocates and was responsible for investigating war crimes, apprehending alleged war criminals, gathering evidence
for war crimes trials, and maintaining trial records for review by a war crimes
board of review. The 7708 War Crimes Group continued to function through
the investigation, trial, and review process, and was deactivated on June 20,
1948.

Post-trial activities relating to war crimes were continued by the War
Crimes Branch, Judge Advocate Division, European Command (later United
States Army, Europe). The branch's responsibilities included the following:
examination and appraisal of petitions for clemency and appropriate recommendations of action to be taken; processing of written requests for information on cases and individuals; translation of correspondence; reproduction
of material related to records of trial for forwarding to the Office of the Judge
Advocate General; inspection of War Criminal Prison No. 1, Landsberg, Germany; and processing of material for trials before the Military Commission.
The branch also furnished the services of an attorney at all executions of war
criminals for the purpose of appraising any last-minute petitions.

On November 2, 1948, a Special Assistant for War Crimes was established
and charged with the responsibility for all matters pertaining to war crimes
that were formerly the function of the International Affairs Branch. These
included coordination and clearance of all war crimes cases in which the
accused was sentenced to death and scheduled for execution; processing of
all last-minute petitions for clemency filed by or on behalf of the accused;
preparation of memorandums for the Commander-in-Chief, European Command, concerning all war crimes cases in which clemency or commutation
were recommended; interview of attorneys and relatives who presented personal pleas or written petitions on behalf of condemned war criminals; preparation of answers, both letter and cable, to Congressional and Department
of the Army inquiries concerning various aspects of the War Crimes program;

collection and dissemination of statistics; preparation of press releases and, on occasion, answering of individual inquiries presented by representatives of the press; preparation of the history of the post-trial aspects of the War Crimes program; and coordination and liaison with the Office, Chief of Counsel for War Crimes (US), Legal Director, Office of the Military Government for Germany (US), other general and special staff divisions of the European Command, and foreign War Crimes missions operating within the U.S. Area of Control, Germany.

On April 19, 1949, the War Crimes Branch was moved from Munich to Heidelberg and reorganized; on September 22, 1949, it was discontinued. On that date the War Crimes Branch and the Special Assistant for War Crimes were combined as the War Crimes Section of the Military Affairs Branch.

From 1949 to 1966 the office handling war crimes activities of the Judge Advocate Division was known alternately as a branch and as a section of a branch until the records were finally transferred to Alexandria, Virginia, by the International Affairs Branch in 1966.

Many of the trials addressed the abuse or murder of downed American airmen. Other trials addressed crimes committed against non–Germans by Germans and other nationalities within territory that came to be known as the American zone. Crimes associated with concentration camps and their various satellite camps and crimes associated with transports were in the latter group. Concentration camps that fell within the reach of the Dachau trials were Flossenburg, Dachau, Mauthausen, Buchenwald, and Nordhausen. In smaller numbers, other categories of war criminals were tried in the series.

In the beginning of their history, concentration camps were built to house criminals. They were, in fact, an effort to get prisoners out of dank jails and into the sunshine. It was believed that having an opportunity to work was also an improvement over the old system. In some ways, these early camps paralleled similar camps in other nations, including the United States; but German camps were to evolve into something entirely different. As Hitler consolidated power, the camps became attractive as a solution for undesirables and enemies of the state.

During the war years, the camps became an enticing source of free labor for various German industries, and most organizations learned not to be too particular about the actual guilt of the prisoners or to be too concerned about suffering and death among the inmates. As the war continued, the military and its industrial allies became ravenous for the free labor. The war also freed Hitler and his underlings to make of the camps what they would.

The demands made it easy to collect and concentrate millions who were somehow out of step with the German cause — or who for any reason became vulnerable. Records of prisoners of war were "lost" or ignored as men lost their status and fell into the hell of concentration camps. Conscripted laborers from a variety of countries came to the camps to work in the factories for pennies a day; they, too, fell into the pits. Finally, persons of almost any nationality, religion, or political persuasion were subject to "arrest" and "concentration." An examination of the Dachau trials sheds enormous light on the complex that evolved, which permitted the exploitation and criminality associated with the camps.

Transport crimes were companion crimes to those of the concentration camps; they were committed during forced marches (or, on some occasions, railroad or truck rides) while concentration camp prisoners were moved from one place to the other. Many of these moves were made to escape the advancing Allied armies.

Although some Germans and members of the German military treated downed airmen as prisoners of war, many hapless Americans were abused or murdered by a variety of persons. These groups of defendants included villagers, local officials, and military or paramilitary personnel.

With the exception of background information available in any textbook on modern European history (the origins of the SS being an example), this book is written entirely from primary source documents (at NARA II), which are organized into files by case. Except for some multi page documents such as reviews, the papers within files are not numbered, and they are not always arranged in a predictable order. The full records are not microfilmed or collected in electronic formats. Very few papers have ever been published in any fashion. Those wishing to do further study will be obliged to turn to the primary source documents.

As the war progressed and Allied forces moved into territory held by the Germans, evidence of crimes of the type enumerated by the Moscow Conference document was obvious. Troops came across concentration camps and were appalled by what they saw. An immediate campaign to find downed airmen and American prisoners of war began. Investigators collected the reports and affidavits that, together with evidence collected during the war, helped to support charges of war crimes. Warrants were issued, arrests were made, and investigations expanded. These earliest documents became a part of the war crimes records.

Records associated with the trials are kept at NARA II in hundreds of boxes, with most boxes containing thousands of pages of documents and other papers. They are found under "Cases Tried" in Record Group 549.

During preparation for writing this book, I surveyed all files from each of the 489 trials and read the trial reviews from all trials. Based on this preliminary research, I chose a group of cases for detailed study.

In general, I chose cases to present within this book for two reasons: (1) they lend themselves to an understanding of the trials, and (2) they have something to teach us about World War II–era Germany and the tragedy that grew out of the German culture of that time. More specifically, I chose cases because they illustrate a broad group of representative crimes — crimes associated with the camps, the transports, and American prisoners of war, especially those associated with downed fliers. Some have lessons to teach about atrocity. Others were chosen because the personalities were revealing: the doctor who reacted like a kid caught with his hand in a cookie jar during his trial for "marauding" and a Czech named Johann Vican who confounded authorities of several nations. Some cases reveal how schoolteachers moved from schoolroom to criminality with ease and how hidden prejudice among the professional class contributed to the criminal endeavor. The case of Wilhelm Grill is a picture of how the Germans fashioned an idealistic schoolboy into an SS man. the case of Lauriano Navas proves that innocents were caught up in the grinding mill of an imperfect American justice system. and the case of Heinrich Buuck reveals how far the Nazis would go to find kindling for the inferno. Finally, I chose cases that prove for all time that the Nazi scheme could not have reached such a horrific level of brutality without the active contributions of Germans of all kinds.

The Army provided written translations of documents, other papers, and spoken testimony in all relevant languages. If, for example, the defendant spoke Spanish, documents might be prepared in English, Spanish, and German. During the actual trials, oral translators were also provided when needed. Unfortunately, some translators were more skilled than others, but most compromises seemed to result in amusing syntax as opposed to actual judicial damage.

Technically, a document is a legal or official paper that presents information or evidence. Often they are witnessed; sometimes they are "certified" by receiving the stamp of an official. Frequently, writers had simple letters witnessed. Sometimes affidavits were highly formal documents adorned with the full measure of legal contrivances. On some occasions, simple affidavits became the only "testimony" or evidence used to convict defendants.

Sometimes, papers taken from other record collections — including such things as medical records, financial records, or camp rosters — were certified as evidence. The death books kept at camp hospitals fall into this category.

Trial transcripts ranged from a few pages with procedural matters taking up more space than the presentation and challenge of evidence, to documents of several thousand pages. A trial transcript included a read-ing of the charges, a reading of defendant's rights, testimony both for the prosecution and the defense with cross-examination, final arguments, other procedural matters, a finding of guilt or innocence, and a statement of the sentence.

Each trial was reviewed and a report was written. The findings of the trial proper could be approved, disproved, or modified. The docu-ment produced consisted of a list of defendants with their civilian occupations, an exact statement of charges, a summary of evidence as it related to the charges, commentary, and findings. Death penalty cases received considerably more attention than other cases during the post-trial phase.

"Cases Tried" contains hundreds of photographs. Some of the pho-tographs are on "mug" sheets, and other photographs of defendants are preserved as additional identification. Those who were hanged were pho-tographed on the gallows with ropes around their necks. The corpses of the hanged were stripped naked and again photographed as they lay in their wood-plank coffins. Most photographs have been entered as evidence. Many photographs were taken of crime scenes or of scenes that in some way concerned crimes. Other photographs are official elements of investigations or they survive as simple records of the trials. Courtroom scenes were preserved. Photographs of Germans being forced to view crime scenes or aid in the burial of decaying corpses are preserved.

Defendants frequently wrote appeals or pleas. Some attempted to write their life stories. Others wrote letters. The Army preserved all this. Correspondence received by defendants was sometimes saved. Friends, neighbors, clergy, and lawyers frequently wrote letters to the Court or var-ious offices concerned with appeals, clemency, or confinement, which found their way into the records.

Each scrap of paper within the records has the potential for significant revelation. "Cases Tried" contains psychiatric reports, medical reports, prison records, character references, military records, parole documents, petitions, and internal route slips. Letters between and among those asso-ciated with various officers or to and from these personnel and civilians are included along with U.S. State Department records, embassy correspon-dence, U.S. Executive and Congressional correspondence, and Vatican cor-respondence. Memoranda, applications, disposition forms, investigation reports for clemency and parole, maps, drawings, and illustrations, and records that preserve the day-to-day activities of German civilian, military, and concentration camp life are preserved. Many papers and documents are accompanied by a variety of supplements. Even some magazine and newspaper reports pertaining to the trials and the personalities involved are included in the records. The types of documents and papers are vast.

Included in envelopes, bindles, and boxes are such items as bullets taken from a murdered American POW, the diving-woman *Jantzen* neck tag from the tee shirt of the exhumed body of an airman who was shot and buried without benefit of a coffin, and a rolled piece of crepe paper (without color) which was offered into evidence as the type of bandage sometimes used by the Germans. My curiosity enticed me to investigate a tiny bulge in a passport-sized military identification booklet which proved to be a stickpin representing a modest honor some German soldier had secreted within the spine. These bits and pieces by themselves represent hundreds of items of historical evidence.

As the trials wound down, leftover matters from the trials were given over to civilian authority. In the United States, that duty fell to the Department of State. The Bonn Settlement Convention, associated with this evolution in international affairs, set up a "Mixed Board" consisting of three Germans and one representative each from France, Britain, and the United States to attend to matters of prisoners. The records associated with the Dachau trials, which fell within the assignments of the "Board," are preserved within "Cases Tried."

Most cases significant to this book appear in the text by the name of the defendant, and, often, by case number. All cases are listed in the Appendix, and they are collectively cited in the Resources section. If the defendant is one of many and is not the "title" name, I have also supplied that information in the text. For example, Erika Flocken was tried during *U.S. vs. Franz Auer et al.*, case #000-50-136. I also refer the reader to the on-line Avalon Project, sponsored by Yale University, for various documents. I find this an excellent source for accurate information that is sometimes tedious to find in library hard copies. I have also included in the Resources section a few of the books I read to gain background and perspective for this study.

Although a few members of various courts and some prosecutors and lawyers understood the German language, life and death decisions were made on the basis of translations (usually called "interpretations" in the records). For that reason, the translations appearing in the records were used for this book. I have made no effort to correct any of these documents. I found no instances of justice gone awry because of inept translations, but knowledge of the quality of translations is perhaps of interest to the reader. All spellings appearing in the translations have been kept intact, with the rare exception of some obvious inconsistencies. An example of an obvious inconsistency would be the spelling of the city Rottenburg which appears sometimes as Rottenberg. It became a tremendous task to track down the hundreds of inconsistencies in spelling, and, when in doubt, I chose to use the spelling in the document at hand. Names of defendants are spelled as they occurred in charge sheets, trial transcripts, and trial reviews; when spellings conflicted, I used the spelling used most frequently. The names of all other persons and places are also taken from translations and I have not attempted to restore German spellings of words taken from primary source documents. Parentheses appearing within quoted material are original to the material. Brackets appearing within quoted material represent information I have placed within the quotes.

This study is more about personalities and their encounters with history than it is about legal history. The study of military trials is not the goal of this book. For the most part, it is not about the king and his men. To a surprising extent, this study is able to follow the lives of individuals up to the Nazi glory days and to watch them walk through the inferno. It follows those receiving the death penalty to the gallows and those given lesser sentences to prison. It is even able to follow many for several years after they finished their sentences and returned to society. I have always believed that it is an error to consider a top-down, "king's eye" view of history as the only valid view. This study proves that common men and women can and do affect history in mighty ways.

Finally, this study is about reality. When the book reports that the trees were tall and the night was dark, it is because witnesses remembered these details with as much clarity as they remembered horrific details. In fact, they seemed unable to tell their stories without reporting the coincidental minutia. As much as anything else, it is perhaps this strangeness of the mind and the memory that reminds us that the trials were held to find justice for real people.

1

Final Desperation: The Story of Heinrich Buuck

> Then the shot fell. I did not know if the man was dead, but
> the man is no longer alive. As a prisoner I did not have the right
> to look at him.
>
> > [From the testimony of Joseph Weiden in
> > *U.S. vs. Heinrich Buuck*, case #000-Buchenwald-9.]

Heinrich Buuck didn't look directly at the camera when his identification photograph was made. He looked down. It was a custom and a demand almost always followed that the defendant should look directly at the camera. When the profile shot was made, he again looked down. The unconventional pose was only one of the compromises the U.S. military would be forced to accept during its dealings with Buuck.

Heinrich Buuck had only one useful eye. His other eye was covered by an eyelid that drooped to his cheek; the "scars and marks" entry reports that the right eye was "missing." His ears protruded, and the profile exhibit shows a nose flattened against his face.

Across the blocks where his individual fingerprints should be found are the handwritten words, "Subject suffers from nervous tremors to such an extent that it is impossible to take individual fingerprints." The clerk in charge settled for a four-finger handprint.

Buuck's record is peppered with reports from psychiatrists that addressed his potential for understanding that it is wrong to murder. It was guessed by the experts that he probably understood right and wrong, at least to the extent the trial would address the legal nature of these concepts. His IQ was guessed to be in the middle 60s. If his IQ had registered ten points lower, he would have been a true idiot and excused from the consequences of his transgressions. It had been difficult to assess Buuck, his evaluators said; his nervous tremors were so severe he could not speak when he was excited. Lives of concentration camp inmates, some of them prisoners of war, were placed in the hands of this tragically disabled human being.

Those brought to trial in this series were accused of war crimes in Austria and the American Zone of Occupation in Germany.

Heinrich Buuck was born to Heinrich (the elder) and his wife in Bordenau-Hannover, Germany, on September 2, 1913. The afflicted child came late in his mother's childbearing years, and his father was already into middle age. The couple had one other son who did not bear his brother's unfortunate conditions. The family lived on a small, traditional European farm. They cultivated a few acres and used additional land as meadows for pasturing livestock, including cows and hogs. They also cultivated several acres which they leased from the church.

Young Heinrich had trouble from the beginning of his life. He was born with wayward facial features that suggested his mental disability. He was never graceful and he stammered terribly when he tried to talk. He couldn't concentrate, had an impaired memory, and had trouble following a conversation. When he was three, he destroyed one of his eyes while playing with a knife.

School was difficult for the boy. He had to stay behind with younger children several times as he repeated grade after grade. He was forced to endure this torture for eight years and developed a dangerous need for revenge as a consequence. He had not learned as much as the average first-grader of today knows when he enters school from a respectable kindergarten. Although he could provide loops and flourishes to sign his name, he remained officially illiterate.

During his mid-teens, Heinrich left school to work on his father's farm. By his late teens and early manhood, posters were placed in public places telling the nation what the proper German boy should look like, and that boy was not Heinrich Buuck. The German boy was tall and handsome and athletic and smart. He belonged to the Hitler Youth and engaged in outdoor activities. Heinrich never joined the Hitler Youth or any political group, and no one seems to have pushed him in that direction.

By the time he was fully grown, Buuck was of normal height — about five feet nine inches tall — but he remained quite thin at about 130 pounds. He had brown hair and blue eyes.

He had his first sexual experience at 21 — an experience his psychiatrist described as "normal." Other similar experiences followed. The term "normal" is not defined in his records. At any rate, psychiatrists assured the court that his sexuality was not a determining factor in his behavior during a war situation.

Late in the war, Buuck became a member of the Waffen SS. Not only was he *permitted* to join the Waffen SS, he was *drafted* into the organization.

The Schutzstaffel, the SS, headed by Heinrich Himmler, was originally Adolf Hitler's personal guard, but over the years it expanded to become a private army. In the early years, every member was hand-picked for intelligence, physical proportions and appearance, and racial purity — perfection in the eyes of the German Nazis; a wonder in the eyes of impressionable youth who looked upon their

Heinrich Buuck

dreadful beauty. Unlike the regular German army, the Waffen SS could recruit, or refuse to tolerate, virtually whomever they chose. They could and did take advantage of possibilities in conquered territories and recruited men of Nordic heritage who met their standards. As war losses increased, they began to lower their requirements.

Soon after his induction into the Waffen SS, Buuck was sent to the Sonnenberg concentration camp, a satellite facility of Buchenwald, as a guard. He was not the only man with disabilities who carried a weapon and determined the fate of inmates. German criminals had been elevated to the level of capo and given authority almost equal to that of the guards. Mental patients, persons with severe chronic illnesses, and men too old for any other use by the Nazis worked in the camps. Often men who had been severely wounded in battle and could not return to the front were sent with their pain and impairments to work alongside men like Buuck. Until a month before the war ended, Buuck drew no special attention to himself and he would not be accused of crimes during that time.

In April, 1945, just after Easter and only five weeks before Germany would capitulate, guards at Sonnenberg were ordered to move a large number of inmates to the Sudetenland (a region in western Czechoslovakia). The specific reason for moving the inmates was hardly important for purposes of Buuck's trial. In those last days of the war, Germany was hemorrhaging hope and it appears that cumbersome moves to plug holes in the crumbling Reich had become routine. The Germans sometimes moved prisoners to replenish labor at a factory, or to repair roads and bridges. Inmates were forced to dig tunnels and caves to hide important materials and factories, but that could have mattered little in the spring of 1945. The Russians were coming; their gunfire could be heard in the East. From practically every other direction the British, the French, and the Americans were advancing. The order came down to evacuate the concentration camp to avoid being overrun by the enemy.

Sonnenberg was not the only camp trying to outrun the advancing forces. While Adolf Hitler in the Führerbunker was counting down the last days of his life, lines of sick, hungry prisoners along with their ragtag guards kept moving — all over Germany, Austria, and other geographical regions that were in their hands for at least the moment.

At the camp, rumor was spreading fast that a march was in their future. Abraham Brilliant, thirty-two, worked in the kitchen of the camp. He cooked for the guards and served them coffee — he even knew Buuck well. He was peeling potatoes when he saw first one man and then another slip into the nearby cellar to get a potato or two to take on the journey. He saw Buuck walk to the small cellar window, place the barrel of his gun through the opening, and shoot. The whole kitchen vibrated. He was supposed to be boiling potatoes with the skins on instead of peeling them, and he was directed to go to the cellar for more potatoes for the SS men. There he saw a corpse with a bullet hole in his forehead. Buuck's first official murder was witnessed by several others who wandered through the courtyard. Restlessness and anger spread through the camp after Buuck shot the man in the cellar, but the guards took little note of the murder. They were preparing for the march.

The next morning, with Easter just behind them, the guards and almost five hundred men set out toward Bavaria. Two days later and a few kilometers out, they heard the sounds of battle coming toward them. They were warned that both Americans and Russians were close. The prisoners were forced to make the trip back to the camp in a single march. They marched all day and all night down a path with deep woods on both sides. The sick and weak prisoners began to falter. Buuck shot two prisoners who fell out of the column.

After two days back at the camp, the officers in charge decided the march would again be attempted. When the prisoners were put back on the road, they noted that very few guards had been assigned. The master sergeant, highest in rank, was in front of the column. Buuck, lowest in rank, brought up the rear. The guards arranged the inmates four abreast, and they averaged about fifteen kilometers per day. Almost immediately their suffering began because there was not enough food and water to go around. Each man received two potatoes at the end of each day's march. The walk would become a death march.

Although rain would plague the transports of April at least part of the time, the Sonnenberg transport began under an uncomfortable spring sun. Most prisoners on the way to the Sudetenland were strong enough to walk, at least in the early days of the march, and their strength was a danger to the guards. Their hunger and desperation would become an even greater danger. The few able-bodied officers had to mind both the prisoners and the compromised guards, and, if they faltered, the inmates might kill them to a man. Guards and capos would become targets for violence during the surrender process.

Sudeten-bound prisoners included Jews of several nationalities. In addition to Jews, evacuation transports included other Poles, Spanish, Italians, Russians, French, Dutch, Hungarians, and Americans. They did not share a common language. Although they could respond to basic German commands, most had no way of understanding German conversation or extended directions.

The Sonnenberg prisoners began their march in the columns that represented good German order. Juda Thau, a medical doctor, began to notice Buuck and his weapon. Thau was a Jew born in Bamberg in 1907, and he would become one of the millions of "stateless" persons at war's end. He was marching in the last line of the column when he saw a teenager falter. He began to try to help the boy when he could no longer walk by himself. Buuck forced him to leave the boy in the middle of the road and move on. Thau walked about thirty meters and turned around to see Buuck shoot the boy. The mayor in the next village they passed was instructed to bury the boy, and the transport struggled on.

Buuck was aware that he was not pleasant to look at. He also understood that he lacked normal intelligence and that he was clumsy and ungraceful. He resented the reactions of others to his disadvantages. He would let this be known during interviews related to his trial. Near Eichenbach a prisoner made a remark about him and Buuck shot him. This was also the same day he beat out a man's teeth with the butt of his rifle.

Four weeks into the march, Buuck was still killing. On one occasion, he took a man about ten meters into the woods and shot him. He forced four other men to use sticks to dig a shallow grave to cover him. During the night, he shot his rifle; at whom and for what reason, no witness could say. With other guards, he forced about twenty men into the woods, and the column of prisoners heard shooting. The guards came out of the woods; the prisoners did not. On another occasion, Buuck shot a man whose body fell down a bank toward the river. Still another man was shot for trying to pick up a potato lying beside the road. To do his killing, Buuck used a carbine in the beginning and later added a sidearm.

At one point along the route, they came across a store that stocked military uniforms. The guards stopped to rob the store and put on the Wehrmacht uniforms they found there. If they were overrun by the Americans, members of the Wehrmacht, the regular military, would be treated with the respect soldiers accord other soldiers. Always, however, all the guards wore the insignia of the SS, a witness testified. While the guards were robbing the store, several prisoners made a successful escape. Others were trapped in a canal near the store and were shot by the guards.

In those last weeks of the war, while the endless columns marched across the war zone, guards began to walk off and go home. No record was made in the trial transcript of guard or capo walk-offs on the Sonnenberg-to-Sudetenland march, but it was another thing all together with the prisoners. As conditions became worse, more prisoners began to slip out of the ranks and run for the cover of the woods. Sometimes, when the sun came up, a score or more would have melted away during the night. Guards did not attempt to find them.

The march lasted about five weeks. On May 7, 1947, the prisoners were liberated by American forces in Praseles, Czechoslovakia. There were only 200 men left of the approximately 500 men who departed Sonnenberg just after Easter. No one could say for sure how many had escaped and how many had been killed. As soon as the guards were disarmed, the prisoners demanded that the Americans kill Buuck. When they refused, the prisoners set upon him and tried to do the job themselves. Buuck, bloody and limping, escaped over a fence. That was the last the men of Sonnenberg saw of him — except, of course, for those who came to his trial with their memories and their anger.

Heinrich Buuck was tried during the Dachau series of trials. Trial records and other documents from his case file, and documents from similar cases, gave the world a lesson in the criminal nature of German transports.

Buuck was the only witness for the defense during his trial. In answer to a question about shooting the man in the cellar, he said, "No, no, never."

His lawyer asked, "Will you tell the court what happened on that transport?"

He answered, "We took the transport — it was a transport on foot — further and further — yes."

Buuck admitted to shooting one of the men on orders.

"Do you know why Sergeant Biedemann gave you the order to shoot a prisoner?"

"Because I received the order to do it."

"Do you remember where you were captured by the Americans?"

"It was in a small village close to a city."

Witnesses were questioned about the kind of weapon Buuck carried. They answered that he carried a carbine and, toward the end of the march, a pistol.

The president of the Court asked him, "What kind of weapon did you carry?"

Buuck answered, "That high — a weapon that high." He demonstrated the length of the weapon by indicating how high it had been.

When the prosecution and the defense counsel began to make their final statements, Buuck began to interrupt. The president of the Court stated that Buuck's interruptions of the arguments should be allowed and should be recorded unless they became too much out of order.

His lawyer began his argument: "The accused has entered a plea of not guilty to the charge of killing ten or more non-German nationals."

Buuck interrupted. "No, no, that is not correct."

"The accused, in his written statement, and also on the witness stand, has admitted shooting one prisoner."

"Yes, on orders."

Three basic arguments were brought forth by the defense during the trial. In the beginning, the defense lawyer was concerned that his client was unable to understand that pleading guilty to crimes for which there was corroborating evidence would likely gain him a life sentence as opposed to a death sentence. By pleading not guilty he was more likely to get the death penalty. Because he had been found to be competent to stand trial, the president of the Court judged that counsel's concern did not represent a mitigating factor. Precedent countered the argument that he acted on orders during a war situation. Issue was also taken with Buuck's "written" statement when the interrogator stated that he had found it necessary to "formulate" sentences and write them down for the defendant based on what he could get from the defendant by asking questions over and over. It was determined by the Court that no promises or threats were made to the accused and that everything was freely and voluntarily stated; the statement stood. The defense, additionally, simply wished to state that in spite of the psychiatric reports Buuck was not intelligent enough to be given the death penalty.

Before lunch on the day following the end of the trial, the Court found the defendant guilty of a "violation of the laws and usage of war, in particular that he did, at, or in the vicinity of Weimar, Germany, in or about April 2, 1945, wrongfully encourage, aid, abet and participate in the killings of approximately ten non-German nationals, inmates of Sonnenberg Concentration Camp, who were in the custody of the German Reich, the exact names and numbers unknown."

The president read the sentence: "The Court in closed session, at least two-thirds of the members present at the time the vote was taken concurring, sentences you, Heinrich Buuck, to death by hanging at such time and place as higher authority may direct."

By March 1948, Buuck's trial had been reviewed, and the death penalty had been approved and ordered for execution. In May, a petition for clemency was considered, and he was given an administrative stay of execution. In September, Buuck's new lawyer requested further mental evaluation. He was told that the review board was considering a recommendation that his sentence be commuted to life imprisonment; he might not have been fully responsible for his acts after all. On January 19, 1949, in response to an inquiry, Buuck's father was informed by letter that his son's sentence had been commuted to life imprisonment on December 8, 1948. During August 1951, an act of clemency reduced the sentence to fifteen years starting on July 25, 1945. Buuck had served six of the fifteen years by this time.

Buuck served a total of about nine years and was released on parole in February 1954. His father was anxious to have him home to help on the farm. It was recorded that Buuck was in good general health, had good self-control, was trusted to work outside the prison without supervision, understood and accepted the nature of his incarceration, and could do simple work. A supervisor and a sponsor were found for him and he went home.

By the end of summer 1955, things were very different. Officials attempting to determine why he had not filed his monthly reports visited the farm. They found three milk cows, three hogs, and a calf on the land that had been in the family for generations. His mother and his aunt were "about eighty." They were unable to communicate with parole supervisors and were too sick to take care of Buuck or help with the farm work. His eighty-one-year-old father was in bed, dying of intestinal cancer. Buuck himself was "beyond communication." His "imbecility" was so bad he could not comprehend nor comply with the terms of his parole. He had been eligible to apply for good conduct relief but had not been capable of doing so. He needed constant care, but his insurance had been disapproved and the parole board could not be responsible for helping the father get him into a hospital for the mentally diseased. His brother was afraid for his parents and tried to help out on weekends, but he was employed and was unwilling to give up a good job and retirement pension to run the farm and care for Buuck. The brother had no interest in the farm, anyway; Heinrich Buuck was the heir. The parole board wanted him released but the parents wanted him kept under parole so someone could share responsibility. The parents were concerned for their safety while the son lived on the farm. This was judged not to be the problem of the parole board, and because further supervision would be pointless, they recommended commutation to time served. It was so ordered. In this way Buuck and his tragedy exited the records of the United States of America.

2

Marauder: The Story
of Dr. Max Schmid

Punishment of marauders: Robbery and maltreatment of the wounded or dead on a battlefield are outrageous offenses against the laws of war. It is the duty of the commanders to see that such offenders, whether members of the armed forces or civilians, are promptly apprehended and brought to trial before competent military tribunals. Like other serious offenders against the laws of war they may be sentenced to death or such other punishment as the trial tribunal may be legally authorized to impose.

After every engagement, the belligerent who remains in possession of the field of battle shall take measures to search for the wounded and dead and protect them from robbery and ill treatment.

[*Field Manual 27-1C on the Rules of Land Warfare*,
specifically Chapter 5, Paragraph 176, as offered
in case #11-514: *U.S. vs. Dr. Max Schmid.*]

In some instances, a defendant, in spite of his best effort to do otherwise, explains himself better than any historian ever will. Dr. Max Schmid is the perfect example.

Schmid was born June 18, 1908, in Enzerdorf, Bavaria, a district of Passau in lower Bavaria. "My father was a country schoolteacher," he told the Court. Schmid was inclined to color his testimony at every opportunity; in fact, his testimony seemed to be a stream of colorings designed to elicit empathy from the Court. He wished the Court to understand that he had come from humble origins and that he had worked hard to overcome his lack of opportunity. He had been apprenticed to and worked with

Epstein, a local bank. He had used the money he earned to further his education. "This was necessary because there were two brothers of mine who were also going to college besides myself. One brother was at this same time studying law at the University of Munich and the other brother at the same time was going to Classical High School." He was, in other words, a self-made man.

Beyond describing his father as a "country" schoolteacher, he had little to say about his patrimony. He did not, for example, enlighten the Court as to his father's political leanings. This might or might not have been important. The trials would show that many schoolteachers were either sympathetic to the Nazi cause from its beginnings or at the least had no objections to enjoying the advantages membership in the party brought them.

Despite the modest background he described, Schmid had been able to acquire a remarkable education during a time when high school graduation was considered an achievement. "I attended elementary school at home for four years and after the fourth year I entered the Catholic Seminary in Passau. I spent one year at the Classical High School in Passau and after one year I was transferred to the Benedictine Monastery, Schweigelberg, in lower Bavaria and I stayed there until the end of the tenth grade." He claimed that he "was to be sent to America [and] then to a Benedictine house on the St. Louis River." He claimed that his mother did not want him to go to America and that he had continued his studies at the "Classical High School in Straubing on the Danube River ... I stayed there until I finished my thirteenth grade and then I graduated in March 1928." Then he began his apprenticeship at the bank.

At the beginning of the winter semester in 1932, he entered the University of Munich. After a semester he transferred to the University of Erlangen and continued there until he earned his degree. During the winter semester straddling 1932 to 1933, he passed a pre-medical examination and went into his first semester of clinical studies at the University of Munich. He passed his state medical examination in 1936 and began his practice at Munich. He divided his first real service between the medical clinic and the "surgical" university. He then served as an "assistant doctor" for two years. "In the meantime during that period I was called up for maneuvers by the Air Corps District Headquarters in Munich and I went through three maneuvers of about four to eight weeks each."

The prosecution had information that he had once wanted to become a priest and they were interested in why he might have given up on that profession. "I did intend to become a priest but I was not quite positive whether I would be able to set an example to my men as a priest should for all my life."

The prosecution wondered what part religion had played in his life. He stated that "coming from a purely Christian and Catholic family my attitude was always one of Christianity and Catholicism." In fact, witnesses stated that he had once been described as "first chaplain" because of his conversion activities. "Yes," he said. "That was in the prisoner of war hospital in June 1945, at the occasion of the arrival of the American troops. On that day I received a shot in my abdomen by my own troops because I had informed an American captain how many troops were in the area and because I had flown a white flag half a day before that together with a Pole at my aid station. I was with this Father there and I won back to the church two men who had been with the SS, and I helped a Protestant soldier to be converted to the Church."

The questioner wondered if he had ever given up on that attitude.

"No" he testified. "On the contrary I was always an active member of the Catholic Church. In 1939, I was threatened to get out of the church. I said that I wouldn't do that. My whole family and my ancestors had been Catholic and I would remain a Catholic. Upon that, this particular gentleman told me, 'In that case you will have to expect that we won't have need of you anymore.' To that I replied, 'In that case I'll be able to earn a living some other way.' In 1939, as I was getting married my priest in my hometown asked me whether I wanted a Catholic wedding. To that I said, 'Yes, I want a Catholic wedding.' The priest said to that, 'But that might have some adverse consequences to your profession.' Upon that I said, 'Father, that doesn't make any difference at all. I'll remain a Catholic and I want to be married as a Catholic.' He said to that, 'In that case I'll have to post your marriage application at the church in public.' I said, 'Yes, Father, you go ahead and do that; I'll always stick to my religion.' Upon that, the priest said, 'You are a brave man.'"

Schmid joined the NSDAP (the Nazi Party) during the early part of May 1933 while at the University of Erlangen. His explanation had much in common with that of other professionals: "We received our meals at the student house and persons were constantly urging us to join the Party and when we didn't, they said, 'You students want to stand aside. You want to be something better than the laborers.' We were publicly ridiculed and insulted. Anybody who wouldn't join would be kicked out of the students' house and wouldn't get a chance to get cheap meals there. That kept going on constantly until one had enough so one joined." In other words, he joined because pressure had been put on him, and, additionally, he would receive professional and personal advantages by joining.

Schmid admitted to joining the medical company of the SA (the "Storm Troopers") in 1934. "Yes, that was at the University of Munich."

He remained in the medical company from March 1, 1933, until August 15, 1937.

He also had a quick explanation for his service in the regular military: "That was in September 1937, upon orders of the Air Corps District Headquarters. I had to serve for five weeks in Munich. After that I was discharged as a Private First Class. In 1938 I was again inducted and served six weeks ... not as a soldier, but in the Medics."

After the war began, Schmid was to serve serious military time. He testified that "on the second of August 1939, I was inducted by means of receiving a draft call."

He progressed rapidly and became a captain in 1942. "That was normal," he told the Court. He also told them that he served on every sector of the front — even on the Russian front.

The prosecutor noted that being assigned to the Russian front was often considered a form of punishment. Schmid explained his service: "I had been on convalescent furlough because of pneumonia after having been in Russia for one year before that. In the fall of 1942 in the Artillery School I came in contact with a certain doctor Raschert who had been here before. He called me in and asked me, 'What do you think of Hitler?' I told him that he is a real bad son-of-a-bitch. He is the man responsible for the war we are having. In a rage he jumped up from his chair and said, 'I'll have you arrested right now and you'll pay for that remark.' He reported me to the Commanding Officer of the school. I went up to him and I told him what I had said, and he then reported me to the Air Corps Headquarters in Munich. I had to go to Munich and report there, and the man there pointed out to me [that] that type of statement coming from my mouth could cost me my life. He told me that he was going to refrain from doing this since I was married and young and because he assumed I said this in a rage. Two days later he came to the school and told me that as of tomorrow I was transferred to the Russian front. I was still a convalescent and still had hemorrhages in my lung, and in that manner I was sent to the Russian front in 1943 under the worst weather conditions."

Schmid was then sent to Marquise (in France) in November of that same year and served there until the middle of August 1944. He testified that it was a part of his duties in Marquise to care for American fliers who had been shot down. He had treated about thirty men. "There were two cases of death during that time," he said. (Schmid was charged with killing two American fliers by injection. He was acquitted of those charges. He had actually been sent a letter of gratitude from an American who felt Schmid had saved his life.)

And then the prosecutor wanted to know how Schmid got the idea to cut the head off a dead body — an *American* dead body.

"That happened as follows: An order from the Air Corps Headquarters arrived on the fifth of May, 1944, stating that the medical officers would at once give orientation lectures on litter bearing and medical assistance." The students expected to take the course were "German soldiers, Flemish, and French. I was demonstrating these matters scientifically as it is done in the university. For that reason I tried to do it well, and I went to my superior in Lille and asked him whether he had any anatomical charts. He told me that he couldn't help me out [because] he didn't have any of his own. So I went back to Marquise again and a few days later I went up to my first superior in Brussels and I asked him to please give me some anatomical charts and special aids for my courses. He didn't have anything either so I had to go back home without having accomplished anything. Then after a lecture one man who was taking the course from the bearer detail said, 'Why don't you try to get a head? There are plenty of dead bodies around Germany, both German and Allies.' So I said, 'Well, maybe you can get me a head.'"

He also described further plans for the head: "I wanted to keep it in an honorable position so it wouldn't get all dusty. That is why I sent it home. I also wanted to use it in Red Cross instruction."

The Americans had heard something else; a French witness had told them the doctor wanted the head as a present for his wife. Schmid was quick to tell them why that was incorrect. He had the "head wrapped up," he said, and he thought the French witness might have mistaken this act as an intention to present it to his wife. He told them his wife had no interest in medical work and would have "thrown him out" if he had sent the skull to her as a gift.

Then the prosecution demanded to know whose dead body he had used for his scientific and medical purposes. He tried to get around the brutal details. He told them he had gone to a place were dead bodies were collected by the detail whose duty it was to do such things. The point of collection had been "in a cellar in Marquise."

The American prosecutor wondered if German heads had been unavailable to him. Schmid again postponed the moment of having to admit that he had committed an act of marauding against an American: "The man in charge of this detail told me that in this room there would be bodies lying and for me to take the head off one of them."

The prosecution demanded to know if his choice of an American was a sign of low regard for them.

"It wasn't in any way a sign of hate, malice, or viciousness. The unfortunate part was that this man came around and pointed it out to me. And thus for scientific reasons I took and prepared this head for demonstrations during lectures," he told them.

French witnesses involved in the case had stated that the doctor hated Americans and the British. In his defense, Schmid said, "I never had any such thoughts in my heart nor did I ever talk about it." He stated that "on the contrary I had nothing but respect and esteem" for Americans and Brits.

The prosecutor demanded to know if the doctor had not realized that desecrating the body of an American flier would violate the rules of land warfare.

"I did it purely with scientific intent."

To train his litter bearers?

"Yes."

The prosecutor wondered what the litter bearers needed to know that required the aid of the head of an American. Schmid was never short of an answer, and he explained patiently. "For the reason that these assistant medics should be properly orientated on anatomical structure of the head as far as the location of blood vessels is concerned in the case of hemorrhages. For instance, so that hemorrhages could be stopped in time by the use of tourniquets and for a better understanding of fractures of the skull and in order for them to better visualize the parts of the skull and in order to explain to them the various bones and vessels along the head so that they would be better able to take care of a person who was wounded."

The Americans had some evidence that instruction given to field medics concerning skull fractures and hemorrhages did not always require the use of a human skull.

"Well, you probably did in larger outfits if it was taking place in a town or in a town with a university. In such cases, they would probably take the men into the anatomical department of the university and show them," Schmid told them.

The prosecutor then suggested that perhaps he simply wanted the skull as a souvenir. He denied this emphatically. He insisted that he had actually used the skull while lecturing his litter bearers. "I started on the first of June, 1944, and, of course, continued until and including the first week of July, 1944."

The prosecutor was still confused as to why he had sent the skull home to his wife. "I sent it away so it wouldn't gather dust and so that it would be kept in an honorable place and for that reason I had it wrapped up by a medic and sent home for possible medical use back home," he said.

Did he consider it more humane to instruct his classes with a bare skull rather than with a head with the skin on and eyes still in it?

The defendant described the general untidiness of doing such a thing. He also had an explanation for what he would have done with the skull when he no longer had a need for it: "If I would not have any use for it anymore I intended to bury it in a Catholic cemetery."

Why in a Catholic cemetery?

"Because it is part of a body, which as the other parts of the human body is supposed to be buried in a cemetery."

After the questioning and cross-questioning by the prosecution and defense lawyers, the Court, somewhat awed it appears, required some information. What, for example, they wondered, had he done with the American flier's eyes, skin, and hair?

"I cremated these, Sir."

When questioned as to why he hadn't buried the excess parts of the head in a Catholic cemetery, he said, "There happened to be a fire burning in the washroom in the furnace."

The Court questioned him as to why he thought it would be important to bury the skull and not the fleshy parts he had boiled away from the skull.

"The fleshy parts I just cremated."

Why not cremate the skull later?

"Well, I wouldn't have considered cremating the skull. It was my honest intention to put the skull into hallowed ground later on."

Dr. Max Schmid was sentenced to ten years in Landsberg Prison and served every day of it except for the reduction in time given automatically for good behavior. He was released upon expiration of sentence in June 1953 and became a hospital orderly.

In September 1959, the Chief Public Prosecutor at the District Court at Landshut wrote the War Crimes Section of the Judge Advocate Division in Heidelberg that: "I have been ordered to verify if subject individual, Dr. Schmid, has committed national-socialist atrocities which are still subject to prosecution. Please would you inform me if, according to the documents kept in your files, this suspicion is justified? In case suspicion exists, I request that copies or photostats of the pertinent documents be forwarded to me."

Apparently, Doctor Schmid had to explain himself at least one more time.

3

A Very Contrary Czech:
The Story of Johann Vican

What happens to a Russian, a Czech, does not interest me in the slightest. What the nations can offer in the way of good blood of our type, we will take, if necessary, by kidnapping their children and raising them here with us. Whether nations live in prosperity or starve to death interests me only insofar as we need them as slaves for our Kultur, otherwise it is of no interest to me.

Whether ten thousand Russian females fall down from exhaustion while digging an anti-tank ditch interests me only insofar as the anti-tank ditch for Germany is finished — we must realize that we have six or seven million foreigners in Germany — they are none of them dangerous so long as we take severe measures at the merest trifles.

[Statements attributed to Heinrich Himmler, quoted in the opening statement of the prosecution in *U.S. vs. Georg Walter Degner*, case #000-Flossenburg-1.]

The jury's deliberation at the trial of Johann Vican took ten minutes, but for years Vican managed to bedevil the governments of four nations: Austria, Nazi Germany, the Federal Republic of Germany, and the United States of America. He confounded the parole system, various supervisors and paper pushers, the local law authorities, his employers, and the general population of Landsberg Prison. He managed to stay in the confinement of the four nations for nearly two decades, and it's possible the worst he ever did was enthusiastically rumble with people who messed with him — until desperation forced him to become a capo. He was one of the last war criminals to be released from prison in June 1958, when, "under

date of 12 May 1958 the German Government, acting pursuant to the provisions of sub-paragraph c, paragraph 3, Article 6, Chapter One of the
Bonn Settlement Convention, requested the Mixed Board to consider
whether clemency would be appropriate in the case of Vican, Johann."
The Mixed Board agreed in a "unanimous and therefore mandatory recommendation," and accordingly General H. I. Hodes ordered that the
unexecuted portion of his sentence be remitted. Vican (case # 000-Flossen-
burg-3) then disappeared from American war records.

Outside a thin upper lip that gave him a minor look of insolence,
Vican didn't look the part of the war criminal he might have been — or the
petty criminal he surely was. His features weren't heavy, but they were
not refined —"common" is the word that comes to mind. The curve of
Vican's upper and lower eyelids echoed each other exactly; but one must
look closely to discover this small strangeness. His ears flared a bit.
His chin was long and slightly pointed but not enough to give him that
"Prince of Europe" appearance. He didn't look particularly defiant. He
would not have stood out in a crowd.

Johann Vican

Vican was born in Czecho-
slovakia in 1913, as the son of
Wensel and Marie, but he was
living in Linz, Austria, by the
time he began to come to the
attention of authorities. Later
reports by a parole officer incorrectly stated that he was born in
Linz and had only three previous arrests; however, his official
record from Linz, because it is
an original document, would
seem to be more accurate. He
identified himself at the time of
his trial as a weaver. Whether he
had been trained in the skill as a
teen or had picked up the trade
in prison is not clear. His parole
supervisor sarcastically questioned whether he actually possessed that skill, but he certainly
became petulant about having to
put up with other employment.

Vican's records from Linz show that he was first arrested in 1930 when he was seventeen years old. He was arrested again in 1933 and in 1934. He was arrested twice in 1936, five times in 1937, twice in 1938, and once in 1940 when he was twenty-seven. His arrests appear to be for disorderly conduct and general hooliganism.

Vican was a fierce enemy of the Nazis, and he paid the price. When the Germans invaded Austria in 1938, Vican climbed the flagpole and cut down the flag the Germans had raised to fly over Klein-München near Linz. Some time after the flag offense, the Gestapo expelled Vican from Austria, possibly into Czechoslovakia. In 1940, the Gestapo picked him up for going back into Austria to visit his mother. He was sent to Dachau as a common criminal. In 1943, he was released on the condition that he would join the SS. After three days and no move toward the condition placed upon him, the Gestapo arrested him again and returned him to Dachau. As a welcome back to Dachau, he received the "twenty-five," meaning that he was put on a table in front of the roll-call line-up and given twenty-five strokes with a stick. He was also sent to work in the quarry to be "finished off." The diminutive hothead survived. He was beaten several times a week and his weight dropped to about one hundred pounds. He became a "Dachau skeleton." Still he survived.

In October 1944, he was transferred to Lengenfeld, an out-camp of Flossenburg, where he worked in a factory. He was among the several prisoners who became victims of acidone poisoning, and he lay in a bunker for four weeks near death. Again he survived.

He must have seemed an amazing animal to the Germans, and they rewarded him by making him a block eldest in January or February of 1945. The next month, he was made a capo—just in time for one of the end-of-war transports. Another written statement declares that Vican had been made a capo two months earlier, but no claim was ever made that he acted as a capo over an extended period of time. His war crimes were committed during December and January. On April 2, he was one of 650 prisoners from Lengenfeld who set out on foot to Munich. The transport was "dissolved" on April 24, near Wureken, Czechoslovakia. On May 2, he was among several inmates taken prisoner by the United States.

After Vican was picked up by the Americans, he was housed with those whom he would be accused of abusing. No one attacked him or gave him a hard time in any way. When prisoners were given the opportunity, hated capos received a brutal payback.

No testimony was given at his trial; a few inconsistent written statements would suffice as "evidence." Vican was accused of beating up to fifty inmates with a rubber hose, a fact he readily admitted on the longest last day he was in custody. It was alleged that three of the prisoners died from one to several days after one of Vican's beatings, a charge he denied until the last day he was in custody.

Vican pleaded guilty to all charges. He would always say that his lawyer advised him to do that because the tribunal tended to spare the lives of those who pleaded guilty. If Vican had had a good lawyer it could have been pointed out that a man five feet five inches tall who weighed less than one hundred pounds would have had a difficult time beating three people to death with a hose. It could have been pointed out that people died in obscene numbers at the concentration camp and a cause-and-effect situation would have been impossible to prove. It could have been pointed out that the "statements" were inconsistent. All of this was noted by one of Vican's lawyers in years to come. The Court must surely have had doubts about the accuracy of the statements because he was not given the death penalty.

In an interesting aside, some time after the trial, Vican would not remember the name of his trial lawyer and a subsequent attorney would have to make inquiries of the Judge Advocate's office to learn his name. Vican wanted to write him a letter, almost surely to give him a piece of his mind, but the Judge Advocate's office could supply only the lawyer's name from records. They could not give his address. He had returned to America and moved to parts unknown to them. The review board would also take strong exception to Vican's later claim that he had not been properly represented.

Other than the commonsense arguments that were never made, Vican would have had little to offer in his defense. About all he had in his favor was a short statement from a fellow capo, which offered more insight into the concentration camp than help for Vican. He pointed out that beating was the standard form of discipline at the concentration camp and that Vican administered the beatings without malice or sadistic leanings. Inmates of concentrations camps were at the mercy of members of the SS staff. Some were also at the mercy of other inmates. Common criminals were housed with the general camp population, and, together with other desperate prisoners, they made the fight to survive vicious and brutal. Some stronger prisoners, especially Poles and Russians, according to the capo, took food and clothing away from the weak, causing the weak to die of starvation or exposure. An extraordinary picture of the compromises humans had to make to survive as prisoners of the Germans is painted in several books by Primo Levi, the revered Italian writer and chemist who survived for a year in Auschwitz. Gitta Sereny in her disturbing book *Into That Darkness,* also records the first-person testimony of prisoners who went to bloodchilling lengths to finance the breakout at Treblinka. Other testimonials and ordinary knowledge of the nature of humankind tells us that, beyond any doubt, this capo was telling the truth. Even when prisoners were not forced into diabolical criminal acts, alliances developed and competed, and the weak were used to satisfy cravings beyond the simple need for food and warmth. Vican had volunteered to try to keep order in this snake pit in exchange for food and clothing. The fact that he accepted the beating of his fellow humans as part of the deal also tells as much about the concentration camps in general and desperation in particular as it tells about the man Vican.

Without argument, Vican joined the ranks of the martyrs that never were. He never once said, "I will not beat people so just shoot me." Martyrdom in the cause of compassion was a scarce commodity in the camps. Vican, however, had it tough.

After a ten-minute recess, the Court found him guilty on all counts and after a five-minute deliberation determined that he should serve twenty years at hard labor. Prisoners with similar convictions usually served five years or less of twenty-year sentences. Vican went to Landsberg Prison.

A lawyer filing an appeal on Vican's behalf tried to make arguments that should have been made at his trial, but the review board would have none of it. He had admitted guilt after much explanation of his situation, he probably was guilty, and he received a light sentence. However severe the court might have been, Vican was definitely his own worst enemy.

Vican's new lawyer tried his best, but in 1951 he received the following admonition from the review board:

> I should like to point out to you that it is a waste of your time and my time to submit petitions requesting a review of cases which have already been considered by the Modification Board until all cases have been considered. Unless some very unusual circumstances arise which are beyond the scope of ordinary petitions, I merely propose to place such petitions in the file and promptly forget them until I have completed the review of those cases which have not been considered by the Board.

By the mid-fifties, most war criminals who had been sent to prison were out on parole. They went home to families and obeyed the laws of the land. The system actually seemed quite eager to release prisoners as soon as possible and to remit sentences with any degree of encouragement. The political climate in the United States leaned toward more normal international relations, and the prison at Landsberg was not a positive factor.

Toward the end of 1953, in a prisoner interview, Vican let it be known that he was interested in getting parole. He told the interviewer that he wanted to live in Bavaria, that he had no relatives, and that he could do only light work. At least part of this was true. He had been diagnosed with heart valve insufficiency and suffered the usual symptoms. He had no parole plan, however.

A parole plan was an important step toward being released. It consisted of getting documents vowing that someone would employ the prisoner, that he would have a place to live, that someone of standing would act as his supervisor, and that he could take care of himself and contribute to society. If all this was satisfactory and he had convinced the prison officials that he understood punishment and assumed moral responsibility for his acts, he would almost surely get a parole. Vican couldn't accomplish this.

By April of that year, Vican submitted another plan. A gardener with a rather large business would employ him and provide him a place to stay even though it was "primitive and modest," was located in the basement of the business, and would have to be shared with an eighteen-year-old assistant gardener. The employer would feed him and pay him DM20 per week. The Division Chief of the Municipal Welfare Office in Augsburg would sponsor him, and Vican agreed to limit his travel to the environs of Augsburg.

In June, the parole application was denied. The board was concerned about the prison supervisor's remark that Vican would require "excellent and close supervision" if he was granted parole. Further, it was noted that he had not cleared up questions about his nationality, and his work plan was of such short duration that it had already expired by the time the application was reviewed.

The potential parole supervisor was prevailed upon to intervene with the prospective employer to extend the employment period, and Vican was released during November of that year. Almost immediately, Vican was in trouble.

By December 20, his parole officer wrote that he had "knowingly sent his report to the wrong office." He was telling his employer that he wanted to change his employment after half a year and that he felt he was being supervised worse than in a concentration camp. The officer had checked out the possibility that Vican had been badly treated and found no basis for the complaints. The officer reported that Vican "drinks more than usual and, in this condition, gives way to remarks which, most probably, he would not otherwise make."

The U.S. parole officer (USPO) didn't delay in trying to bring Vican to heel. To Vican, he wrote, "I have information to the effect that you are drinking entirely too much alcoholic drinks and talking too much. Further, you are employed by a very social-minded employer and your remarks about your supervision are only showing your true character. Unless you prefer to spend the balance of your sentence in prison, I direct you to immediately cease drinking any alcoholic content drinks and adjust yourself to civil life."

By February, things were tougher. The assistant USPO was writing the head USPO that he had gone armed with a warrant to arrest Vican. He visited the Parole Supervisor, Herr Moegele, and learned that Vican's employer was ready to fire Vican. The parole supervisor told the assistant parole officer that Vican would probably have to go back to jail because it would be "practically impossible to secure another job" for him. The assistant USPO wrote the head USPO that, with the parole sponsor, he had visited the employer. Because Vican returned from his weekends in a bad frame of mind, Mondays were damaging the employer-employee relationship. But the employer was willing to give the relationship another chance.

Vican wanted four things: to drink beer, to go to the beer hall, to visit Frau Koninger, and to visit his mother in Austria. The team visited Vican and he appeared to be humble, attentive, and cooperative. He was reminded that he had agreed to refrain from attempting to go see his mother as part of his parole terms. Vican said he'd try to adjust.

Vican had an explanation about the Gasthaus (beer hall). He had gone there because he had "been especially invited there to play the accordion." The committee visited the Gasthaus. A waitress said she knew of no particular accordion player and Vican's name was unfamiliar to her. As to the Gasthaus "Pferseer Hof," they learned that "the owners are of good reputation, but that the clientele often includes persons of dubious reputation."

Vican had an explanation for Frau Koninger. She did his laundry. He complained that, with other arrangements, his laundry cost DM7.50, more than a third of his weekly salary. The committee advised that he "could certainly get his laundry done much cheaper elsewhere."

Then the committee went to the Sixth Precinct Police Station and talked to the officer on duty. They learned at the station that "Frau Kreszenzia Koninger lived at Augsburgerstrasse 37 in concubinage with one Josel Studener, born in Munich in 1915, who is separated but not divorced from his legal wife." They learned that the "character of these two persons is not such that good citizens would wish to associate with them."

The committee, while speaking to Vican, reminded him that "Parolee Gartner had been recently returned to the prison for parole violations."

The committee reported that this had a noticeable effect upon Vican and he emphatically "replied in the negative" when asked if he would rather return to Landsberg.

The USPO found Vican to be "childlike" in his failure to comprehend the seriousness of the situation. However, Vican promised to do better and the assistant USPO pocketed his warrant and went home to write the head USPO that he was giving Vican another chance. But, again, Vican could not avoid trouble.

For one thing, he couldn't seem to get his dates right on his bimonthly reports. He dated his first report from November 29 through December 15 instead of from December 1 to the 15. For the period of December 16–31, he went back to November 29 and ended his report as of December 27. By the fourth period, he was still going back to November 29 as the beginning date and the end date was always off a bit. During the first period of March, Vican submitted two separate reports covering the same period of time but differing in content. He sent his April report in on the 25th instead of the 30.

He addressed his first report through a "person other than his parole supervisor; he stated his address improperly; and he entered the name of his employer in the space provided for the parole supervisor's address." In the next report, he "entered his own name and address in the space provided for the parole supervisor's address; he stated his address improperly; he failed to state the number of days he had worked; and he signed the report in the space provided for the parole supervisor's signature." A dizzying display of errors continued in report after report.

On one occasion, Vican "knowingly and improperly submitted the said report to the Bezirksfuersorgeverband Augsburg-Land" instead of giving it directly to the parole supervisor as he had been specifically told to do.

Vican did take time out to write a couple of complaints on his report. In January, he said, "at present time I have no difficulties with my employment, however, I would like to have another employment." He wanted to work at a spinning mill and follow the weaver's trade. In February, he said, "I would like to ask … if I could not be allowed to drink one glass of beer, why should I have prohibition for alcohol, I did not drink in excess, I am no drunkard."

Vican could explain at least one lapse — why he didn't file a report in the days after the committee visited him and gave him one last chance. First, he stated that he did not receive the forms for the monthly report until a "few days ago," and his employer was willing to back him up on that one. He also said that his sponsor was not able to fill out the questionnaire with him because he (Vican) "alleged that he had cold hands and desired to fill out the forms independently in the evening." The sponsor said he had advised Vican fully. It seems that three days after the visit of the committee, Vican "unfortunately left his home on Saturday and did not return earlier than Monday, failing to inform his employer of his whereabouts or to apologize for his absence." Still the employer was willing to stay the course.

In May, without telling anyone, Vican quit his employment without reporting to his parole supervisor. Authorities picked him up and Vican went back to Landsberg Prison. In prison he played the accordion and had only one close friend. He said he had beaten prisoners while in the concentration camp, but he still said he did not commit murders. He did not take advantage of opportunities for schooling offered by the prison. Otherwise he was cooperative and was a willing worker in the metal shop.

In late October 1957, Vican was ordered to be released. He was in his middle forties. Perhaps he went to live with his mother and settled down to a quiet life in an Austrian spinning mill. Perhaps he continued to raise hell until his frail health put an end to Vican, the very contrary Czech. Records don't follow Vican beyond his last steps outside the prison.

4

Murder in a Stable:
The Commando 99 Ruse

On November 3, 1950, Congressman Augustine B. Kelley of Pennsylvania, using the letterhead of the U.S. Congress, wrote a letter to the review board concerning a group of war criminals and one criminal in particular:

> I wish to express my interest in behalf of the defendants in the above-identified case [*U.S. vs. Berger et al.*], in particular one Joseph Bresser.
>
> This man's case was brought to my attention through a relative in Germany of a close and respected friend of mine. His sentence of fifteen years seems highly excessive for his crime, and the sentence of the other defendants in the case seem equally out of line.
>
> I would, therefore, urge in your review of the case that consideration be given to some reduction in sentences or other appropriate leniency for these defendants.

He signed his name followed by the letters "M. C."

Here, in 1950, Congressman Kelly was attempting to generate consideration for those who participated in the Buchenwald "Commando 99" episode. Other young men in Congress, such as Richard Nixon and Tail Gunner Joe McCarthy, began to think that America should stop spending so much time on the old Nazis and turn attention to the Russians. While their hearings were not always popular, many of their ideas had sympathizers. As this case unwound, the Cold War would become a factor in the pursuit of justice.

At Buchenwald's concentration camp, in a place described by witnesses as beyond the kitchen and behind the music building, a long narrow structure stood that had once sheltered horses. It continued to be known as the "horse stable" long after its functions had changed—long enough for the horse stable to find its way into infamy. The telephone number of the building was "99" and thus the special detail that came to work there was called the "Commando 99."

In the horse stable, Germans developed a ruse that rivaled the "shower" deception of the gassing process at Auschwitz. The building was renovated to look like a clinic. Rooms on each side of a long hall were given names like the "examining room." Posters of naked men illustrated skeletal and muscular particulars of the human body. A row of letters suggested eye examinations might take place. Men stood around in white coats and they seemed to be doctors, or, at least, medics.

The clinic had a large radio which was hooked up to loudspeakers. The music was so loud, those in the building could not hear each other speak. It was impossible to hear what was going on from one room to another.

This clinic served Russians and only Russians. It was alleged by Americans that they were prisoners of war. Marian Zgoda, the inmate "stretcher bearer for corpses," knew that, he said, "because they were wearing Russian uniforms." To the best of his memory, he thought this special group of prisoners had begun to arrive at the stable on November 23, 1941.

Zgoda used a prosecution exhibit to point out a center swinging door that allowed entrance into the building. Then, "they went through here and they entered this room here." He indicated a passageway and a large room on the right side of the exhibit. "When they entered the room, a small table was set up with a Russian General who was to tell the Russian prisoners of war they should undress."

The Russian General Kushnir Kushnafef was a prisoner of war at Buchenwald. Evidence showed that he acted only as an interpreter for Commando 99 and perhaps, because the activities were so far away from him and because the loudspeakers covered other sounds, it is possible Kushnafef did not actually know what was happening. It is also possible that he suspected. Records do not suggest that he cooperated willingly with the detail.

Zgoda testified that "one doctor was present. It was Doctor Schidlavsky or Doctor Hofen or Doctor Platzer." In fact, all the SS men in the detail were "dressed as doctors, and they were wearing white coats." They also wore SS caps and boots.

After undressing, the prisoners were led to a room Zgoda described as an "examination room." He pointed to a position that was labeled on the exhibit as a "counseling" room. As the questioning continued, the prosecutor referred to the room as the "consulting room."

In this room, the prisoners were examined. "They had to open their mouths and say 'Ah.'" They also had to lift their arms so the examiners could check for lice. "Then they were led on."

The prosecutor then asked Zgoda about who did the examinations. The interpreter quoted the witness as saying, "That was one of the noncommissioned officers. I don't know whether it was Berger, Bresser, or Dittrich."

The prosecutor challenged the translator: "The prosecution wishes to make correct the translation. I believe the witness said, 'whoever was there.'"

Zgoda replied that "they were all there: Berger, Dittrich, Bresser, Hilberger, and Bergt."

For the moment, the prosecutor did not note the additions to Zgoda's list, but he again took issue with the interpreter: "There is another correction of the translation. I believe the translation should be, 'whoever was there'." The interpreter said that he believed his understanding and the prosecutor's understanding were the same. "No, it isn't because they were not all there at the same time." The specific reason for his attention to detail was likely to make sure that Zgoda's list did not provide grounds for deniability among suspects. It was also interesting for other reasons. It is noteworthy that the prosecutor had such a good command of German that he could challenge translations. It is also to be noted that some trial documents reveal sloppy translations which went unchallenged, particularly on the part of defendants.

Having made his point, the prosecutor asked the witness to continue to describe the progress of the prisoners through the stable. "They were taken to the height gauge so their height could be measured and then they [were] taken to be bathed into the bathroom."

Against one wall of the height gauge room was a series of marks with measurements written beside them. Alongside the measurements was a vertical slit a foot or so in length. Zgoda confirmed that a model of the structure exhibited in the courtroom was correct. One by one, the prisoners went in to be measured.

Zgoda testified that he knew precisely what happened because he was on duty in the room directly across from the "measuring room" and could see exactly what was happening. "They were led by the hand and whenever they entered through this gate they were led along here with their backs to this instrument." (He continued to use the exhibit to illustrate his testimony.) "The SS man who was standing next to him would tap against the wall with his foot. And at that moment, the shot was fired and the prisoner would collapse."

The prosecutor wanted to know precisely from where the shot was fired. "Through the slit," said Zgoda. The SS men in back of the slit wore cellophane shields in front of their faces "so the blood wouldn't splurge into the face of the SS man."

This Buchenwald installation, which worked so well, was copied exactly from an installation at Oranienburg (the headquarters for the entire concentration camp system in Germany).

Although there was a high rate of efficiency to the procedure, inopportune events did occur. Frequently, the men failed to die as planned. The bodies were thrown on a heap in a special room called "the way of the corpses." Those on top of the pile who still showed signs of life were shot again or stabbed with a dagger. Those lower in the pile lived until the next step in the procedure. One Russian managed to run out of the room "quarreling" after he was shot; he had to be chased down and killed.

As the corpses piled up, a truck came to pick them up. Josef Bresser, the concern of Congressman Kelley, sometimes drove the truck. Witnesses Kelley would also say that Bresser sometimes wore a white coat and played medic in the horse stable, an allegation Bresser always denied.

Zgoda testified that he knew Josef Bresser, and he identified him in the courtroom. Zgoda testified that Bresser was sometimes behind the height gauge. He was there "from April 1942 until 1943." This was in direct opposition to Bresser's claim that he had only driven the truck that carried bodies from the horse stable.

Zgoda testified that Bresser did indeed sometimes drive the truck, just as he had claimed. He described the vehicle as being a five-ton truck of special design. "It was the same as trucks generally only there was a special box inside the truck." He said the truck was lined with zinc plates so "the blood would not be dripping out."

After inmates loaded the bodies onto the truck, the bodies were taken to the crematory. For their help, the inmates were allowed to have time out to warm themselves at the crematory on cold days. Later in the evenings, after the executions were finished, the inmates were called back to work. They had to "go into the room at the other end and to clean up and wash—clean up blood which was sprayed around and [they] had to load up the clothes of the people who had been shot to death."

Serving on the Commando 99 detail was profitable for the participants. They were given special rations: bread, butter, sausage, cigarettes, schnapps—and DM50 for Christmas. They were also given citations, which left written records that would be entered into evidence against them at their trials.

The detail sometimes had a special visitor: Karl Otto Koch, the commandant of the camp. Koch gained infamy for being executed by the Nazis near the end of the war for plundering the coffers of the camp. Koch has another claim to fame; he was the husband of Ilse Koch, the "Bitch" of Buchenwald.

The Russians arriving at Buchenwald in trucks from Weimar were taken directly to the horse stable. Some days the trucks would bring about thirty prisoners to be shot. Other days there were so many — several hundred — that the shooters had to relieve each other.

Witnesses, representing the prosecution and the defense — some hostile and others cooperative, some helpless inmates of the camp and others criminals who were already awaiting executions for their own war crimes—confirmed the activities of Commando 99.

Each of the accused offered an explanation. Bresser's explanation was that he only drove the truck and never stood behind the execution slit. He was more or less believed. The other defendants attempted to put forth evidence that they were carrying out orders. Precedents had already been set that disallowed the "superior orders" defense; however, these men claimed they had orders of a different kind. The Russians were not prisoners of war, they said. The Russians were commissars and political people. Commissars were "personnel attached to the Russian army for the purpose of assuring that party policies were carried out and also to instruct as to party policies," according to defense testimony. They were not legal soldiers and had ordered the killing of German prisoners of war in Russian hands. Commando 99 was following orders to execute only duly tried and sentenced criminals, said the defense in its struggle to justify the deeds done in the old horse stable.

Several prosecution arguments contradicted the "legal execution" claim. It was highly unlikely that such an elaborate ruse would have been used to fool men being led to a firing squad. It would not have been necessary to keep the operation top secret if it had been a legal action, and every effort was made to maintain secrecy. It would also have been standard procedure to read the prisoner the charges along with a statement relating his conviction to his sentence, according to the prosecution.

Zgoda testified that he had never heard any orders read with respect to the prisoners. He did say, however, that on one occasion he had seen a legal officer present — one "Adjutant Schmidt" to be exact.

Hermann Helbig, chief executioner at Buchenwald during the period in question, insisted that the executed were commissars and political people. They were brought to Buchenwald by the Gestapo, Germany's "political police." The prosecution would attempt to deflect this defense. He asked Helbig what kind of uniform he thought the prisoners wore.

Helbig testified that "at the beginning these commissars were usually clothed in uniforms of the German police or Wehrmacht and later on they were clothed in rags, many of them." He also admitted that sometimes they wore "a uniform with the color of the Russian prisoners of war. The commissars had caps, gray with a red stripe."

Other evidence revealed that identification tags bearing the word "Stalag" ("prisoner of war camp") were found in the drains of the horse stable, and one inmate testified that he saw Russian uniforms in the laundry at the camp. The prosecution offered a strong wall of evidence.

Helbig could still counter. He testified that the commissars had been hiding in disguise among prisoners of war and that they had been reported by their own comrades. He knew it firsthand — not merely from camp rumor or supposition. He had also seen an order from Berlin. It was a document from the main office of the National Security Service and on the top left the word "secret" was printed. The text read as follows: "The following Russian political commissars whose names are mentioned below are to be executed as soon as the transport arrives. Receipt of execution asked for." The "commissars" were listed by name. He could not remember whose signature was at the bottom of the order. He had seen such an order only once, but he had witnessed the executions forty times. He could also remember that on one occasion the order had been read at the executions. For his testimony, Helbig had been transported to Dachau from Landsberg Prison where he was awaiting execution for other war crimes.

Although the trial review found that it was unlikely an elaborate scheme such as the Commando 99 detail would have been necessary for legal activity, most defendants in *U.S. vs. Berger et al.* were given relatively light sentences, notwithstanding Congressman Kelley's evaluation. Josef Bresser received fifteen years.

Although many of the trials at Dachau were uncomfortably complex, it would seem that *U.S. vs. Berger et al.* would have provided for an exercise in black and white. If the Russians had been convicted in a German court, no matter how flawed that court might have been, the defendants would have been acting legally and none should have been convicted. If they were being murdered according to some arbitrary order and without the benefit of trial, most of the defendants should have received the penalty of death by hanging. The Court managed to find a gray area. The Commando 99 unit had some moral responsibility to question what was going on around them; that responsibility was not written into law, however.

In 1946, when the review board was evaluating the case, they upheld the Court's decision suggesting that the Russians were probably prisoners of war with all the rights and protections recognized by civilized societies. By the early 1950s, a strange contradiction had occurred.

In September 1950, a defense attorney presented a "Summary of Facts for Pardon of the Defendants." The attorney, William O. Miller, argued that it should be kept in mind that "the accused had not harmed one American soldier, nor one true American ally, for at the very time this case was being tried, Molotov walked out of the conference with General Marshall in London." The Cold War was being personified and was becoming a presence in the process. In this statement the presence was named Molotov.

Miller further felt it was to the advantage of his clients to point out that Russia "never was a member of the Geneva Conference and consequently did not deserve any of the protection set up under the rules of that body." Miller also offered the criticism that only one man with legal training served on the five- to nine-member Courts at Dachau. The Nuremberg Court had been composed of distinguished jurists.

In June 1955, within a disposition form addressing the application for good conduct release of Bresser, under the heading "Discussion," the following is found: "Bresser was convicted of participation in the unlawful execution of Russian prisoners of war at the Buchenwald Concentration Camp." The very next sentence reads, "the Russians were executed pursuant to a judgment of conviction imposed by a Nazi Party court having jurisdiction under the then German Reich." In *U.S. vs. Berger et al.*, morality, the law, and American politics combined in a strange way.

Josef Bresser was an almost ideal prisoner. He sat out his time without drawing undue attention to himself. He participated in the sports program and applied himself "toward preparation for employment upon release." In 1953, he applied for parole. His only problem was his employment plan. He wanted to pick up the profession he had left off before the war and open a driving school. The parole supervisors had to point out that he didn't have the resources to open the school and that he had no guarantee of customers. He submitted an alternate plan that included employment in an "electro-firm." He was released in February 1954.

At home, Bresser had a loving wife. He had a good relationship with his daughter and grandchildren. By 1955, he had renovated his home, established a successful driving school and garage business and had become the employer of a few unskilled persons. His business was "lucrative" but he still "wanted more." This need to make up for the lost years was guessed to be the cause of his slight nervousness. He didn't participate in community affairs and showed absolutely no interest in politics or political parties.

During that same year, Bresser applied for "Good Conduct Release." This meant that he would have to continue to live up to all major conditions of his parole but would not be supervised. If he kept his nose clean, he was "out." Because of his excellent record and great potential, in 1955 he was granted the release.

On May 2, 1957, pursuant to the Bonn Settlement Convention, the German government requested that the Mixed Board grant clemency for Bresser.* Clemency was granted and his final release became effective on June 22, 1957.

By this time, an American ambivalence about the Russians had developed into suspicion and the Cold War, and "West" Germany had become an ally and friend.

*As the tribunals associated with the war wound down, the various military entities were given over to civilian authority. In the United States, that duty fell to the Department of State. In the Bonn Settlement Convention, associated with this evolution in international affairs, a "Mixed Board" consisting of three Germans and one representative each from France, Britain, and the United States attended to matters of prisoners including various petitions.

5

Education: Schoolteachers at Work in the Fields of Evil

> We believed this to be the right method because of our education and because our educators and our idols—teachers, masters, etc.—were in complete agreement with this ideology.
>
> [From the "life story" of Wilhelm Grill, referring to Nazi "gospel."]

Friedrich Lutz, a highly respected teacher, gave two versions for joining the Nazi party during the early years. His short answer was that teachers were forced to join. His trial explanation was that he could not get justice in a dispute with a Nazi colleague unless he too joined. He suggested that he understood and disliked the Nazis, but his career was also important to him. (Lutz's case is described in more detail in Chapter 15 of this book.)

Karl Schopperle was different. He believed. He thought Germany needed a new direction and he placed his hope in the Nazis when he joined their movement in 1933. According to a friend of fifty years, when Schopperle witnessed the "exciting" political movements, he "saw only the renewal, the good, for he himself can only believe in the good, and he joined the NSDAP and the SS hoping to be able to rebuild a new Germany."

When he was younger he had joined the Wandervogel (the "Wanderbird Movement") and had "passionately devoted himself to their ideals: keeping alive old manners and customs, nature study, comradeship, love of home, and the like." The Wandervogel was a movement that carried on some of the traditions of traveling storytellers and minstrels. They affected a costume and championed causes ranging from nature to social issues. Typically, the members tended to be very idealistic.

He devoted time to the problems of education. "He was sitting around the campfire, discussing, teaching handicrafts, inventing and telling stories and fairy tales and found his joy only in the good, the true, and the beautiful at a time when his friends were taking exercises playing football or indulging in other sports." He had talked to his friend about the political developments during that time, and he had learned that Schopperle only "wanted to give the young people a better future, one

Friedrich Lutz

like the Wandervogel had tried. He always labored unselfishly and did not perceive how other people got jobs and worked to line their own pockets." After World War I, when he became a teacher, he was eager and enthusiastic. He was a volunteer for the fire department and the choral society, among other things. He built bobsleds, canoes, and sailboats with his students. He put the skills and learning he used as a trade school teacher into bettering the lives of the community's youth.

The parson of the Protestant church in his hometown who gave religious instruction at the school found Schopperle strong in person but enjoying a "general popularity" among his students. He was, in spite of his strength and position, benevolent. Among his colleagues he was "rough, but cordial."

During his time as a community leader, he gained the admiration of his neighbors. His friend said specifically that Schopperle "never attacked anyone on account of his religious or political convictions and he respected everyone's opinion." The friend did not say that Schopperle didn't discriminate on the basis of race, and he did not mention his reaction to the obvious religious/racial propaganda of the Nazis.

The friend suggests that Schopperle was brave. He wanted officers of the Court at Dachau to know he (the friend) was never a member of the NSDAP or "any of its organizations." He was a Freemason, a member of the "Rupprecht at the Five Roses Lodge" and "under special observation" for that, but Schopperle had remained his friend.

To be sure, the war was not easy on Schopperle. His son came back from the war "half-blind and badly wounded." His son-in-law disappeared from the face of the earth while serving in Russia. One of his daughters was "made a prisoner of the French by virtue of her being a private in the Women's Labor Service." After the war his wife was placed in custody for ten weeks during the "deNazification" phase of the Allied Occupation.

Schopperle went into service in the concentration camps as a billeting administrator in 1940. After that, he was in charge of construction at a variety of camps. Eventually, he became commandant of Gross-Raming where he was involved in the hideous death of a prisoner named Ilic.

Ilic had been working on a detail located twelve or fifteen miles outside the camp when he escaped. The other prisoners had to go back to the camp and stand at attention during most of several nights until the prisoner was captured again. After two days and two nights during which the prisoners endured a thunderstorm, Ilic was captured and was returned to the square with a sign around his neck which read, "Hooray! I am here again." He had been beaten severely. Schopperle gave orders for Ilic to be tied down on two chairs placed in the center of the square where he was again beaten. When he fainted, cold water was thrown on him until he regained consciousness and "then they started it all over." Then Ilic was thrown on the electrically charged barbed wire in Schopperle's presence. Ilic was thrown back from the wire but he was

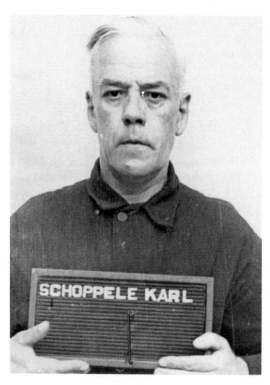

Karl Schopperle (Note the misspelling of his name on the card.)

still not dead. After that, he was thrown to the dogs that tore him to pieces.

Finally, in 1944, Schopperle became commander at Linz III, an out-camp of Mauthausen. Among the crimes for which Schopperle was charged, other than that of being a common conspirator, was giving an order in front of a general roll call in reveille square in March 1945 to hang three Russians who had been caught trying to escape. About two weeks later the inmates were called to the reveille square to witness Schopperle supervising the hanging of another inmate. The capo complained that the noose was not fastened in a way to cause a quick death, but Schopperle refused to adjust the noose. He ordered the body left hanging in the square all night and all the next day.

About one week later, the camp was bombed and one of the capos was assigned to a cleaning detail when he came up missing. When he was found, Schopperle ordered him to hang himself in a supply room. Instead, the capo ran from the supply room, disappeared, and had to be found again. The inmate was shot in reveille square.

In his defense, witnesses gave testimony that he was not a cruel man and tried to take care of prisoners in his care. This could have been true because inmates testified that they sometimes found a mixture of benevolence and barbarism in the methodology of Nazis. Schopperle had translated the skills of a teacher — compassion mixed with firmness, leadership mixed with perceived responsibility — into traits often found in camp commanders and war criminals. He was sentenced to death and was hanged at Landsberg Prison.

Ludwig Stier, sentenced to death on June 23, 1947, was the son of a stonecutter who struggled to support his family. He grew up in a small village in the Palatinate in southwest Germany and appears to have wanted nothing more in life than to be a teacher in a village school. For most of his life, he was able to accomplish his goal. He went to the teacher's college at Kaiserslautern and immediately joined the military during the early years of World War I. He was wounded but survived to become a lieutenant in the reserves. He married, happily it appears, raised three children, and taught in the village schools of his homeland. He was unselfish, kind, and good, his wife said. He was a local education leader and an early member of the Nazi Party. He had joined the first of March, 1932.

"The situation in Germany was so bad," he testified, "that everybody was longing for some improvement and according to this when I heard the propaganda meetings of the Party, I believed that the Party would be able to help." He said the general situation improved beginning in 1933, and, "in the beginning," he had remained in complete agreement with their goals.

The prosecutor wondered if he had ever changed his mind.

"When the war started," he replied.

"Not before 1939?" he was asked.

"No."

The prosecutor wondered if he had happened to notice that minorities were being oppressed between 1932 and 1939.

"Yes," he testified.

He was then asked why he didn't leave the Party. The prosecutor also suggested that he might have agreed with the oppression.

"No, I did not leave the Party for the single reason because as an official employee I couldn't do so; otherwise, I would have lost my position or at least I would have been prevented in making any progress in my career."

"So to further your ambition you were willing to participate in the oppression of minorities, no matter how long it lasted. Is that true?"

"I did not understand one foreign word, 'ambition.'"

The interpreter stated, "I explained 'ambition' to him in proper German."

The prosecutor asked if he remained a Party member for purposes of ambition.

"I only remained in the Party because I feared that I wouldn't get along in my position."

Stier was a really sick man. He had severe high blood pressure and was able to stay at the front only a short time at the beginning of the war. He had been serving in the Flack Regiment 49, First Section, as an officer in charge of nutrition. He was confined to a hospital for eight months in 1942 with skin disease and a kidney ailment associated with his hypertension. By this time, he was a captain in the Luftwaffe and was assigned administrative duties in various places. In 1944, he was assigned to the position of Company Commander of the guard troops, which consisted of fliers, at Wiener-Neudorf, an out-camp of the brutal Mauthausen concentration camp system.

"I was the disciplinary authority over these guard troops," he testified. "The guard troops had the duty to guard the work camp as such and to guard the prisoners on their individual work details."

Stier and the troops he supervised were quartered outside the camp. "It was prohibited for us to enter the camp," he said. Actually, he would admit, he had been in the camp three times. Once, he had come in to be shown where the prisoners lived and where some of them worked. Again, he was brought in by the camp leader to see how much worse shape the prisoners were in who were arriving new from Mauthausen proper as opposed to the resident prisoners at Wiener-Neudorf. A third time he was "invited" to the Christmas roll call of prisoners.

According to his wife, Stier had been terribly upset when he learned he would be taking control of guards at a concentration camp, even if those guards were of some stature and functioned only to prevent escapes from the work places. "I remember very well that all his nature revolted against this assignment which for the first time in his life brought him into contact with a sphere of activities which conflicted with his sensitive, balanced, and harmonious inner self. He began to have trouble with his superiors and his health suffered." The "frightful events of the war situation depressed him to such a degree that he had lost his peculiar and gay nature completely." Frau Stier believed Americans, coming from a free country, couldn't understand what it was like to be a German teacher. Her husband was the "prototype of a small German official. His advantages are dutiful loyalty, diligence, incorruptibility and loving devotion to his job." These conditions, given his place as a cog in the wheel, resulted in "timidity and fear." Her husband never "dared to oppose an order by a superior." Obedience had become a part of his life, she said, and his sick condition was so severe "he was simply unable to master a situation which fate had imposed on him."

Investigations and evidence from several trials proved that Mauthausen was about as bad as concentration camps ever got, and prisoners had a terrible fear of it. The camp was known for working people to death. Among the enterprises the camp served was the German Earth and Stone Works, Inc. Heinrich Himmler visited the camp two or three times a year. According to Alois Hoellriegl, who had been a guard at both Mauthausen and Wiener-Neudorf, Reichsführer Himmler had a special interest in the infamous quarry; he owned "a large amount of shares." In 1941, Dutch Jews had become the special draft animals of the quarry. They carried the stones up a flight of stairs "consisting of 180 steps." Sometimes they would fall and get beaten until they got up and continued. If they became too ill to work, they were disposed of by any number of methods incorporated into the Mauthausen discipline. Hoellriegl had himself witnessed Jews being driven to the cliffs of the quarry and told to jump. "The prisoners clutched to the ground and tried to hold on, but were hit with sticks until they fell from the cliff and fell down to be smashed." One of the dog handlers felt free to set his "snappish dogs" upon prisoners "when he felt like it."

As the camp leader had told Stier, Wiener-Neudorf was probably better than the main camp if degrees of hell can be said to have significance. Nevertheless, said Hoellriegl, Mauthausen kept the best men for itself.

Among the types sent to out-camps were "professional criminals, sex criminals, priests, murderers, etc."

"You can imagine what went on in those camps," he said. "All imaginable sexual perversions took place because many men had been imprisoned for tens of years." The out-camp prisoners worked among the civilians, including women, where they applied their illegal trades. The prisoners preyed upon each other and "everybody was spying." Guards and prisoners alike were always betraying each other to Hoellriegl, the block leader. He testified that he tried to maintain a middle-of-the road position, but he found it impossible and stayed in trouble with his own superiors because of his "reluctance to make out reports." He testified that weaker men broke down completely or committed suicide. Added to the brutal activities of the prisoners—the professional and sex criminals, the priests, the murderers—was an almost never-ending string of air raids. Sometimes an air raid warning would sound just after the men came back to their barracks, necessitating a forty-five minute walk to the shelter. During a typical 24-hour period, in April 1944, alarms were in effect from 0930 hours to 1300 hours, from 1600 hours to 1730 hours, and from 2200 hours to 2400 hours. Sometimes the men would have to stay up all night and return to the factory to work their twelve-hour shift, literally under the gun, and start all over again the next night. After work, they were harassed by the German obsession with long roll calls that might or might not be related to delousing or bathing. "We had to stand around completely useless sometimes until the hours of the morning and we lost our sleep," a witness testified.

Walter Gaedicke had been imprisoned at Wiener-Neudorf because "I am a religious socialist, a Quaker, and I have been active in the peace society formerly and I have been taken into custody without a trial." He knew of the brutalities at the camp. In fact, he had a friend from Linz, Austria, who had been a stage designer. His friend, a prisoner, had to make a sketch when someone died. His friend had shown him sketches of men hanging on the electric wire that surrounded the camp — or from the rafters. The guard troops functioned at the work places but were not in direct contact with the prisoners. Other guards did that. The guard troops formed a ring around the factory and prevented the escape of the prisoners. They witnessed the hellish society but were slightly removed from it.

Their function as guards came to an end, officially, on the night of March 31, 1945. The Russians were coming, and the camp commander called his staff in, including Stier, to tell them that "evacuation and retreat" was in their future. Like other camps, Wiener-Neudorf would hit the road on Easter Monday, April 2.

The meeting seemed not to be a secret. Several orders involved assignments to middle-level administrators about securing and distributing rations and about providing for transportation for the top camp officials. Stier was asked to determine routes, campsites, and resting places. The camp commander also said that any who fell out of the column and could not go on were to be shot. An order was given that no one was to be left behind in the camp, and several prisoners in the hospital at Wiener-Neudorf who were not fit to travel were taken to the potato bunker and shot on his orders.

Stier testified that he informed his guard troops of the orders. He told them, he said, that it would be none of their concern; the dog leaders would do the shooting.

Before six o'clock in the morning, about 2,500 left the camp in rows of five and in groups of about 100 each. The commander of the transport, a "certain Dr. Taff," rode ahead of the transport on his horse. One of the dog leaders had a small cart pulled by two dogs; he did his killing at the end of the column for the most part. Stier rode up and down the column on his bicycle. The transport was on its way to Steyr, another out-camp of Mauthausen.

Although evidence indicates that the camp larder was very well stocked, the prisoners were issued meager rations to take along. A typical ration was two pounds of sausage, a quarter of a kilo of margarine, and one and a half loaves of bread. Once, on the fourteen-day march, the prisoners were issued a half-liter of very thin semolina soup. Sometimes the men were able to barter for supplies from farmers. Some prisoners exchanged cigarettes for a sheep, and some Russians "cut out parts of a dead horse lying on a roadside." One reason more food was not brought along was that the camp commander used one of the larger trucks to transport his personal belongings.

Hoellriegl was with the column, riding his bicycle, but he had no particular duty. On the first day of the march, he met a woman he knew who had worked in the laundry shop at the camp. She was riding a bicycle, and she asked Hoellriegl if she could join the transport as she too was trying to flee the onslaught of the Russians. Hoellriegl said that "behind our transport a hundred thousand women were fleeing from the Russians because they were scared." Well enough they might have been scared for behind the transport Russian troops were being turned loose on the civilian population to create terrible pain and suffering. Whether the Russians in their counteroffensive inflicted as much suffering on the Germans as the Germans had inflicted upon the Russians during the invasion is a matter of debate, but the Russians had much ground to make up if they were going to even the score. Hoellriegl was not exaggerating. Stier saw Hoellriegl and the woman. He "reproached" Hoellriegl, asking him why he was riding "along all over the place." When he told the captain he had no orders and no functions, Stier ordered him to ride along with him and to assist in finding resting places for the column. Stier allowed the woman to stay with him.

The Wiener-Neudorf transport was not the only march in progress on that particular route. Ahead of them were other transports (one in particular made up of Hungarians) that left their executed dead along the roadside. Sometimes the road was so "cramped" the column could not proceed and had to sit beside the road.

On the first day out, the transport marched forty kilometers. The killing pace was established to pass the point at which the column was vulnerable to attack. They believed the Russians were in a valley which intersected the road on which they were marching, and they set the pace to pass this point before the potential attack. Except for the Russian inmates, neither staff nor prisoners wished to fall into the hands of the Russian Army. After the first day, the pace slowed considerably.

For eight or ten days, the column marched west-southwest toward Steyr, but then they received new orders. The column was ordered to turn directly north and to march to Mauthausen. Steyr, it was feared, was vulnerable to the Russians.

According to Stier, the rest days were generous; another transport had made the march in seven days. The prisoners were not the only ones who needed help. The older, weaker, sicker guards, together with the weaker prisoners, were allowed to hang on to a cart that was being pulled by other guards and prisoners. In spite of the fact that the prisoners' welfare was the concern of the doctors, Stier took it upon himself to encourage prisoners to help each other. Weak guards and ill prisoners were allowed to ride on the kitchen truck to get a rest. Stier wanted everyone to know that he had been compassionate to prisoners. Stier, however, solved tough problems without mercy. He ordered prisoners who could not go on to be shot, and he ordered burial details.

Stier's attorney tried to make much of his disability, but a doctor who was expected to defend him testified that he was in the early stages of his illness during the march. During that period, patients are often highly energized and motivated to work hard and make quick decisions, the doctor said. He could not make an excuse for the teacher-turned-criminal.

By the time of the trial, Stier was extremely ill. He complained early into his cross-examination that he was having trouble concentrating, and he asked for relief. The doctor examined him and said he could detect nothing that would prevent his continuing to testify and otherwise aid in his defense. Nevertheless, the president of the Court ordered a recess on June 20 to give the defendant an opportunity to rest. When court was reconvened on June 23, the doctor testified that Stier had had a heart attack. The trial continued with the consent of the defense, and Stier returned only to hear his death penalty read.

Stier did not make it to the gallows; he died in the hospital shortly after the trial ended.

Alois Hoellriegl had continued with the transport on to Mauthausen, arriving there in the middle of April, but he "deserted" on May 2, just days before the general capitulation of the Nazis. The reasons he gave for his desertion, which he considered a rather daring act, were that he was in danger because he had helped two prisoners escape in late April, he feared the camp commander would order force against the prisoners, and he did not want to fire at Americans if it became necessary to defend the camp. He hid out with a farmer until the SS discovered his whereabouts. From there he fled into the woods. He climbed a "steep fir tree, climbed over to another one until I found a dense spot" and stayed there twenty-four hours living on food the farmer had given him. From his position, he watched "troops of prisoners move about, armed with rifles and machine pistols." When he came down on May 7, the shoes he had hidden in a bush were gone. The farmer who had helped him had been mistaken by the angry prisoners as an SS man and had been shot. Hoellriegl regretted the shooting because the farmer had been giving food to the prisoners as they escaped.

Hoellriegl secured his bicycle from the farm and headed in the direction of Vienna. The roads were crowded as they had been on the march. Guards, escaped or released prisoners, civilians, and members of the German armed forces struggled along the road in a general and desperate chaos. During that time, no one had time to stop and settle old scores. As he neared the Danube ferry on May 8, he heard about the capitulation. "It was a wonderful day in every respect. I was relieved now; I felt like a free man."

As he approached the ferry, he observed whole columns of the Wehrmacht cross the Danube. "They were throwing all their equipment into the Danube; so much radio equipment and so many weapons were flying into the water that a dam was formed almost. The enlisted men were laughing, but the officers had sour expressions on their faces. Everybody was going to Linz, into American captivity." Hoellriegl had heard, however, that "everything up to the Enns River would be Russian by 2400 hours." He turned and rode back to Mauthausen — in a direction where inmates were taking out their revenge on guards. He was recognized by a band of prisoners from the then-defunct Mauthausen camp wandering outside the city Perg. The inmates shook his hand, he said, and did not harm him at all because he had tried to be decent to them. One of the prisoners, a fourteen-year-old boy who had been the youngest prisoner at the camp, told everyone in the group that Hoellriegl had been a good block leader. The wandering prisoners gave him cigarettes and advised him not to return to Mauthausen: advice he declined. Hoellriegl, along with virtually all guards, was later arrested by the Americans, and although he gave statements and testified in many instances, supplying an important picture of life in the work camps, he was held accountable for his own crimes. Evidence would reveal that his accounts of his own movements were self-serving and perhaps suspect. He was hanged for his own murders.

Clemens Wiegand managed to bring dishonor upon himself without going into the snake pits of the concentration camps. He also received one of the most unusual sentences at Dachau. His mother was born in the United States, and he had a brother living in New York. He wrote a rather interesting composition, his Lebenslauf, or life story, for the record. He was well educated and was, like Schopperle and Stier, one of many schoolteachers who disgraced themselves during the Nazi era.

Wiegand was the leader of the local version of the Nazi Party, the Ortsgruppen. He had joined the Storm Troopers in 1933 and joined the Nazi Party in 1935. He soon thereafter became a principal in the local office of the Ortsgruppenleiter and served there until he was drafted into the regular army in the summer of 1939. He was named a sergeant later that year and served in the French campaign. In the summer of 1940, he was discharged and resumed his teaching and Party activities and finally became Ortsgruppenleiter in Frankfurt-am-Main in January 1944. In the early winter of 1944,

Alois Hoellriegl

an American plane was shot down near Ginnheim and several of the crew parachuted safely from the burning plane. One of the airmen, Anthony B. Martin, was being led away with his hands in the air when Wiegand shot him in the head. Wiegand left the scene thinking the airman was dead. Later, someone told him that the airman was still alive. Weigand became "upset" and returned to where the flier lay. A crowd was gathered, several of whom wanted to take the wounded man for help. Weigand and the police drove the crowd from the scene. Then Wiegand and a Wehrmacht officer discussed the man, but the officer eventually left. Wiegand was left alone with the flier with the crowd at a distance. He lit a cigarette and walked around. When he seemed to think no one was noticing, he walked up to the airman and shot him twice in the head with his pistol. It took the airman three hours to die from the wounds.

Wiegand was subjected to an early justice and was tried for his war crime in Heidelberg, Germany, on October 15 and 16, 1945. The review board was to find that his acts were "not committed in the heat of sudden passion, but were planned, deliberate, and vengeful." Wiegand admitted what he did and offered no defense other than to say that he was angry and bitter because of the Allied bombings. He also said that part of his anger was fueled by Nazi propaganda, which told the public that airmen were paid murderers. The Court was equally inflamed by the cold-bloodedness of his act and gave him the highly unusual sentence of death by decapitation.

The review board upheld the death sentence but changed the method from decapitation to hanging, although decapitation was "consistent with German criminal law." They believed decapitation "might offend the sensibilities of the people of the United States."

* * *

Several defendants were tried in Mauthausen case #000-50-5-1, perhaps the most senior being Schopperle. One defendant in particular offered a sad counterpoint to Schopperle and his ilk. His presence at the scene also counters any argument that the Heinrich Buuck situation was unique.

Alfred Richter was the son of a farmer who was owner of a small plot of fields and woods, and he was his father's main workman. He also sometimes worked on a neighboring farm for extra money. Two of his brothers had been killed fighting the Russians in the East.

Richter had been drafted into a construction battalion in 1939 but was sent home in 1940. He was wounded on the eastern front and became unfit for infantry duty. In 1944, he was drafted into the SS and was transferred to guard duty in the concentration camp near Linz. Being unfit for combat, or any number of other activities, did not at this point make him unfit for service in the SS, as was noted in the case of Heinrich Buuck.

A psychiatric report on Richter said that he suffered from "innate imbecility to a considerable degree." Richter could read only his name, could do almost no sums, and actually knew little about farming. "He can only partly grasp the meaning of questions and therefore the answers he gives are mostly wrong. He is unable to follow the course of conversation, cannot concentrate on a subject, and is abnormally forgetful."

The psychiatrist believed he could not "discern right and wrong, good and bad." He was not capable of understanding a trial and should not be held responsible for anything he might have done.

In the chaotic last years of the war, the impaired Richter was only one more burden for the prisoners among the old, sick men, the criminals, the wounded, the insane, and the intellectual misfires who had dominion over them. It was suggested that other guards amused themselves by taking advantage of his limitations.

Witnesses testified that Richter had trouble with everyone. "He always spurred prisoners on to march faster and in this way he threw the column out of order and then he complained on this ground and beat prisoners with his rifle butt."

Richter tried to testify in his own behalf. His lawyer asked him when he had been assigned to Camp Linz III (also described in the testimony as Camp Klein-München).

"'44."

"What part of '44? Can you remember?"

"When I came to Camp Linz III."

"Was that early in '44 or late in '44?"

"'44."

"When did you first know you were accused of beating a man with a rifle butt?" his lawyer asked.

"No, nothing," he answered.

"It was testified here by a witness that you struck somebody with a rifle butt, causing serious injury," his lawyer stated.

"No," said Richter.

"How far did you go in school?"

"School?"

"Yes."

"I didn't get far in school. My mind is too limited."

"Have you noticed any improvement since you went to school?" his lawyer asked.

"I never could get along in school. I never could do the work. I didn't move on."

"Did you get promoted in the army?"

"What am I supposed to say?"

When his lawyer rephrased the question, Richter gave a mangled description of his promotion over the years from private to corporal. "Can you tell the Court why you have no witnesses here for you?" his lawyer asked.

"I can't bring any witness. I am alone. I am independent."

The prosecutor had only three questions for Richter. He inquired as to when Richter had become a member of the Waffen SS and whether he knew it was wrong to beat a prisoner (the second question being asked twice). Richter was unable to give answers to the questions.

The Court had no questions and the president of the Court excused Richter and sent him to the dock while the trial continued. Before the sentencing, Richter was asked if he wished to introduce evidence of extenuating circumstances or make any further statement to the Court.

"Everything is true, and I didn't go voluntarily, and I never was punished while in the Wehrmacht, and then I went to the SS from the Wehrmacht," was his answer.

The Court gave Richter life imprisonment, but on review the sentence and conviction were disapproved.

6

Everybody Believed It: The Story of Wilhelm Grill

Although no explanation seems readily available — no associated career or even education — young Wilhelm Grill was a masterly writer. His writing is further enhanced by the work of a translator so skillful that the researcher must read, far down into the paper, a translator's note that a verb is missing in the text to recall that the paper was not originally written in English. Grill's work is self-serving and blame-placing, but it gives a vivid, compelling picture of how young people were consumed by the Nazi culture and, step by step, of how they became disillusioned.

Grill was only a baby when World War I ended. He was a little boy when the NSDAP gained a foothold in Germany. When the breathtaking Nazi flag became a ubiquitous feature of the cityscape, he was an adolescent — wide-eyed and easily impressed. He joined the Hitler Youth because he liked playing in the band. He knew nothing of politics at that time, he said.

He wrote that young Germans had never learned the "difference between democracy and dictatorship." The older men who had fought in World War I defended the Nazis, and young Germans were taught to respect their elders. "They enlightened us constantly about the disgrace Germany had suffered in 1918" and they told young Germans "that from now on this would be changed." It was an emotional argument, he said.

When Grill became a very young member of the SS, the German people would greet them "with deafening cheers." This had a deep emotional effect on the young men and further convinced them they were doing the job their nation needed. He wondered how those who formulated the the-

ory could be wrong. "Our own people succeeded by means of propaganda in drumming into our
minds that our method of living,
our views, and our aims were in-
fallible. Everything foreign was
vilified and ridiculed." This was
possible because of their youth and
the ignorance of those hearing the
message, he believed.

Further, the young people
could see dramatic examples of
progress, including road building
and industrial development. Germany was always signing agree-
ments with other nations leading
them to believe their nation was
making an "everlasting peace with
the rest of the world. If anyone had
said to us at that time that everything was done in preparation for a
future war, we would have considered him insane."

Wilhelm Grill

Looking back upon his younger years, he believed the regime realized
that youth are basically good; they had appealed to their conscience and
sense of honor. Adults had a responsibility to perceive the truth, but "the
people, everybody believed it." Then everything was too late. He said the
"Chauvinism started" and Germany became a "flexible tool" in the hands
of the Nazis. Because "the few opponents were arrested, a warning voice
never made itself heard."

During his youth, Grill apparently did not identify the persecution
of Jews as being a direct aspect of the Nazi philosophy. He seemed to think
of it as a social problem outside the cause for which he would give his
honor. He wrote that he was opposed to this behavior, found it revolting,
did not ever participate in it, and kept up contacts with his "partly Jewish" acquaintances even up to the time of the Dachau trials.

In 1934, the eighteen-year-old Grill lost his job and one of his friends
suggested he consider the Armed (Waffen) SS. He joined, in part, because
"conscription was instituted in 1936 and I would have been drafted anyway." He didn't bother with politics in the SS at the time but "understood
my job to be a strictly military affair." Grill claimed that he was taken into

the NSDAP at Dachau "without his knowledge" several days before he arrived there personally. "At that time all young age groups were taken into the Party according to their duties. As an SS man, one could not very well refuse without being discharged immediately." (This attitude would be in contrast to attitudes that developed later in the war; the SS could not have cared less if men like Buuck belonged to the Party. And not all members of the SS belonged to the Nazi Party.) It is likely Grill, given his support for the Nazi policies, would have had no objections anyway. In 1937, when Grill went to Dachau, he believed the inmates were legal detainees — as most of them were, at least according to German law — and, further, he believed "the guarding of opponents of the regime belonged in the [military] category."

In 1938, he joined the Reich's Labor Service (RAD) to fulfill his obligation to the state. Later he joined the regular German army when war broke out and was severely wounded. His recovery lasted a year and a half, and he was left with a useless right hand with painful nerve damage.

Grill displayed some confusion as to when (at what age and experience) German citizens should have understood the true nature of the Nazis and their allies. It's also a bit unclear as to whether disappointment with the failure of the system or an awareness of the immorality of the corrupt culture first inspired his disillusionment — or indeed the disillusionment of the collective German society. Grill simply believed that mature individuals should have detected those flaws. His summary was that awareness came with disappointment, and cold, hard knowledge came with disaster and failure. The disillusionment that began to grow among the young as the unthinkable war gained momentum became an avalanche of hatred for the failed Nazis after the war, according to Grill. On the other hand, thousands, younger than Grill, who were teenagers and adolescents near the end of the war, (members of the Hitler Youth in particular), were rabid in their enthusiasm for the cause and tried to keep fighting after the capitulation.

For Grill, there was an uneasy feeling when, in 1939, he found himself in a war he never believed would happen. His terrible war wound hardened his heart further. By the time he was thirty years old and subject to the trials at Dachau, the very camp where he had been a guard as a teenager, he was ready to paint sweeping strokes of guilt on many segments of society. He would even at some point assume his part of the guilt.

The Nazis used a technique of governing that could roughly be called "organization." Unlike other dictators who attempted to hold all power, Hitler distributed power — real power. Ian Kershaw in his book *The Nazi Dictatorship* refers to Gauleiters as "regional chieftains" and says, "Hitler invariably sided with his Gauleiter (or, rather, with the strongest Gauleiter) in any dispute with central authority or government ministries, protecting their interests and at the same time securing himself a powerful body of support, loyal to him and to no one else." Party leaders in small villages, frequently constables or police chiefs, held so much power that people feared them. Village guards dressed in beribboned, spectacular uniforms, and they preened, strutted, and gave orders almost as they pleased. Much of what happened in Nazi Germany was not due to direction; it was due to opportunity provided by the peculiarities of the system. Grill would look back upon this and recognize it for what it was.

As Grill matured, he wrote, he began to see that "generals and leading men" took advantage of this power and opportunity. "All these gentlemen were thrilled about the bloody successes wrought by the young Germans true to their country. The ordinary soldier, bound to his oath, was like a toy in their hands." They believed they were defending their homeland. In retrospect, he believed his superiors knew very early on that they were involved in a "criminal undertaking." After the war, he said, the leadership to a man claimed they had been merely the recipients of orders. They claimed to be "small clerks, as small and wretched as they had once been great and unapproachable." He believed insanity determined the orders passed from desks at the home front, and his superiors handed down their orders in the same manner. At the end of the war, "those very gentlemen who are the most eloquent in denying their guilt are the ones to be blamed. All political threads of that time unite in their hands." Just as the common soldier had borne the burdens of the ugly society and its war, the youth were, at the Dachau trials, bearing the burdens of punishment that should have been placed on their superiors. The generals had had an opportunity to understand, evaluate, and denounce the culture whereas the youth had not. "If, in 1939, they would have prevented everything, this terrible misery affecting all the people would not have started. The very same holds true for the world of politics. The leaders knew the plans for future power very well." He wondered how it came about that Germany wanted to conquer "everything." He also wondered how those who joined the Party as far back as the late twenties, when Nazis had no significant power, could plead compulsion and coercion. Unlike the youth, they were not transferred into the Party without knowing it. In fact, those who should have known better plunged straight ahead. They moved upward in their careers, enjoyed the spoils of leadership and opportunity, and indulged whatever grievances and perversions they might have harbored. Grill wanted the world to know that because Nazism was the invention of and had the support of mature, thinking adults, it was a conspiracy and a deliberate, criminal act.

In one sense, many of the walking wounded who could no longer function on the front line were destined to be transferred to the concentration camps. Being assigned to a concentration camp meant a meeting with an even more profound destiny.

Those being assigned duties at concentration camps were subject to continuing propaganda. They were told of the criminal nature of Poles and Spaniards and how these people endangered Germany. This was easy to believe, and it was only years later "when I had established closer contacts with many inmates that everything [began] to appear to me in a different light."

By the time Grill went to Gusen I to serve at the post office installation for the infamous Mauthausen concentration camp, he was married. Because of his injury and its associated difficulties, he spent his nonworking hours at home. Life was not easy for returning veterans. The camp personnel had established a hierarchy, and those who were flawed in any manner were put upon by more able guards and administrators. The hard time even extended to wounded veterans. His superiors hated him because he secluded himself. He was told that he was "half a man, too soft, cannot be used for anything."

Grill began to watch the concentration camp change in other ways. When the war against Russia started, he began to see the hated Russian POWs arrive. He recalled that twenty-eight Dutch Jews arrived as a result of the "Night and Fog" decree. Then prisoners from other conquered and occupied lands began to arrive and fill up the camp.

One of Grill's main assignments was to try to maintain camp secrecy. "Strict supervision had to be exercised because all affairs had to be kept secret [labor methods, sickness]; that held true for the SS men also." Grill was responsible for censoring the mail of those who could send and receive mail. "Any prisoner, regardless of where he is, will always try to evade the given instructions. He has to expect punishment if he is caught." People tried to relay accounts of what was happening in the camp, using the mail as their method. Every time anyone was caught breaking the rules, he was given twenty-five "strokes" and sent to a "penal company." Grill took the order seriously and tried to carry out the duty. He also knew he was subject to punishment if he did not do the job properly. Sometimes letters were checked again by officers. "Cases of negligence would have been severely punished." (It was just so for American operations. However, America, with all its mistakes, never set up anything that resembled the Mauthausen concentration camp.)

Understanding Grill's attitude toward beating-as-prison-control is difficult. Out of a sort of kindness, Grill usually did not report infractions.

He punished the culprit by withholding mail for a month and "in serious cases with a few strokes" with his clumsy left hand. Prisoners begged him to administer this punishment instead of reporting them, he would write. He seemed to know that beating was wrong, and, if his statements are to be believed, he tried to avoid the practice. His claim that beating the prisoners was to their long-range good is offset by the deduction that the beatings were to his own long-range good. Other defendants tried to justify their acts as walking the fine line between good and evil as best they could, but Grill, because of his gift for expressing himself, could easily set the moralist to pondering the situation. The Court would not be impressed by the arguments in Grill's case, although they were apparently swayed by similar arguments in some cases as noted in this book.

For the most part, prisoners were not allowed to receive parcels during the early years. When it became more difficult to feed the prisoners, parcels from families were again allowed. Although Grill had not been allowed inside the camp (the post office was an adjunct operation), when parcels began to be allowed he had to go inside the camp to supervise.

In 1942 and 1943, only Germans and Poles were allowed to get packages, and all mail had to be written in German. The prisoners were not limited in the amount that could be in their parcel, but they could only receive what they could eat in two days. The excess was taken from them and distributed to those who received no parcels or to "heavy laborers." Young Poles or Russians (many were in their middle teens) and sick prisoners were also given these "excess" resources — all this according to Grill.

The standard procedure was for those receiving parcels to come to a table and open their packages while inspectors watched and made decisions about the contents. Much of the parcel contents had value beyond the calories that could be provided. The prisoners used it for barter, sometimes trading for favors from the guards.

One of the charges against Grill was rifling the mail. He insisted that he only censored the mail — an honorable thing for a wounded soldier to do. "Not a single prisoner can accuse me of having benefited financially during the entire time of my service. I was too much a soldier for that sort of thing, and as such I always acted according to my instructions. I was never punished during the entire time of my service; in line with my education I would have regarded it as disgrace." Opportunity existed for Grill, just as it did for the superiors he despised, to take advantage of rank and situation. Such opportunities even existed for prisoners, especially those who handled the plunder taken from transports entering the death camps. Did Grill serve for years amid parcels containing food and other hard-to-get items without taking anything home to his young wife during desperate times? He swore he never did — that he never put need ahead of duty. Perhaps he was human; or perhaps he was extraordinary. Independent evidence was never offered to tip the scale in either direction.

Grill said he got into trouble for not making reports about parcel smuggling. They needed to know that in Berlin. His superior mentioned escape plans hidden in walnuts as being a possibility. "If nothing of that sort has occurred, you will have to make up some cases yourself. I do not care how you do it, but I need the material," he was told. He refused and was told he was stupid and useless.

He had little respect for certain kinds of prisoners. "There were prisoners at the camp who constantly destroyed human life." He knew that a camp senior — a flunky of the administration — was responsible for the deaths of up to eighty fellow inmates by drowning or beating. He recalled that others were responsible for drowning "hundreds" in barrels. Prisoners stabbed and hanged other inmates, or chased each other into the electric fence. The strong "had the law on his side in cases of gambling, prostitution and the camp brothel, of informing, of homosexual activities or purely personal hatred." Most of these activities took place at night (when day workers would not have been present). These criminal sorts were often the ones put in charge of other prisoners by camp supervisors. The prison flunkies had too much freedom, he believed. A large number of these criminal inmates were murdered by other inmates in the concentration camps and on transports during the chaotic liberation phase.

Grill definitely did not like duty in the concentration camp post office. Most especially, he did not like officers. He wondered that they were not expected to offer excuses for being drunk "for days" while the subordinates worked sixteen or eighteen hours straight. They met every fourteen days with the commandant and discussed happenings in the camps. They had no excuse for denying they knew everything going on. "The camp did not extend for miles; it can be regarded as a small two-family house where everyone knew everyone else." The officers took morning coffee and their noon and evening meals together. They talked at the officers' club. Every detail reported all incidents to them every time they returned from work. He begged for understanding for the ordinary SS man. "Should those who defiled us spiritually and emotionally, who deprived us of every joy of life, who added fright and fear to the heavy duty, be less guilty today?"

When the general-duty SS men were sent away to more important service in 1943 after severe losses in the East, Grill volunteered for front-line duty in spite of his injury. That met with much disfavor. "Then I tried in a different way. I absolutely had to leave." He tried to get a discharge, but his superior interrupted that move. However, he did find a way to be away from the post office almost full-time. He took charge of the National Socialist Welfare (NSV) office. His office began sending children to the country, secured Adolf Hitler scholarships for youth, made collections and took care of people who were bombed out. In name, he was still in charge of the post office. Soon the superior he disliked most wanted to get into charity work. He added these responsibilities. He tried to help refugees from the Eastern conflict and the relatives of war casualties. He stayed in charge of the post office in name until July 1944, when he was relieved by a new postal chief. He continued his social work until May 2, 1944, and managed to help 1,700 refugees. He was captured by the Americans on May 5, 1945.

Grill's heavy criticism extends to the Americans. While as self-serving as his other statements, it is still possible that he gave an accurate picture of what it was like to be awaiting trial for war crimes.

After he was captured in May 1945, he was sent from prison camp to prison camp in Austria. His weight plummeted to 44 or 45 kilograms (less than a hundred pounds). All his personal possessions—watch, ring, fountain pen, underwear, and the glove used to cover his hand for medical purposes—were taken. "Our hair was shaved off and we were painted yellow." They were worked more than thirteen hours a day and they were mistreated "constantly." He wrote that they slept on concrete without blankets, and when an American interrogated them in a building with water standing on the floor, the Americans said, "No dog lives like this in the United States."

From May 1945 until early 1947, Grill readily admitted hitting prisoners, and he believed he and his fellows deserved punishment "for having believed our leaders and having served as their tools." During all this time he was never accused of anything more serious than hitting the prisoners. He, perhaps conveniently, never used the word "beating" to describe his assaults. Suddenly, in 1947, line-ups began. He was accused of brutalizing and killing people. He was shocked and never varied from his plea of innocence in these matters. He never tried to cut a deal.

Again, he found someone to blame. He blamed professional witnesses. Former prisoners, he said, gave testimony for trade. For a few packs of tobacco, the blame for murder was shifted from one person to another. He said the rate of exchange between internees and commission members was one liter of schnapps to twenty packages of tobacco, a statement which seems not to make sense (given the syntax) unless he is saying commission members gave former prisoners and guards rewards which ranged from schnapps to tobacco for giving incriminating evidence. It cannot be denied that trials were rushed and defendants had little opportunity to present a sophisticated defense, but bribing witnesses would seem an unlikely and unnecessary activity for commission members; at war's end, decaying bodies lay in piles all over Germany and were even scattered along the very walks prisoners and guards traveled to get from one part of the camps to another. These bodies alone provided enough evidence to support the claim that atrocities had occurred. Prosecutors had thousands of witnesses to choose from in occupied territory. Grill also claimed that those who refused to give in were threatened with incriminating evidence. This seems within the circles of possibility with investigating personnel interpreting the action as legitimate pressure and the defendants, with their experience and traditions, seeing it as a life-threatening demand.

Then came the next phase of his ordeal, according to his recollection. He was informed of the new charges on May 20, 1947, and his trial began on June 13. Except for one charge that he received two days prior to the trial, he did not know the charges to be placed against him until he went to court. He had no opportunity to determine which witnesses he might need. Those he did call could not appear because of such short notice. He was given no interview with his American lawyer but could only write notes to him. His German lawyer interviewed all six of the defendants in the trial together, only once, and then for not more than five minutes. The trial happened so fast it was "breathtaking." After he was condemned to death and the penalty confirmed by the review board, his elegantly written, well-thought-out petition for additional review seems to have been lost. His lawyer "could not find this petition of review or its English translation at the War Crimes Group of the Military Government of Bavaria."

Grill sent a copy of his original petition together with a new, more organized petition that would seem the equal of any lawyer. He claimed infringement of several rights: (1) the right to receive a copy of accusations before the trial, (2) reasonable access to an attorney, (3) adjournment for purposes of acquiring witnesses and planning a defense, and (4) the right to bring with him or have summoned by the court those whom he would have named as witnesses.

In his petition, Grill countered the testimony of all witnesses with arguments his defense attorney had not made for him. Several witnesses testified that they had seen him "at the door" of the bathhouse and inside the house where "death baths" were given. Grill countered that for the brief hours he was there, the "bath" had no doors, walls, or windows; it was an open-air facility while he was at the camp. A witness said Grill was present when inmates were drowned in water twenty inches deep when the height of the basin was only about ten inches. The bath could not be seen from the blocks where the witnesses said they were watching. Two months before the trial, a witness had said he knew nothing of Grill except that he was associated with the post office, but at the trial his contradictory statements were accepted. A witness said Grill had joined in beating inmates with another SS man at a time well after that SS man had been transferred out of the camp. A witness claimed to have seen the death baths during a time when he (the witness) was actually working at the stone quarry. A witness testified that on a particular Saturday, Grill had chosen for punishment between two and three thousand inmates from an invalid's block that could, at capacity, hold only three hundred people. Finally, he objected to the fact that an accused person "may be sentenced to death by reason of written depositions whose origin cannot be controlled [and by a] witness who had been guilty of the robbery-murder of a seventy-six-year-old woman [but] was not made available for cross-examination." Trustworthy records do not exist to prove Grill's appeal statements correct, but it's difficult to believe that all the testimony and depositions entered into the trial record would have stood up to a good cross-examination.

Grill also claimed that his trial lawyer wanted to hurry things up and told the defendants that if they tried to call witnesses, a "chief witness for the prosecution" would be called against him. Grill objected to the tactics and his lawyer "declared without my having asked him to do so" that the defense would rest.

"I have never made any secret of what I had done; but I shall defend myself to the very last breath against the suggestion that I had committed any murders, or that I had taken part in any, or that I had perpetrated any cruelties. I am ready to take the penalty for what I did."

Mauthausen was one of the most brutal societies ever created by human beings. Humans were shorn of any bit of human dignity and were humiliated and brutalized unmercifully by the SS and by their fellow prisoners. Thousands were worked to death or murdered outright. It took many willing persons to do the evil deeds, and, to be sure, everyone charged claimed blamelessness or innocence. Was Grill one of the most brutal of all, or was he a helpless, innocent man caught up in a feeding frenzy represented by the military trials?

As time would have it, Grill did not exit history in the throes of a Shakespearean tragedy. He would drift back into society as a relatively young man and join the company of many other young men who escaped the gallows. Together with his lawyers, Grill put together a collection of affidavits to rival that of any of the other defendants. His affidavits would fill a sizable volume. He had statements affirming that he was indeed a very good person and could only have participated at the low level he admitted because of the stranglehold Nazi education had over the youth of Germany. The review board was no more impressed with the statements than with his excellent memoir. His folder contained a stack of statements from fellow SS men and assorted fellow workers. These, of course, had no impact. His plea for clemency was rejected because this was not new evidence. Former prisoners wrote many letters saying he had been at least as good as he had stated in his own defense. The review board was almost never impressed by these testimonies. Finally, the right letter came in. A prisoner at the camp who was assigned to the infamous bath house, an educated and distinguished gentleman, a professional pathologist who evaluated the degree of life left in abused fellow prisoners, wrote that he was at the bath house during all the period in question and that never — not even once — had Grill been in that part of the camp. The review board at last believed there was doubt about Grill's part in the torture deaths. His sentence was reduced to twenty-seven years. He was saved.

During his years in prison, Grill failed to get the least bit of sympathy from the guards and administrators. He whined constantly. He fumed that he was not guilty of anything that would merit the imprisonment. He did attend school and received a certificate as a locksmith, but he was reprimanded for repairing the watches of fellow inmates and pocketing the money. His supervisors said he used his imprisonment to gain sympathy. He was also "nervous." He was not an easy person to like, and he had the ability to get on the nerves of everyone around him merely by being present.

In 1954, he was finally allowed to admit he had done some things that were wrong, to say he was sorry, and to assure those in charge that he had benefited from his imprisonment. These statements were required from those who had any hope of being paroled, and it worked for Grill as it had for others. During this time, most remaining prisoners learned the lesson of confession and expressed guilt. He went home to his young wife, to his baby who had become a nine-year-old schoolboy in his absence, and to his elderly parents.

7

Laws Governing Land Warfare: Americans in the Hands of an Angry Mob

It is settled law that civilians of one belligerent nation may be tried and punished before a duly constituted tribunal of another belligerent nation for violations of international laws governing land warfare. When a civilian wrongfully assaults enemy persons who have fallen into their hands as prisoners of war, or aids, abets, or participates in such wrongful assault it is an offense falling within the scope of this rule.

[A summary of concepts offered in argument against German citizens who had killed or abused prisoners of war.]

As the war progressed and the balance of power began to shift to the Allied Forces, warplanes were a constant threat to Germany and occupied France. With the initiative, a rain of airmen from disabled aircraft began falling over villages and fields. They were falling into trees and onto the roofs of houses. They were falling into the hands of civilians who were infuriated by the destruction they were causing. Hardly a German in the area of a bombing target was spared personal injury or the injury or death of friends and family. This anger was compounded by real, or perceived, directives that promised civilians they would not be prosecuted if they killed airmen, especially Americans. In fact, many local officials believed they were under direct orders from Berlin to execute airmen.

As the trials associated with the murder or abuse of downed airmen continued, the orders or directives that permitted (or required) attacks on airmen were variously attributed to Martin Bormann, Heinrich Himmler, or Joseph Goebbels. They came to the population by way of secret orders or they were announced in newspapers or on the radio, according to those offering excuses. Most likely, the facts and rumors were intermingled and did not originate from a single source. The secondary sources were speeches, comments, and written opinions or interpretations by various German officials of some significant rank. Trial reviews show that the directives were secret *and* published abroad, depending upon origin, and Bormann, Himmler, and Goebbels were indeed major sources of the initiatives.

In the villages, women and older men tended fields and shops. Children beyond kindergarten age had duties around the homes, shops, or farms. Most villages had a local version of the Nazi Party with the leader being a mayor or some other village-level authority who took his job and his status seriously, and almost everyone who could limp about was in the home guard. Villages had a certain number of discharged soldiers so badly wounded they were unfit for military service — or even service at a concentration camp. Each village had a constable or small police force. Crime was apparently quite low but the police were kept busy in the last years of the war rounding up deserters and returning them to military authorities. Mobs that gathered around downed airmen sometimes contained displaced persons or "refugees." Many of these foreigners were among those who tried to provide some protection for airmen. All village idiots had not been sent to guard prisoners; many were at home tending farms as best they could and doing other jobs within their capacity. It was the same for the mentally ill. Sometimes military men were home on leave. It was also suggested by trial evidence that some men too old for real fighting enjoyed strutting and playing the part of local men of significance. Virtually none of them were fit for combat. However, hundreds, perhaps several thousand, to one extent or another, either killed, abused, or abetted the death and abuse of downed airmen.

In late April 1944, an American flier bailed out over Micholfold, Germany. His parachute collapsed in midair and he fell on soft dirt, making an indentation nearly two feet deep. Karl Mack, who townspeople testified was gravely impaired mentally, rushed up to the airman and hit him in the head with a pole. Three witnesses testified that Mack was not at the scene, but Mack himself admitted he was. He also stated that he hit the airman with the pole to make himself look more important before the public. He said the airman was already dead. In fact, the airman was taken to a hospital where he died later the same day. Mack was acquitted.

When a plane went down near his farm, Wilhelm Paland was working in his field. He ran over to the pilot and tried to hit him, but he thought he missed because the pilot bent backward. A witness thought he missed also because the pilot was so tall. Karl Stieg was just entering his barnyard with a wagonload of wheat. It was August and harvesttime. By the time he got to the pilot, about ten people were already gathered around. Hermann Linne had been the first to get to the pilot and he had taken him into his custody. He was cursing at Stieg and the others around who were trying to hit the airman. He bodily separated them from the pilot. He told them if they wanted to fight Americans, they should volunteer to go to the war front. Fritz Teuteberg was there too. He said the "pilot threw himself to the ground and I slightly tapped him with my knee." Paland got two years for whacking the tall pilot. The court interpreted Teuteberg's "tapping with his knee" as kicking; they gave him four years. Thanks to Linne's interference at the scene, Stieg's swinging arms had not connected and he was acquitted.

In June 1944, a four-motored American bomber crash landed near Mittenwald, and the nine crewmen aboard were taken into custody by members of the German Armed Forces. A huge crowd, perhaps up to 1,000 citizens, gathered around the airmen, many of them screaming, "Beat them to death!" More than "80 percent" were women. The soldiers were evidently making some effort to protect the airmen, but they were outnumbered by the inflamed crowd. Several citizens assaulted the airmen. They kicked and beat the airmen with their fists. The assailants, when brought to trial in 1946, seemed not to be repentant. Charlotte Battalo had become "madly" angry when she saw the airmen walking along chewing gum, she said. She had been bombed out of her home in Berlin and had not been able to recover any of her belongings. When she saw the excited crowd, she rode her bicycle over and pushed through the crowd to the airmen. She screamed insults at them and began hitting those airmen marching at the end of the column as they were being taken into custody by the soldiers. She thought she was the first to assault the airmen.

Other evidence suggested that Battalo was wrong, and she did not get the ultimate credit for being the first to strike an airman. Georg Gruendel had been in the military but had been discharged because of a nervous condition. He threw clumps of earth at the airmen and hit them with a piece of rotten wood he found lying along the road. He also slapped and kicked them when he could reach them. His excuse was that he was "overly excited" because of the air raids that day over nearby Munich.

Maria Hegele was also mad as hell. She had been bombed out of her house, could not stay in the air-raid shelter because of fumes, and joined the crowd out of curiosity. She jumped at one of the fliers, "shouting hysterically." She spat at him and hit him in the face.

Mathias Schandl was a farmer who was sheltering evacuees. Some days he had to feed fifty or sixty persons. The downed plane had flown within one hundred meters of his home. He became excited by the situation and grabbed an umbrella from a woman in the crowd and hit an airman several times with it. He also kicked and beat them "to move them forward." He claimed the soldiers had asked for his help with the airmen. He also ripped a pair of earphones off an airman because someone mistook them for a portable radio.

Erhardt Erdt, a butcher in the town, picked up a bicycle pump and hit one of the fliers until it was bent. The noisy crowd was angry that he didn't hit more and hit sooner. They spat on him because he didn't. He also pleaded excitement as his defense.

Only one of the airmen received a significant injury, and all were able to walk away from the scene to the custody and fragile protection of the German Armed Forces.

On July 28 of that same year, flier Peter Mandros escaped his bomber when it crashed near Bauerheim, and he was picked up by a local farmer. Mandros was uninjured and offered no resistance. The farmer took him into the village where he left him with the wife of the village mayor. Shortly thereafter, Willi Rieke and Karl Schenk, both home guard officers, came to the mayor's office. Rieke, fifty-six, gave his occupation as a "sports instructor." He was a member of the NSDAP. He was also the commander of his home guard unit.

The two men took the flier away in a car. Rieke drove with Mandros at his side while Schenk rode in the back seat and held a carbine on Mandros. Schenk said that as they drove over a bridge, Rieke stopped the car and ordered the flier out of the car. "I then heard Rieke load his pistol." The flier stood beside the road with his hands raised above his head. Rieke fired two or three times at Mandros and the flier fell to the ground with a wound in his left chest. Then Rieke got down beside the flier and fired two or three shots into his head behind the left ear.

According to the several witnesses who saw the shooting, Rieke got into his car and drove on. People stayed in the vicinity and watched as the flier kept moving. Within a few minutes, Rieke drove back to the scene and fired yet another shot into the flier's head. Mandros was taken to the morgue and later that afternoon to the cemetery where he still showed "nervous motions."

Rieke told Schenk that when he got back to the office he was to report that "the flier was shot while escaping or while trying to escape." It might have worked for the short run, but Schenk and several other witnesses testified against him. In February 1947, Rieke was found guilty and was sentenced to death by hanging.

Eric Mette and Otto Peters were military men home on leave. Both were twenty-three years of age, both had a grammar school education, and both had been in the Hitler Youth organization as teens. Mette had had no real life outside the needs of the German government. He was drafted into the Labor Service when he was sixteen and was then drafted into the Waffen SS where, over almost five years, he served on both fronts and was wounded in action on four separate occasions. He said he had received training concerning his conduct as a member of the "German race." He had been taught to obey orders and that the death penalty would be invoked if he did not. Sergeant Mette had heard on the radio and read in the newspapers that Goebbels said it was the duty of every German soldier to treat American fliers as criminals. Mette's house had been destroyed by an American bomb.

Peters had volunteered for the Navy in 1941, was a corporal, and served until the end of the war. He would offer no complicated explanation or defensive justification for his actions.

The procedure for military personnel on leave was to report to the local authority as soon as they arrived home, and they were to obey his orders while on leave. In their town that man was one Herr Kremling. Both Mette and Peters followed that order.

A downed American airman was apprehended in the village and taken to a restaurant while Mette and Peters were home on leave. Later that day, he was seen sitting on a bench outside the restaurant between Mette and Peters, both of whom were in uniform. Kremling gave Mette a pistol and told him to take the airman in the direction of a nearby town and shoot him on the way. Mette and Peters walked. The airman pushed a bicycle on which his parachute had been placed. It was unclear whether Peters actually knew Mette had orders to shoot the airman. He said Mette did it while he (Peters) had stopped to tie his shoe. Mette said that Peters did not know that he was going to shoot the airman at the exact time, but Peters, later that day, when he was asked what had happened to the airman, said, "We shot him." Mette reported the shooting at the police station and was given twenty cigarettes.

Peters's father testified that his son cried about the incident. He had said, "Yes, father, I know what I did. We did unjustly. I am sorry we did it but I can't change it now."

Peters was born in April 1923, was baptized a month later, and was confirmed in the Evangelic Lutheran Church in 1938 when he was fifteen.

He went to the village school where learning came somewhat slowly for the good-natured, pleasant boy. He had lots of "playmates" and played with neighborhood children in the yards of family friends. The entire Peters family dressed up and went to church regularly, and the congregation was always impressed by their kind, polite children. Peters grew up as the proper child of an old, respected family of excellent reputation. They lived a gentle life among family and friends.

On the contrary, the village had been terrified of the local Nazi leader, Kremling, who ordered the killing. He was described as "a brute," and he "ruled the whole community by his violent reign of terror." On the day of the murder, Kremling ordered Bernhard Heinemann to build a coffin for the airman. He specifically ordered something "crude." Heinemann instead built a coffin that was decent and in keeping with German customs for Christians. Kremling became angry. "I was roughly and mean[ly] insulted by this man" for having built a decent coffin, Heinemann said. Kremling would not allow the coffin to be used and ordered the airman to be buried without a coffin. Heinemann thought young Peters was deathly afraid of Kremling.

The Lutheran pastor testified that Kremling was ambitious, false from his heart, and an ardent Nazi. Kremling had ordered a plaque placed above the airman's grave that read, "Here lies a murderer pilot."

Heinemann and everyone else around town were relieved when the criminal Kremling hanged himself in 1945, supposedly to escape the sure justice that was expected to be his lot. Mette's father testified that Kremling, who had taken advantage of the boys' position as servicemen, was "not a man, but a bandit."

Mette, perhaps because of his experience, was more mature and had a greater understanding of the world than Peters. He had seen the face of war up close, and killing an enemy might not have seemed an improper act to him. When he was 30, he would say that he could not comprehend the person he was as a young man. Mette, however, enjoyed the same affection of his community as Peters had. The communities would join together to pass a resolution asking for mercy and understanding for their young men.

Although Peters was given life imprisonment and Mette was given the penalty of death by hanging, America would be kind. Peters's sentence would be reduced considerably, and Mette's sentence, through clemency, would be reduced to life imprisonment, and then to twenty-seven years. Their crime, however heinous, was not to be compared with those of mass murderers, and the review board would also note the part Kremling had played. The factor most cited in deliberations was the age of the men at the time of the crime. If mercy was to be given anyone, Peters and Mette probably gave the board as good an excuse as anyone else.

Both men progressed well in prison. Mette was reprimanded for failing to keep his tools properly listed, and Peters was reprimanded for running in the cell block, but that would not be held against them when they applied for parole. Both men had some trouble during the early weeks of their parole, however. Peters was warned for taking a short vacation in the mountains after he was released. He said his doctor told him he was "sick" and needed a rest, but he apologized and resumed proper parole behaviors immediately. Mette had become engaged to a young war widow with a child who lived in the Eastern Zone. He also took a short unauthorized "vacation" and left his first employment without permission. He was told he would not be able to marry and might even be returned to prison if he couldn't straighten himself out immediately. He secured approved employment and his parole supervisors blessed the marriage plans. Peters and Mette were among thousands of young men who escaped the ultimate punishment and were allowed to return to society upon the simple promise that they were sorry and would make good citizens. Most apparently made good on their promises.

Technically, to be a Nazi was to belong to the NSDAP; however, the word became a derogatory term for those who belonged to any organization that furthered the Nazi cause, or to persons, party members or not, who by acts of commission or omission furthered the cause. Thousands, even millions, of Germans identified with the Nazis in one fashion or another. Still, "Nazi" and "German" are not synonyms. As Wilhelm Grill said, many were fooled and caught unaware. Many found it virtually impossible to resist without risking their lives and the well-being of their families. Many tried to stay out of the mire. Others resisted in underground groups. According to Dietrich Orlow in *A History of Modern Germany*, at least 11,000 persons were executed by the Germans between the beginning of 1943 and the end of the war for participation in anti–Nazi activities. Some resisted actively and openly. Johann Friedrich Wilhelm Loser had such a background, and that background earned him the benefit of the doubt when his enemies suggested his name to the Americans as a war criminal.

Loser served in the regional government. He had been a member of the NSDAP, but was expelled in March 1945. He had disobeyed orders to turn over prisoners of war, including downed airmen, to the SS and the Gestapo to be shot. He had instead delivered them to the Wehrmacht where he believed they would be recognized as prisoners of war with the protections of the Geneva Convention. The prosecution was never able to prove to the Court that he was anyone other than a responsible mid-level politician.

Late in the war, four downed American airmen were being held near Budensheim. They had made one escape only to be recaptured and returned to custody. On a second escape, they overpowered, beat, and disarmed their guards. They were apprehended while attempting to break into what they thought was a school. It was a mistake. They were really breaking into a Hitler Youth building. (By the time the war was in full swing, the Hitler Youth represented real soldier material and fought as savagely as any other element of the German Armed Forces.) The Americans were taken to a nearby police barracks where they were beaten. Some of those assaulting the prisoners testified that Loser beat the airmen with aluminum knuckles.

Loser pleaded not guilty. He said he shook the Americans and interrogated them, but he had stopped the others who were doing the beating. He said he had a broken hand at the time which was in an aluminum cast, but he would have been unable to beat anyone without damaging his injured hand further. He also claimed that those whom he had stopped from beating the Americans had accused him because they thought he had died at the hands of the Gestapo. They would have considered it safe to protect themselves by accusing a man who was already dead, he said, and accusations were looked upon kindly by Americans at that time.

The review board would later say, "There was introduced sufficient evidence to have supported a finding of guilty, but the Court evidently believed the theory of the incident as contended by the accused and acquitted the accused." It's possible he was indeed innocent. It's also possible the Court rewarded him for saving the lives of the Americans earlier that year by risking his own life.

In August 1944, a big air battle started over the house where Ludwig Blasius lived, and it continued into the afternoon. The air was full of puffs of smoke, burning planes, and parts of planes falling to earth. Ludwig was 11 years old. Later that afternoon, he and his cousin Hans had to "guard" the cows. They had seen airmen bail out of planes, and they knew that several had been taken prisoner. They carried out their job in a meadow that was bounded by a hedge. Beyond the hedge was a field and then the road. As time went by, they saw an American walking up and down along the hedge. He was limping. They understood that he had not been taken prisoner. Then they saw a motorcycle approach with two men riding on it. The men stopped the motorcycle and got off. One of the men shot the airman. The boys heard the airman cry out several times. Then the men got back on the motorcycle and left.

In late spring 1944, Arthur Jetzinger, the fifty-one-year-old chief of police in Dessau, Germany, read a shocking direct order at a daily morning conference with his subordinates. The order, supposed to have come directly from Heinrich Himmler, stated that local authorities were ordered to shoot downed airmen. In other words, they would not be granted prisoner-of-war status in accordance with the Geneva Convention. They would not be put on trial; they would simply be shot. This supposed order is in some contrast to what others in Germany believed; they believed the order stated that no one would be prosecuted for killing or abusing airmen. The latter notion would have given local officials an option; the former did not. Additionally, Jetzinger read a directive that stated that any who refused an order to kill airmen would be "taken before the SS police court and shot."

In the summer of 1944, Jetzinger called police officers Fritz Pohla and Ernst Vogler and a third man into his office. He ordered them to go to a nearby town and pick up three airmen being held by the Burgermeister. They were to shoot the Americans. "You know the order," he said. "Go out and take the fliers over and do your duty."

The policemen picked up the fliers, took them into the woods, and Pohla and Vogler each shot an airman. There was some dispute over who shot the third airman, although it was generally thought to have been the action of the third policeman present. Pohla went to tell the Burgermeister to attend to the burial of the victims while Vogler and the other policeman guarded the bodies. The Burgermeister had the bodies removed by horse cart and buried in a common grave later that day in a "secret way."

Both Pohla and Vogler confessed to what they had done, but they offered in their defense the Himmler order. They believed they were obeying a legal order. As previously noted, precedent had denied that superior orders could be used as a defense in most cases although mercy seems to have been granted to some who were hopelessly caught up in the system, and it could become a mitigating factor in sentencing. The order the policemen received did not even qualify as a military order, having come from a civilian—the chief of police. These were common-law murders and would be treated as such at the trials of those involved.

Although the Dachau trials exhibited several flaws, if they could be faulted for only a single thing, it would be the fact that in many instances the accused did not have a proper opportunity to offer a defense. It was unlikely that anyone could have offered sufficient evidence to sway the court, although the third policeman in the case could not be located at the time of the trial; his statement would be entered as prosecution evidence. Further, the Court relied on statements from other witnesses who could not be cross-examined because they were unavailable. Two witnesses were thought to be residing in Russian territory. The reviewing committee said of the trial that: "taking into consideration the results of this investigation, the confession of each accused and their testimony, any error committed by the court in admitting the statements of [the third man] and the other witnesses was not prejudicial to the substantial rights of the accused." It was clearly a death penalty offense and the defendants were so judged and sentenced by the Court in April 1946.

The murder of American airmen would generate many of the activities in the Dachau series. While some understanding was usually given to the outbursts of angry citizens, premeditated murder frequently resulted in death on the gallows.

8

Cassius' Dagger:
A Mob in the Hands
of Angry Americans

Look! In this place ran Cassius' dagger through;
See what a rent the envious Casca made;
Through this the well-beloved Brutus stabbed,
And, as he pluck'd his cursed steel away,
Mark how the blood of Caesar followed it.

> [From Mark Antony's funeral speech in *Julius
> Caesar* by William Shakespeare; quoted as part of
> "General Comments" by the Army Judge Advocate's
> review in case #12-2422: *U.S. vs. Peter Kohn,
> Matthias Gierens, and Matthias Krein.*]

By the first week of June 1945, Americans were already bringing Germans to trial for war crimes. The trial of *U.S. vs. Kohn et al.* was intense with witnesses piling on evidence, and the review board found it necessary to offer some note of the length of its assessment: "This review has been necessarily long. It is the first trial of a German civilian within the confines of the once German Reich by a Military Commission for crimes denounced by the conventions and treaties solemnly entered into by the two warring nations and recognized as sacred and binding." The prosecutors, the Court, and the review board were in a vile mood, and the case of Kohn, Gierens, and Krein, together with a second case two weeks later against Peter Back, who was still at large during the first trial, frames this anger with as much definition as does the more famous case at Nuremberg — or even by later cases in the Dachau series. The *Kohn et al.* trial opened on June 1, 1945.*

During August 1944, Nicholaus Nospes, a seventy-four-year-old pensioner, was cutting wheat when he saw a parachute. An airman fell into a tree and was caught there by the parachute. While he was trying to free himself, an angry crowd gathered including women and children. Two German soldiers in uniform tried to help the airman, but there was so much anger, excitement, and confusion, they were unable to prevail. Peter Back rode up on a motorcycle and fired two shots at the trapped airman, all the while shouting for the crowd to kill the airman. One of the shots hit the airman in the head. He fell to the ground, wounded, but struggled to his feet. Back held off the soldiers with his gun. He fenced off the crowd and would not let those come close who wanted to protect the airman or participate in the killing.

Neighbors knew that Back had a reputation for being impulsive and for taking up the excitement around him. A teacher in the community remembered having him in church choir when he was a teenager. He remembered that he was of a simple nature and not able mentally to judge things clearly. He also remembered times, in church, when he would become ecstatic and pale and would begin to shake.

In a statement relevant to his trial, Back said he was sorry and that he had acted impulsively. He knew he had done wrong, and he and his wife grieved over it. He had decided never to do such a thing again.

Peter Kohn had acquired a piece of wood about three feet long and several inches thick. He used the wood to beat the airman around the head and shoulders. Kohn's excuse was that he became so excited by the enraged Back that he forgot himself. Just at that moment, he later testified, he remembered Goebbels's speech to the effect that "the one who kills them [foreign airmen] and the one who brings them off this world will not suffer punishment." He also said he was afraid of Back. Kohn had served in the Germany military and spent two winters as an infantry soldier at the Russian front where he was badly wounded. He had three children and a pregnant wife at home.

Matthias Gierens used a large rock-crushing hammer to beat the airman until his head was a mass of clotted blood. Gierens came from an unfortunate family. He had both a brother and a sister die in the insane

*Much is made in this case about its being the first war crimes case. Actually another trial, U.S. vs. Bruns, case #6-56, had been held on April 7, 1945, almost exactly one month before the official capitulation. Hauptmann Bruns was sentenced to death "by musketry" for killing two downed German-speaking airmen of Jewish descent. Bruns was the only defendant in the series to die by firing squad.

asylum. His priest testified that he believed Gierens was without control and was insane, although he had only come to the latter conclusion at the time of the trial.

According to Joann Jacob, a farmer and mayor of a local village, Matthias Krein had special responsibilities. Jacob and Krein were members of the rural police, and it was their responsibility to check out crashed planes, record markings, turn pilots over to the nearest police, and protect airmen. Jacob was not at the scene of the crash because he was off investigating a downed plane. Krein, however, was at the scene. He stood by and made no more effort to do his duty as Jacob understood it other than to say mildly to Back after the deed, "You shouldn't have done that." Witnesses testified that Krein had a carbine and could have stopped the attack if he had seen fit. Krein said in his defense that the weapon was unloaded, but the Court was unimpressed by the excuse.

By the time Jacob arrived at the death scene, the body was covered with straw, but he could clearly see what had happened. He and Krein took the body and buried it in the local cemetery "for Christian reasons." They did not put it in a coffin nor did they seek the services of the clergy. They understood that the Nazi Party prohibited the coffin and clergy.

Leonard Heidt, a local farmer, was part of the crowd. He protested the beating the men were giving the airman, but Back "jumped at him and told him to remember Goebbel's [sic] speech." For trying to protest, he was imprisoned by the Gestapo. The German people had not done this sort of thing in the first war, he said.

The tribunal sentenced all participants to death: Back, Kohn, and Gierens for the actual deed and Krien for failing to use his authority to intervene.

The review board was no less livid than the Court had been. They were also aware that their exercise in justice might be examined by future generations. They made every attempt to create a work of literature as they understood it, even to the point of quoting Shakespeare. The following are excerpts from the "Comments" section of the reviews of case #12-2422 (the trial of Kohn, Gierens, and Krein) and case #12-2422-1 (the trial of Back).

> [As to the defense argument for Back]: His argument is learned, but it is the time-old cry of those who would claim that someone else "beguiled them and they did eat." The War Crimes trials of post–World War I heard this whining excuse time after time.
> [As to the argument that Back might have been insane]: If Peter Back was mad, it was the madness of a people who had taught themselves to believe that the crimes of the citizen were the virtues of the Reich, a perversion to which German philosophy has shackled itself for years.

[As to the character of Back]: Athwart this entire case falls the shadow of Peter Back. That he was the moving genius, the motivating impulse, the whip-master urging his weaker colleagues to follow their savage instincts is not denied. It is unfortunate that he cannot be found at this time [on the occasion of the first phase of the trial]. Even as his diabolical Führer has been swallowed up by an uncertain oblivion, so has the disciple. Crippled in body from infantile paralysis, but sadistically ruthless in his contorted mind, he finds a helpless victim to torture and kill in this American airman and he adds to his country's ignominy and shame another instance of shocking crime against the rules and usages of war. The search will go on for him, unrelenting and thorough. Whether he bides for a time in some mountain fastness like a predatory beast who fears contact with the avengers of his victim, or whether he cowers in some hidden wine-cellar with other creatures of darkness to avoid detection matters little. Sooner or later, he will be taken and pages of this record will be useful in bringing to ultimate justice this typical prototype of Hitler's "Master Race" and Nietzsche's [sic] "Superman" bent only upon ruthless domination of those weaker than he in spirit. It is to be regretted that he may not lead the procession of murderers at this time to the gibbet that is the fitting end to their bacchanalia of blood on 15 August, 1944.

[As to Peter Kohn]: In this character we have a mobster type as old as Caiaphas' judgment seat and as recent as a creek bottom lynching bee. Guided by no master morality of a Back or the morbidity of a Gierens, Peter Kohn, a railroad worker, joins the quickly gathering mob about the defenseless aviator who has already surrendered and adds his fury to that of his cowardly compatriots in crime. He picks up a club and belabors the wounded airman who is still standing. The American tries to ward off the blows but falls to the ground from which he never rose again. Kohn's excuse is the age-hoary one: Back urged me, Goebbel's speech [sic] beguiled me, I became excited, I was "out of control." He testifies that he cannot say "that the shots alone or the beatings alone would have killed the airman." Who can tell whose blow caused this death of this young American 2nd Lieutenant there that fateful August day? As we try to reconstruct the event, as we calculate upon the effect of Back's shots, Kohn's bludgeon-blows, or the possible coup de grâce by Gierens' iron hammer, we yield to the law that says that each must share the guilt of ultimate death. They are mute evidences on the corpse of many vengeful wounds.

Then followed the quote from Shakespeare concerning the rudeness of the blows that fell upon the body of Caesar by Cassius, Casca, and Brutus. The explanations then continued.

[As to Gierens]: Here we have the morbid embodiment of all that the Nazi philosophy exemplifies. He does not testify for defense counsel have sought to ascribe his actions to "Madness."… The completion of the macabre design, formulated by Dr. Goebbels and his degenerate Nazi associates and extending into the very lowest stratum of German national life, even down to Gierens in the tiny Trier village of Preiest, is not yet realized. Does one need more than to read Gierens' own statement to decide as to his guilt or his deserved punishment? The philosophy of his reasoning demonstrates the morbid predominance of organic sensations that have enveloped German thinking since 1933 and of which this is but a by-product. His instilled, insatiate hatred was, as Spinoza said of Avarice, "a species of madness, although not enumerated among diseases."

[As to Krein]: Here we have the case of one who did not strike a blow, who did not beat or shoot or hammer, but whose shame is as flagrant and whose crime is as dastardly as those who did. A peace officer's duty is to save his prisoner from the fury of the mob. His duty lies in venturing his own life and safety that the law of the court may be applied and not the will of the mob. If he goes along with the lynching party, stands by while it vents its unrighteous spleen upon the helpless victim, makes no effort to stop the violence or the mobsters is he not as guilty as they? And if he keeps back the crowd with his menacing gun to prevent others from aiding the victim, if he himself encourages the murderers, shall he not share with them the blame? ... Truly Krein was another Saul "consenting unto his death," not merely "standing by" and "keeping the raiment of them that slew him," but lending his sanction to this deed by holding back any possible interference with his gun.

[On defense counsel]: He was diligent to the highest extent and adhered to the finest standards of an advocate at any bar. One may review this acquaintance with him with the hope that there still lives in Germany, amid the blood-dripping ruins of what was once an altar of Justice, an abiding basis upon which some semblance of the pro–Nazi system of government-by-just-law may be rebuilt.

[On the seriousness of the crime]: The Saturnalia of blood there in that simple Rhineland village on that August noonday takes its place beside the butcheries of Buchenwald and Dachau. There bemedalled and high-ranking over-lords decreed torture and death that Attila would have hesitated to essay. In Preist, ordinary citizens of the Third Reich ... joined together in their bloodlust to slay an unresisting, unarmed, trussed-up young American who is their captive. The gory annals of the Comanches have no more brutal sequel.

The "comments" of the review board reveal prejudices, innocence, and hubris. Here also is an early awareness that justice for the dead could not be delivered in adequate measure.

On review, Krein's death sentence was commuted to life imprisonment on June 24, 1945, and much was made of the American effort to be magnanimous. The other defendants were hanged.

9

Americans as Slaves of the Third Reich: The Agonies of Berga

ARTICLE 10. Prisoners of war shall be lodged in buildings or in barracks affording all possible guarantees of hygiene and healthfulness. The quarters must be fully protected from dampness, sufficiently heated and lighted.... With regard to dormitories ... the conditions shall be the same as for the troops at base camps of the detaining Power....

ARTICLE 11. The food ration of prisoners of war shall be equal in quantity and quality to that of troops at base camps. Furthermore, prisoners shall receive facilities for preparing themselves additional food which they might have. A sufficiency of potable water shall be furnished them. The use of tobacco shall be permitted.... Prisoners may be employed in the kitchens.

ARTICLE 12. Clothing, linen, and footwear shall be furnished prisoners of war by the detaining Power....

ARTICLE 13. Belligerents shall be bound to take all sanitary measures necessary to assure the cleanliness and healthfulness of camps and to prevent epidemics.... Furthermore and without prejudice to baths and showers with which the camp shall be as well provided as possible, prisoners shall be furnished a sufficient quantity of water for the care of their own bodily cleanliness.... It shall be possible for them to take physical exercise and enjoy the open air.

ARTICLE 14. Every camp shall have an infirmary where prisoners of war shall receive every kind of attention they need. If necessary, isolated quarters shall be reserved for the sick affected with contagious diseases....

ARTICLE 15. Medical inspections of prisoners of war shall be arranged at least once a month.

ARTICLE 29. No prisoner of war may be employed at labors for which he is physically unfit.

ARTICLE 32. It is forbidden to use prisoners of war at unhealthful or dangerous work.

ARTICLE 33. The system of labor detachments must be similar to that of prisoner-of-war camps, particularly with regard to sanitary conditions, food, attention in case of accident or sickness, correspondence, and the receipt of packages. Every labor detachment shall be dependent on a prisoners' camp. The commander of this camp shall be responsible for the observation, in the labor detachment, of the provisions of the present Conventions.

[*Geneva Prisoners of War Convention of
27 July 1929,* as cited in case #12-1836:
U.S. vs. Erwin Metz et al.]

Toward the end of the war, about seventy Americans were being held at a prisoner-of-war camp at Berga, an out-camp of Stalag IX-C, Bad Sulza, Thuringia. The Americans were in the charge of a German noncommissioned officer named Erwin Metz and were guarded by a variety of German nationals. The camp was associated with L Company, Home Guard Battalion 621, as shown by the shoulder epaulet marked 621-L.

Metz was a fair-haired man of average height with ruddy complexion. He wore thick glasses of the sort that make the eyes appear large and bulging. He was burdened with a complex speech impediment that included a lisp and a strange sound to his words. The Americans thought he sounded like Donald Duck.

Americans at the Berga camp, including Pfc. Meyer Lemberg, were being furnished as war labor to a construction firm commanded by the SS. Lemberg had been captured with several others by the Germans on December 17, 1944, after only one day into the Battle of the Bulge. The American POWs were marched from one small town to another with the transport picking up other prisoners along the way. They were given very little food, and the Germans took all their money. After several days, the transport counted about 985 men from a variety of nations. At the town of Gerolatein, they were put on boxcars with about 60 men in each car. They rode on the train five days, until the day after Christmas, and during the first few days they received no food or water. The train would stop at sidings during the night. On one occasion, the train stopped because of an air attack. Some of the men ran into nearby fields and an American was shot. When they reached Camp IX-B, they brought the total up to nearly 4,000 inmates. This larger camp housed men of many nations including about 1,000 Jews. By this time, the number of Americans had grown to between three and four hundred men who were assigned to a barracks about 20 feet wide and 100 feet long. Many had to sleep on the floor without blankets. After a time, each soldier was issued one blanket. They had no personal items at all.

American Pfc. Stephen Schweitzer spoke German and tried to use his skill for the benefit of his fellow prisoners, and the Germans put him in charge of his fellow countrymen. He was from New York City, was 32 years old, and had spent three years in college at Fordham University. He was captured with several others by the Panzer Grenadiers in Belgium on December 19 during the Battle of the Bulge. Although the Germans took everything from the Americans they could find, he was able to hide a notebook in his boot on which he used to record data about sick prisoners. Schweitzer's little notebook, which was marked as evidence in the trial, still remains a part of the records at the National Archives and Records Administration.

Erwin Metz

These men, like Lemberg, eventually fell into the hands of the Wehrmacht troops of L Company and were forced to endure the journey by train. By coincidence, the German officer in charge was also named Schweitzer.

There were no sanitary facilities on the train and the men had to urinate on the floor. Men with diarrhea had to use their helmets. The men begged for water but were denied it. A German guard even slapped a container of water from a German civilian who tried to hand it to the men. When the train came under the air attack described by Lemberg, the guards left the men locked in the cars while they took shelter. About eight men were killed in the car ahead of the one Schweitzer was riding in.

After they reached their intermediate destination, an American slapped one of the workers in the kitchen, and in retribution 3,500 prisoners were forced outside into the January snow with machine guns trained on them. The temperature was below zero, and they were forced to stand on top of a hill where the wind was "blowing strongly." Some of the men had overcoats and some had managed to take their blankets with them, but most had to go out in their boots, trousers, shirts, and field jackets. They stood on the hillside over six hours before someone identified the boy who had hit the guard. When they went back to the barracks and to work they were not given food or fuel for 36 hours.

On February 8, the Americans were sent to the construction site at Berga where they would also come under the control of Metz. For the trip, each man received one-third of a loaf of bread and was to share one can of meat with three others.

A construction firm was attempting to build a series of tunnels near Berga. The Nazis had decided that tunnels should be constructed in many places. Sometimes they functioned as air-raid shelters but usually they were used to conceal war machinery or factories. The camp where the Americans were sent to work was believed to be for a factory or gasoline plant. Although the construction firm directly supervised the work of the prisoners and was responsible for making sure the work was safe, the prisoners were the direct responsibility of the parent Stalag. Metz was in charge of the Americans.

Eighteen shafts were being tunneled into a small mountain at Berga. The mountain rose abruptly from a flat plain which was maintained as a more or less typical construction site. On the opposite side of the small, narrow plain, the Elster River flowed, and across the river the Germans were moving earth to construct a railroad station. It was planned that eventually the shafts within the mountain would be interconnected. The laborers were forced to drill through solid rock with jackhammers to build the shafts.

The project at Berga demonstrated in its own way that lunacy had come to determine the methodology of the Nazi endeavor, as evidenced by trial exhibits. Using persons not physically fit enough to care for their own bodily needs, the Germans had caused great, ragged holes to be made into the side of the mountain. The outside entrance to a typical shaft was not framed by concrete or even timbers. It was simply a hole around which exposed tree roots snaked. Even a casual observer would have understood immediately that the tree roots had not been cut and the entrance "finished" because the project was out of control. The inside of the "tunnel" exhibited little more sophistication. Here and there lay a few cables the workers had abandoned when they left the camp at the end of the war. A large duct hung from the ceiling, and a narrow track was laid down the center, probably for a small car to carry dirt and rock debris through the tunnel. Testimony would confirm the conditions suggested by the trial exhibits.

Entrance to one of the tunnels at Berga.

View of the work site at Berga: Tunnels were dug into the mountain at right.

While Berlin and the other major cities of Germany lay in rubble, at Berga, and all over Germany during the last days of the war, lives were spent in similar foolish efforts.

Like Lemberg and Schweitzer and their fellow prisoners, other American prisoners at the camp were the remnants of 350 prisoners who had been captured by the Germans in the Ardennes phase of the counteroffensive in December 1944. They too had been transferred from camp to camp, finally arriving at Berga in February 1945, about ten weeks before the capitulation. These were the fortunate few because, during the Battle of the Bulge, the Germans had carefully followed military orders to take no prisoners. In addition to POWs who had been murdered outright, the brutal battle had cost the lives of a heartbreaking number of young American men.

The health of the prisoners had worsened as they passed through the camps. They were severely malnourished and were physically unfit for any significant labor. Nevertheless, the men were organized and ordered to work twelve-hour shifts in the tunnels. This work qualified as hard labor, in itself an infraction of the Geneva Convention, and the nature of the labor was intensified by the physical condition of the men.

At the camp, the prisoners received nothing for breakfast and only one liter of soup at noon. They were given about 400 grams of bread in the evening. "Once or twice" a week, the prisoners were given some cheese and 30 grams of meat. One prisoner lost 37 pounds during seven weeks at the work camp, and the exhumed bodies of the several who died were extremely emaciated. Testimony revealed that Metz personally withheld food from the prisoners on several occasions.

The prisoners were first housed in a rough camp and had to walk some distance to work. After a brief time they were moved closer to the work site and were housed in a building they called the "new camp." The camp was practically without sanitary facilities. Eight buckets were placed along the front of the barracks and six along the rear. Additionally, there was one primitive latrine under construction for the 350 prisoners, but it would never be completed. There was no source of fresh water and cholera

External view of the barracks at Berga.

was already a problem at the camp. The prisoners tried to boil water while in camp, but while they were working, the only water available was directly from the river. Dead bodies were left in the open beside the barracks for days before they were buried.

In the tunnels, dust permeated the air. German civilian workers from the nearby town and guards were allowed to wear masks, but this simple safety aid was not allowed for the prisoners—American or otherwise. The prisoners carried the dust back to the barracks with them on their clothes. The result of this dust exposure was numerous deaths from pneumonia.

In the barracks, the men slept three to a bed in bunks one and a half meters wide stacked three high, making a total of nine men who occupied a space less than sixty inches wide. The barracks, which housed the 350 prisoners, was itself only ten meters wide and 40 meters long. Outside, it resembled a giant, backyard clubhouse built by thirteen-year-old boys. It lacked a true foundation but sat about a foot off the ground on slender posts. The cold coming through the floor must have been brutal. The building framework was covered with raw lumber, and the raw, knot-stippled reverse of the exterior lumber formed the inside wall. The bunks were

Inside view of the barracks at Berga.

placed so close together it must have been difficult to walk between them. Even the tiny, six-paned windows were partially covered by the bunks. The men slept directly on sacks of straw. The dirty straw spilled through splits along the poorly executed seams. The sacks were unimproved in any way, and not a scrap of anything resembling bed linens was provided. At the camp, each man was issued a single blanket. No heat of any kind was provided for the barracks, but some were allowed to build fires in the open during the day. Blackout rules disallowed fires at night.

For most of the time the prisoners were at the work camp, they were exposed daily to freezing weather without adequate clothing. In fact, the camp provided no clothes at all, and the prisoners continued to wear the clothes they wore on the day of their capture. They were given neither caps nor gloves but were still forced to carry rails that stuck to their hands. They were beaten when they took a "loose hold to avoid having their hands stick to the rails." Pfc. Maircel R. Ouimet suffered the horror of the forced labor from February until April and lost over 30 pounds in the process. He said that when the guards beat them, the Americans would sometimes threaten to tell the Red Cross. The guards laughed. The Germans were confused as to why the Americans did not understand that they were under the command of Hitler, their leader.

Beatings were a common occurrence at the camp. Schweitzer himself had been hit with a shovel handle, and he had watched from ten feet away as a boy in his teens was beaten to death by a guard for failing to remove his hat when the guard walked by.

Metz was personally responsible for numerous beatings of prisoners and was also accused of shooting a prisoner of war who was placed in his custody after he tried to escape.

All prisoners who could walk, including sick prisoners, were forced to work, a practice which resulted in the deaths of many. "The guards dragged dying prisoners out of bed and threw them outside to die." Seven to ten men collapsed every day on the job site. When they did, they were kicked to make certain they were not faking. If they did not come around, a helmetful of water was thrown on them.

The prisoners received no routine medical care at the camp. A physician came to the camp once a week and the prisoners asked for his services, but Metz denied them attention. Prisoners died from infection and gangrene or diphtheria. At one time 300 of the 350 prisoners had dysentery. During all the time at the camp, Metz allowed only seventeen prisoners to go to the hospital and two of them died before they reached the facility. Schweitzer tried to fashion an isolation area for men with contagious diseases, and he tried to keep a record of his little dispensary in his notebook. Only those who were totally unable to walk were allowed in the dispensary. Anyone who could walk at all was forced to go to work. A German Jewish doctor who was a prisoner in the camp was given the job of putting up a barbed wire fence, and he would sneak into the dispensary to try to give Schweitzer diagnoses that he could write in his book, and with which he could request specific help from Metz. Help rarely came. Many died in the dispensary.

The moment the Americans rescued the POWs, they immediately began an investigation of the stories the prisoners were telling. Of the many bodies exhumed one was a soldier buried at Berga from whose body they recovered the two bullets that still remain an official exhibit in the case. One of the bullets is almost pristine in shape; the other is somewhat flattened.

The following transcript is taken from an interrogation in preparation for the Metz trial. An American interrogator to a German, a former guard: "We know all about your experiences with prisoners of war. This is the reason why we didn't question you until now; we collected all the evidence before interrogating you. You better tell us the truth, and I remind you that you are under oath. Do you understand the meaning of an oath?"

The guard: "Yes."

"Tell me of all the cases in which you know the rules of the Geneva Convention were infringed."

"I don't know of a single case."

"You don't want really to tell me that the Poles, for instance, were treated according to the rules of the Geneva Convention?"

"Certainly they were. Of course, in the end there were no Poles there anymore [at Berga]."

"What happened to them?"

"Oh, I don't know."

Did he know of any Americans who died?

"No, I don't know of anything."

But the Americans now have the details. Does he know of any Americans who died?

"I know only of two Americans who died."

And how did they die?

"They tried to escape."

"Now tell us the story in detail. We will see whether it checks with our information or whether you are lying."

"The American escaped, and a day or so later we were informed by the Gendarmerie in the Wilde-Taube that they had captured an American prisoner and they gave us his prisoner number." The matter had been reported directly to Metz, he stated.

So they went to get the American. Did he make it back to camp?

"We wanted to bring him back to Berga, but he [Metz] shot him on the way because he wanted to escape."

He ran with a gun pointed at him?

"Yes."

Was any other military man with Metz?

"Yes."

And who was he?

"I don't recall his name, but his rank was probably corporal. His job was Hundeführer [dog leader]."

"What was his dog used for?"

"He had to use it in case prisoners tried to run away. He had done his job before at Stalag IX-C, and he had been sent to us for different assignments a short time before this American was shot."

Was he sure Metz had been the one to shoot the American?

"Yes, he said so himself."

This soldier was murdered by Metz during the middle of March. Most prisoners who escaped were punished by being made to stand out in the cold without food or water, or by being beaten, but this brought the number of Americans who had escaped in five days up to seven. Metz was furious with the escapes and made it known that he personally intended to pick up the prisoner. He boasted that the prisoner would not return to the camp alive. When Metz picked up the prisoner, he told him he was beginning his death march. Metz would testify that, on the way to the camp, he had stopped to talk to a civilian and the prisoner tried to escape. After shouting for the prisoner to halt, Metz shot him in the back. A guard told one of the prisoners that Metz had shot the prisoner in cold blood, and a passerby would say that the hair about the head wound was burned.

Early in April, the approach of the Russian and American armies prompted an evacuation of all the prisoners and other personnel at the work camp. They were marched into Bavaria on a route "approximately paralleling the Czechoslovakian border." Metz was still in charge of the American prisoners.

The prisoners were given only about half the rations of guards, and the deaths of 30 to 40 prisoners on the march could be attributed to their being "weak, sick, exhausted." On one leg of 21 kilometers, no soup was provided at all and one loaf of bread was given to be divided among 10 men. Seven men died on this leg. As the column passed through towns, the accused tried to prevent German civilians from giving food to the prisoners. The rations consisted primarily of potatoes. They were not provided water at all and the only water they got was from streams they passed.

When they left the camp, most of the prisoners suffered from diarrhea, and their illnesses became worse on the road. Thirty to forty sick prisoners rode in wagons but no medical treatment was given to them. Metz made some of the prisoners get off the wagons and walk. As prisoners collapsed and died, they were piled into a wagon. One living prisoner was thrown into the wagon and before his fellow soldiers could get him out, bodies were thrown on him until he smothered to death. Metz said he did not take the sick prisoners to a hospital because no one had ordered him to do so. At one point a mayor and several citizens forced Metz to hospitalize 32 sick prisoners who were riding in wagons. Four prisoners were sent to a cemetery for burial along the route. It was discovered that one of these was still alive when he was sent into the village, but he received no medical attention, died, and was buried with the others. Two were shot trying to escape, and Schweitzer saw small holes at the base of their skulls, which approximated that which a .25 caliber bullet would make when shot at close range.

Later, 30 bodies were exhumed from graves along the route. Seven had not been found by the time of the trials. As the march progressed, the transport began to break up. Guards would leave and groups of prisoners would be let go. The French were released in one group to make their way in the villages and countryside. They would not have to struggle long; help was on the way.

The Americans were not released, and their march continued. It was believed they might be used as a bargaining chip in the expected peace negotiations. Prisoners were not permitted to take their blankets with them on the evacuation march and could only huddle together for warmth during the night; their misery continued. Sometimes they were forced to march in circles to avoid capture. Their ordeal on the road lasted a little more than two weeks. They left Berga on April 6 and were liberated by the Americans at Bernreid, Bavaria, on April 23. Schweitzer took Metz's .25 caliber automatic pistol from him at liberation.

During the weeks that the 350 Americans were under the supervision of Metz, at least seventy Americans died. It could have been more. The Germans' mania for record keeping had finally faltered. Erwin Metz's death sentence, handed down during the Dachau trials, was commuted to life imprisonment.

10

I Know Howard Hughes:
The Agonies and Conceits
of John V. Case

A trial is a small war ... or to be a bit more accurate, it is like a small war game. Technically, the forces are equal competitors, prosecution against defense, and the judge (in the military trials, the Court) acts as referee.

In the Dachau trials, sometimes hopelessness had a clash with power, or inferior intellect clashed with superior ability. In case #11-96: *U.S. vs. Kirschner and Wolf*, a clash of personalities provided the interest. This was not to be a simple case of side against side; this grew into an ensemble performance with years of sideshows to provide mutual frustration.

On the surface, this would seem to be one of the "flier" cases that falls easily into the pattern. An American airman parachutes or crash-lands safely only to be shot by locals in a village. It was not to be. Apparently the accused convened a tribunal, a "summary" or "quick" court; within moments they found the airman guilty of bombing an ambulance, and they shot him on the spot. The victim was believed to be a young lieutenant, Daniel P. Loyd, but the very identity of the dead man was to be a complicating factor.

The perpetrators, Karl Adam Kirschner and Hugo Wolf, would be given death sentences at the end of the trial, and the sentence, despite some errors in the trial, would stand up under first review. Wolf's later appeals would succeed; it was Kirschner who would hang.

Basic facts show that at about midday on June 10, 1944, Loyd's plane came down at Bois-Arnault, a small town west of Paris, France. Loyd suffered a head wound during the downing. Later, Loyd came into the custody of Kirschner, a lieutenant with the 12th Panzer Division (Hitler Youth Division), and Wolf, a forty-one-year-old baker in civilian life and a sergeant with the same unit; both were members of the SS. Other soldiers were present but were not charged. Kirschner was in his mid-thirties and was a mechanical engineer. He was town commander and headquarters commandant in Rugles, a village near Bois-Arnault. He was also a member of the Nazi Party.

Loyd was first taken to an orphanage in Rugles where troops were stationed and was then taken by Wolf and others to the command post. Kirschner interrogated the flier, held the court, found him guilty, and pronounced the death sentence.

Immediately after the trial and the execution of the sentence, Wolf came across the street and said to a man standing there, "There's one more who will not go back to America." Thereupon, a grave was prepared.

Kirschner's defense was that townspeople had reported to him that four American planes had been shooting at a vehicle on the road. Kirschner would later say that the vehicle was a Red Cross ambulance carrying two German officers who were killed by Loyd's attack. Kirschner had not witnessed any part of the event. Other witnesses would say the vehicle was a "command car" carrying two German officers. One witness said that when he came upon the vehicle, one of the officers was dead and one was still alive. He saw nothing on the car that resembled a red cross. He later said he had seen the chassis of a larger vehicle that might have been an ambulance, but only the car in which the officers were riding was shot up. It would never be exactly determined whether Kirschner rushed to judgment, was misinformed, or whether he simply fabricated an excuse. He would admit that he informed Wolf of the decision of the summary trial and that he ordered Wolf to carry out the sentence of death by shooting.

Strictly speaking, according to trial records, a court would not have been against the law. The court could have been legal if the one who appointed the court had not sat as a member (as had Kirschner), if an interpreter had been present, if the court had had at least three members (as this one had not), and if witnesses had been called before the court (and no evidence was offered that the court heard witnesses). It was also a matter of law that such a court could only have ordered its own sentence executed if the "accused" had been a German soldier. The "court" was not legal; it was simply a variation of the "kill a flier if you can" mentality.

The Americans tried, convicted, and sentenced Kirschner and Wolf for a common-law murder. To this point the "flier" case had been routine.

Then entered one John Virgil Case, uncle to the deceased and brother to the deceased's mother. Case began by opening a dialogue with William R. Corbett of the War Crimes Commission at Dachau, complaining about a number of aspects of the case.

Corbett, attempting to pacify Case, wrote an unauthorized, private letter to Case which opened boxes that would require rather high-level officials to close.

> I request that this letter be considered a private one and that you treat it as such. I ask this not so much for what it contains, but because I am going completely "out of channels" on an official matter, and in doing so, I violate the accepted fact that official matters are handled through official channels.
>
> To this case I feel that a deviation in procedure is merited. Today I had occasion to read your letter to the General in charge of War Crimes matters in Washington, D.C., and noted the frustration, desperation, etc., contained therein. I appreciate very much your feelings in this matter and feel that you do not have a true picture of how it was handled here in Dachau. Of course, I am referring to the murder of Lt. Loyd.
>
> Perhaps I should begin at the beginning and more or less bring you up to date on my interest in this whole matter.
>
> Early in September, 1947, I was given the assignment of interrogating Wolf and Kirschner, confined at Landsberg Prison under the death sentence for the murder of Lt. Loyd, with the object in mind of establishing the identity of the flier killed by these two. Among other things, pictures of Lt. Loyd were provided from which Wolf and Kirschner were to identify Lt. Loyd as being the man they killed.
>
> At this point I should like to point out that in your letter to the General you infer that the interrogation at Landsberg was only a matter of having Wolf and Kirschner "simply write down a statement" on 9 September '47. This I assure you was not done. I questioned each prisoner for well over an hour trying to gain all information possible from each. During this period of time I made notes of any point of interest. At the conclusion of the interrogation I had each write down the information of value in the statements to which you refer. In addition I filed a report myself in summation of the two interrogations which perhaps you did not have occasion to see.
>
> Generally it contained the following. First, Wolf did not see the plane because he received custody of the prisoner from soldiers of an anti-aircraft outfit who captured the flier. This transfer of custody took place at a place other than the scene of the crash. Two, Wolf's claim that he didn't talk with the flier thus not learning his identity may be explained by his inability to speak English. On the matter of the searching and taking of things from the flier, if it is true that soldiers of the anti-aircraft unit made the initial capture, it is only reasonable to assume that they conducted the search which any soldier would make on taking a captive. Therefore, it

certainly falls within the realm of possibility that the French witnesses saw quite another soldier take the possessions from the flier.

Add to this the fact that Wolf tells me at the time he was newly arrived in France having been under treatment in Germany for wounds received on the Eastern Front. He had just reported in a short time prior to the incident and therefore couldn't have been too well known in the vicinity.

Completely aside from this case, I should like to add that experience with French witnesses has taught me to receive their evidence always with a "grain of salt." I've found that in the light of new information a French witness can do an about-face and be just as positive of something new as he was of the old.

I can see you raising an eye-brow at this, but I'm sure you would find the opinion here almost 90 percent in favor of forgetting French witnesses in our cases at Dachau, as their unreliability has become something of a joke here. Such a generalization, I'm sure, is going to sound very stupid on my part, and I ask you to take this only for what it's worth — no more than my own opinion. To an American it is inconceivable that a person can witness an incident and still not be able to give an accurate account, but it's no more unexplainable than many more of the characteristics displayed by various nationalities here in Europe.

To return to the case in hand, Wolf flatly denied taking any valuables or papers from the flier. In view of the fact that he freely admitted carrying out the order of Kirschner to shoot the flier, I see no reason for him to conceal something which is less incriminating in his case.

On the other hand let me stress that Kirschner told me over and over that the flier's name was Lt. Daniel Loyd and that the flier himself gave him his name. I especially questioned on this point as being all-important, and he stated positively that he remembered the name, not as a result of hearing it at the trial, but from the incident of his having interrogated the flier.

The pictures and the inability to identify them are easily explained. Note each picture you sent yourself and see if each might yet be another person due to the differences in lighting, distance, dress, etc. Perhaps not to you who knew him well personally, but to us it was quite apparent and was pointed out by Wolf. Add to this that it is very difficult to properly identify people from pictures, which experience here in War Crimes has taught me, and actually the short time either Wolf or Kirschner were in contact with the flier, and it is easy to believe that they did not willfully fail to identify Lt. Loyd as being the man in the pictures. A general description of the flier as each remembered him did agree, however, and was much as I believe he actually looked — I asked for this description before producing the pictures.

The character of Wolf and Kirschner is itself important in the acceptance of the statements each made. Kirschner is the type of man who clings stubbornly to the idea that what he did was justified. He is an SS officer who would place a cause or responsibility to a cause above anything else. What he did he stands by. It might be even a matter of pride with him that he relates honestly what he did. With him I directly approached the problem of the identification to which he in turn responded by stating as precisely as [he] could what happened and what his own role was. I knowingly made mistakes which he took great pains to explain to me and correct.

In the case of Wolf I found a rather simple man. A typical four-over, and a typical product of a German education. He was a man that did as he was told, and to disobey as a soldier was as remote to him as the wildest scheme a person might conceive. Now he is bewildered, bitter, and feels that he was in no position to have acted differently. With a little sympathy and talk of home and family he talked willingly and very freely. I am really convinced that he "opened up." Especially in the case of the pictures, he seemed to earnestly attempt to identify them.

This of course is my own opinion and is to be accepted as such. In any case, I do not feel that any more information will be forthcoming from either Wolf or Kirschner.

I ask you to accept this letter as a small contribution to you so that at least you are clear on this one point in your own mind. I feel that it will not be necessary to give reference to it at any time in your future investigation, and I ask you not to.[*]

Case was livid. He immediately got in touch with Brigadier General George A. Horkan, Chief, Memorial Division, and perhaps alerted the General to what the real problems in this case would turn out to be. The following text is from his letter, dated November 7, 1947:

Pursuant to our telephone conversation [of earlier that same day], I am enclosing the letter and envelope [from Corbett] received this morning from Dachau, Germany.

If this chap had reviewed the SHAEF [Supreme Headquarters Allied Expeditionary Force] trial transcript he never would have written this type of letter in as much as the SHAEF transcript tears this letter to pieces.

That, however, is unimportant. The important thing about this letter supports clearly what I have said for the past year about the way the WCC [War Crimes Commission] is conducting their official business, with incompetent civilians.

I pointed out to Major MacDuff in General Eisenhower's office that I had contacted over 80 Army officers during the past two years, and, with the lone exception of the WCC, every officer and every department were patterns of efficiency. I was indeed sorry I could not say the same about the WCC. WCC records in Washington only show the SHAEF transcript

Many letters quoted in this chapter were several pages long in their original form. The portions of the letters quoted represent only those excerpts necessary to an understanding of the type of correspondence that passed between and among those involved in the many side stories associated with the trials.

which they inherited, plus whatever data I have given them, or information I have asked them to obtain.

Personally, I feel damned sorry for fine men like General Eberle, Colonel Young, and Lt. Col. Straight, and I definitely do not hold them responsible for the disloyalty and general inefficiency that flourished among civilian employees.

If the Army feels that certain civilians are indispensable, it seems to me the Army should commission such individuals placing them under the strict rules and regulations of the Army.

I'm going to write this chap and point out to him the errors he has made in conducting the examination of the two German SS prisoners and if you have no objection I will send you a copy of said letter. There is no point in me discussing his behavior with him.

After you have finished with the enclosed letter you might turn it over to Major MacFarland for I will be seeing him about Monday the 10th of November.

You, Colonel Busch, and Major MacFarland did a wonderful job of my nephew's case. The results were bitterly disappointing, but Hazelle Loyd and I wanted facts and you certainly gave us what we asked for.

Within two days (on November 9) Case was following up on his determination, or threat, to write to Corbett. He began by presenting a critique of Corbett's abilities:

Among the numerous incivilities by which the civilian personnel of the WCC has irritated and agitated the public, your letter of October 31, 1947, deserves classification among the most unique. The WCC is becoming quite famous. Fiction has its three musketeers, baseball is immortalized by Tinker to Evers to Chance, but the WCC tops them all with its matchless and inimitable combination of Egre to Hubbard to Corbett. When it comes to "muffing the ball" and making "bone head fumbles" you three fellows take the cake!

Case accused Corbett of depending on clairvoyance and supernatural intervention when he predicted that nothing further would be coming from Kirschner and Wolfe.

Within his critique, Case, in a brief few words, addressed the very human concerns of relatives of troops killed in battle. Many had precious little in the way of remains to say prayers over and to bury. Others had nothing at all; their loved ones were simply "missing" forever. In addition to the death of her son, the mother of Lt. Loyd must surely have suffered the special agonies associated with the knowledge of the way her son died and the uncertainty surrounding the identity of his remains. In a short sentence buried amid his pages-long attack on Corbett, Case wrote, "The latest evidence of Lt. Loyd's identity is a tooth cast made from a head that has a deep mastoid scar. Lt. Loyd never had a mastoid [surgery]."

Case didn't remain long with the agonies of Lt. Loyd's mother, however. He went on to other concerns. Apparently, Case was a lawyer. He was active in acquiring information and just as active in giving advice on how the Army investigator should have proceeded—and on how he should proceed in the future:

> Regarding SS officer Kirschner, the self-confessed director of murder, in whose sincerity you express much faith, you point out that Kirschner remembered the true name of "Lt. Daniel Loyd" from June 10, 1944, until September, 1947. If this is true then why did you accept and sign Kirschner's sworn statement of September 9, 1947, in which he confesses he is not sure about the name, and that the name might be "P. Loyd?" Since you denounce with much bitterness all French citizens in general because of inconsistencies, may I ask if you know or can name who is more versatile than yourself in this art? You also state that Kirschner questioned Lt. Loyd in the presence of three other German officers. Did you record the names of these three witnesses? In further defense of Kirschner you say, "it might be ever a matter of pride with him that he relates honestly what he did." This successful imposition by Kirschner upon your own credulity certainly disqualifies you to act in my behalf or in the behalf of Hazelle Loyd. The most important information that Kirschner or Wolf can furnish is the names of other German SS troops who participated and collaborated with them at Rugles. Since you are positive that you have the murderers of Lt. Loyd you might take the trouble to ask them about what was done with the body. If they refuse to tell you perhaps other SS troops who do know will tell you. Now that both are convicted to hang for the murder of Loyd neither could have any reason for withholding such information. Moreover, this information is known personally to Kirschner and Wolf's fellow officers who were stationed at Rugles.
>
> Your letter goes to great length to put more faith in Wolf than in honest French citizens with whom Wolf lived. If you will review the trial transcript of the first trial held at Rugles, on the seventh of November, 1944, and then confront Wolf with the testimony with his old friends with whom he lived, you will understand how little you have accomplished.
>
> If you arbitrarily and prejudicially invoke a boycott against French citizens in general simply because of their native or geographical extraction then how in high heaven do you expect to get convictions where countless crimes were committed on French soil? Crimes that only French mothers and fathers saw? If you are expressing WCC policies it is imperative that some Congressional subcommittee make a thorough investigation at once. Such methods can only sow the seeds of another war and it certainly sets a hideous example of American democracy in the American zone of Germany. Your bitter animosity toward the French people is unfortunate for it comes at a time when our Congress is appropriating billions of dollars in land-lease to keep France as an ally of the United States.

While, according to Case, the French were steadfast in their determination to do right by Lt. Loyd, he suggested that their collective friendship must be bought to prevent another crisis in Europe. America did much to rehabilitate the countries of Europe after World War II, but Americans of that day gave little attention to the possibility that France was a major military threat to the United States. Case hovered no longer over the possibility of warmongering among angry French than he did over the sorrows of his sister. He simply could not give up on being a detective at a distance:

> Hugo Wolf certainly sold you a bill of bad goods when he got you to believe that he was new in the area of Rugles. The facts are, Hugo Wolf was very well known at Rugles, Chronville, and St. Sulpice. You might ask Wolf how well he knows Mme. Cecile Gruart who, on June 10, 1944, saw Wolf as he left the courtyard of the German Kommandature with an American pilot who he said was a "D. T. Loyd." Wolf showed both Mme. Gruart and her husband, in their own home, a watch, photos, wallet, ring, and a silver pilot's insignia which Wolf said belonged to the pilot. Later she saw Wolf and four SS troops take this pilot away in a car. Since you openly pride yourself on finally getting Wolf to "open up" you might again charm him into telling you the names of the SS troops who were on this trip.
>
> No, indeed, Hugo Wolf was no stranger in the state of Eure, France. Wolf was the life of the party at the home of Mme. Franchini where he was billeted. On the evening of June 10, 1944, he arrived at the Franchini home, tossed his machine gun on the living room table and bragged about how he had just shot a pilot who was an American and proceeded to display the very same articles he had previously showed to Mme. Gruart and her husband. On this occasion, Wolf placed the flier's uniform in the hall, on top of a chest of drawers. A few days later Mme. Franchini cut a small piece of leather from the tab and later, at the trial, this piece of leather was introduced as 'exhibit G' and it fit exactly.
>
> If your faith in Wolf's sincerity is still unshaken you might interview M. Eugnen Buchon, Rue Aristide Briand, Rugles, who was Wolf's barber. On June 13, 1944, Wolf went to this barbershop for a shave and reiterated most of what he said to Mme. Franchini and family about the articles belonging to the prisoner. Wolf showed the barber the photographs of the pilot also the ring, watch, etc.

In addition to his skills as a detective, Case imagined himself to be an intimate of a variety of significant military and cultural leaders. In his letter to Corbett, Case suggested that he knew several important men personally and he could call down their influence, power, and services when he chose; but each time he invoked the mighty, he retreated with the explanation that his propositions are only hypothetical.

I presume you are all fed up with living conditions in Germany and like many others you long for the sight of the Statue of Liberty and I cannot blame you for this. But it seems to me you go about it in the hard way by writing such an unheard-of letter to me. Why don't you just go to Colonel Red Straight and tell him your desires. He has a very keen mind and a very keen sense of fair play. The Colonel perhaps does not know me, but I do know him very well by his reputation in Iowa. His home is at Sioux City.... I was there in 1936 with former attorney general H.M. Havner in some prosecution work. Colonel Straight had no connection with our work, but he was active in business in Woodbury County and participated in about all the civic affairs of Iowa, and his work was very outstanding.

Since you have offered me advice I suppose it is all right for me to offer you some. I would suggest that you go to the Colonel and just tell him about the advantages one has here in the good old USA as compared with those in Germany. Just tell him you wrote Mr. Case a sort of screwball letter for provocative reasons, but on second thought you figured it was the hard way to get back. I think you will find the Colonel just like his name — straight, that is. With your keen mind you will just about know when to put the charm on the Colonel. When you have worked him up to the pitch where he is ready to say, "Yes, Jim," just interrupt him and mention casually about the reservations on the new type passenger planes, the meals of which are much more superior than the old type 30 passenger planes. Besides the newest planes are built for comfort where a person can relax and sleep between highballs. If the Colonel shows any hesitancy whatsoever, just come right out and tell him frankly you will not settle for less. All Colonels like frankness.

As your final card just tell him you know a guy named Case in Washington who knows all the Generals and Colonels from Eisenhower's office down. Of course, I don't, but that is beside the point. The big idea is to impress the Colonel you know.

If the Colonel does not provide you with transportation in a manner that a person of your rank is accustomed, I might speak to a chap who is here visiting his old friends Senator Brewster and Senator Ferguson. His name is Howard Hughes. He is an old chum of the two senators, in fact, he last visited them only a couple months ago. Hughes, as you may know, produced the movie "The Outlaw" and he and the two senators are putting on a show here that is to last through the 20th. These three always play to a packed house, and it may be held over by popular demand.

The point is, Mr. Hughes just completed a new eight-propeller plane, and if your Colonel turns you down just tell him your old friend Case in Washington will arrange to have Howard Hughes fly you back. This will really impress the Colonel, believe me!

Then Col. C. E. Straight (called "Red" by his friends and often by the press) was to receive a letter from Col. Edward H. Young, chief, War Crimes Branch, dated November 12, 1947. To "Dear Red," Young wrote the following:

I am enclosing herewith the correspondence that the Executive Officer of CAD brought to my office with the statement that so far as the Graves Registration of QMG [General Horkan] and CAD were concerned this case is closed.

General Horkan stated that he had sent a representative of Graves Registration to the West Coast personally to visit and inform Mrs. Loyd of proof of her son's death, and she had accepted this decision and was satisfied. General Horkan stated further that he cared nothing about starting any controversy over the enclosed letters other than that he would like all war crimes agencies to carefully avoid giving out any private or personal statements that could be erroneously in conflict with official statements. Thus, I am telling you about this in order that you can take what action you see fit to preclude leaks in the future of information outside channels. I think you well might want to talk with Corbett about his letter but corrective action otherwise is clearly a matter I leave to you. When he receives the Case letter (copy of which is enclosed) undoubtedly he'll not try to pacify families of victims in his own private manner. I don't get Case's meaning in his long discourse about Corbett's action was to influence you getting him a luxurious ride home! However, you might be interested.

This correspondence back and forth between Case, and his accusations against members of this office and other civilian members of the War Crimes, is beginning to get under my skin. I don't know what his real motives are since apparently he is the heir of Mrs. Loyd to profit by the proven death of her son. Mr. Hubbert believes that he may be getting fees for continuing his inquiries, etc. Anyway, he is unreasonable and like many others who continue to bedevil everybody with inflammatory letters, a number of which come through this office quite often, I can't understand what results are expected.

I will be interested in hearing any comments you have on the foregoing remarks.

Case certainly was not timid. He had suggested to Corbett that he knew men of standing, and it appears that he took his evaluation of himself seriously. Just after Christmas, 1947, he wrote Colonel Straight directly.

This silence on the part of the WCC in occupied Germany, plus the amazing revelations exposed in a secret letter to me by your own investigator on October 31, 1947, leads to the inevitable conclusion that there is a well organized effort on the part of certain WCC officials in the American Zone of Germany to do an about face in carrying out the convictions of self-confessed Nazi criminals who murdered and tortured unarmed American boys who became prisoners of war. I am further advised that an intensified effort is being waged by Mrs. Hugo Wolf to bring pressure from top Germans who are now influential and work close with U.S. Army officials.

Your chief investigator, Mr. Corbett, in his speaking about the Nazi murderer, Kirschner, allows his letter to beam with such adjectives as "proud," "honest," et cetera, despite the fact that Kirschner not only violated the International Laws of War in ordering the assassination of Lt. Loyd, but Kirschner even violated his solemn oath to Adolph [sic] Hitler in the manner in which "spot trials" were ordered held by the Reichstag.

Colonel, it approaches criminal travesty when WCC officers will deliberately lie or be so gullible as to voluntarily set up such alibis for the Nazi criminals they are under oath to prosecute. This defense by Mr. Corbett comes too late to be of any value to Hugo Wolf. Hugo Wolf has already confessed about his close acquaintance with Mme. Franchini made in two lengthy sworn affidavits at Zuffenhausen, Germany, on February 4 and 5, 1946, in the presence of three U.S. Army officers. Just why these vitally important affidavits were quashed as evidence at the trial of Wolf is a matter I am very much interested in and my sister, Hazelle Loyd, mother of Lt. Loyd, has asked that I make every effort to find out.

After castigating the honesty of French witnesses in general, your chief investigation officer assures me that his opinion is a WCC pattern and says, "I am sure you would find the opinion here almost 90 percent in favor of forgetting French witnesses in our cases at Dachau." If this statement coming from a WCC official is true, then how does the WCC expect to get convictions that will hold water on appeal, since these Nazi murders of the American boys were committed on French soil before the eyes of French citizens? Could this possibly be the reason why the WCC in the Kirschner and Wolf trial picked the two outstanding weakest witnesses out of an available total of sixteen strong witnesses?

I most certainly regard your chief investigator's letter as a warning, and I strongly protest against this practice of the WCC in selecting the weakest possible witnesses for obtaining questionable convictions and ignoring the services of 100 percent eyewitnesses. I am bound to feel that my efforts of over two years securing information from Canada, England, Germany, and France, most of which I have given various Army branches when advised that the Army did not possess such information, is about to be defeated by a WCC policy disclosed by Mr. Corbett, your investigator. I have made my investigation over this long costly period quietly and without fanfare. But I can assure you of one thing, Colonel, if this letter of Mr. Corbett's is to stand without contradiction I will be forced very much against my own will to seek congressional assistance and my rights as an American to the freedom of the Hearst-McCormick-Patterson press.

By this time, Case had Straight's attention. It would seem that he had either underestimated Straight or overestimated his own potential for affecting Army affairs. In January 1948, Straight wrote to the chief, War Crimes Branch, about the Case problem:

It is suggested that a letter be directed to Mr. Case in substantially the following form:

The information set forth herein is in reply to letter of December 30, 1947, to Lieutenant Colonel C. E. Straight, Deputy Judge Advocate for War Crimes, European Command, concerning Daniel T. Loyd, a victim of the war crime involved in *U.S. vs. Kirschner et al.*, Case No. 11-96, trial by a Military Government Court appointed by the Commander-in-Chief, European Command. Most of the contents hereof are based upon information received for the addresses of your letter.

The Deputy Judge Advocate for War Crimes will have completed his Review and Recommendations for the Commander-in-Chief, European Command, in connection with the Kirschner case as well as the balance of the 489 cases tried by 7708 War Crimes Group, prior to April 30, 1948. Information received indicates that, because of your concern in the matter, the Kirschner case will probably be given priority over most of the other cases. Lieutenant Colonel Straight has stated that a preliminary examination of the record of trial fails to reveal any compelling reason for recommending a commutation of either of the death sentences imposed by the Court. Obviously, all those rendering assistance to the Commander-in-Chief, European Command, as to appropriate final action by him as Reviewing Authority will be governed by the record of trial and not an inappropriate and unofficial view expressed by Mr. Corbett.

It is agreed that many of the remarks by Mr. Corbett in his letter to you of October 31, 1947, were inappropriate and improvident. At no time was he Chief Investigator for the 7708 War Crimes Group, nor was he at any time in a position or assigned tasks permitting of his exercising authority over or initiating policies and procedures followed by that unit. Lieutenant Colonel Straight advises that Mr. Corbett's transfer from war crimes work to another agency in the European Command was affected prior to the arrival of any information there concerning his letter to you.

With reference to your expressed apprehension to the effect that officials in the U.S. Zone of Occupation, Germany, are avoiding their duty in connection with the execution of sentences imposed upon convicted war criminals, no official or unofficial reports or information to that effect have come to the attention of the Department of the Army, as a result of field inspections or otherwise.

As to the evidence introduced in the trial, it appears that the chief prosecutor was given considerable latitude to exercise his discretion as to the most effective order and manner to present his case. As you are fully aware, similar freedom of discretion is granted those in the Department of Justice and the offices of United States District Attorneys in the trial of cases assigned to them for trial. The results of the trial demonstrate that the [prosecutor] was successful in convincing the Court by the evidence adduced as to the guilt of the accused. A part of the report by the SHAEF Board of Inquiry was utilized.

That those in charge of the operation conducted by 7708 War Crimes Group do not agree with the ridiculous statement, made by Mr. Corbett in his letter to you as to French witnesses, is demonstrated by the fact that many hundreds of French witnesses have been utilized at Dachau. A quick survey indicates that more witnesses were brought from France than any other European country.

Case had been quick to realize the metaphorical possibilities of Straight's name. In his suggestions for wording a letter to Case that might settle the dust, Straight lived up to those possibilities; not only was he "straight" but he was also to the point. Straight's personality extended beyond control and firmness, however. He also appreciated possibilities. He ended his letter to the chief of the War Crimes Branch with an observation of his own.

> It is of interest to note that he attacks the undersigned [Straight] for the first time. He was quite complimentary as to me in his letter of 9 November, 1947, to Mr. Corbett, a copy of which letter I am keeping for possible future protective and defensive purposes.

Young sent a turnaround letter to Straight in which he said that he would follow Straight's suggestion with a couple of modifications. He decided to give Case only that information which was official and not supply him any personal opinions at all, and he decided that it was neither necessary nor appropriate to reply directly to many of Case's statements because they were "merely derogatory."

In a quick letter to Eberle, likely in reply to the letter Young had suggested, which had incorporated Straight's suggestions, it is obvious Case was not in awe of the words of the nation's mighty. He is not even impressed.

> Receipt of subject letter is hereby acknowledged, being your reply to my Brief of Charges to General Eisenhower, Jan 12, 1948, referred to you for investigation and report.
>
> Your reply was disappointing since you completely ignored my suggestions and charges and limited your reply to irrelevant subjects on "policy" and "tremendous volume of work and limited personnel of the War Crimes Branch."
>
> By taking your letter literally and checking it against pertinent Army Directives I learn that your statements concerning WCC policy are in error and contrary to Orders of July 11, 1947, regarding "Military Government of Germany" copies of which were sent to General Clay upon approval by the Joint Chiefs of Staff of Army, Navy, and State.
>
> The question you pose regarding records "which for security reasons are classified" is very confusing since General Eisenhower made public the statement that "the records of World War II are no longer secret." Adding to this confusion is Colonel Young's of October 29, 1947, stating that SHAEF files of Lt. Loyd have been "regraded and unclassified" at my request, by Order of Secretary of the Army "with British concurrence."

I wonder if you care, or if you appreciate the gravity of the reaction to a four-sided contradiction of this kind has on the mind of a mother who, since June 10, 1944, has spent a small fortune contacting Canadian, French, British, and German sources to learn facts about the assassination of her son, because of the general ineptness of the WCC. If you cannot see this picture, permit me to point it out to you and thus spare you the effort of study:

First, the unpredictable General Eisenhower, through the left side of his mouth, and for public consumption, states that records are no longer secret and through the right side of his mouth tells subordinate officers quite the opposite. Secondly, the British are permitted jurisdiction, no doubt by General Eisenhower's well-known "Lord Montgomery" complex, despite the fact that Lt. Loyd was never a British soldier nor a British subject. But inasmuch as Lt. Loyd gave his life as a U.S. Army Fighter Pilot, in the interest of perpetuating the British Empire (more than from any threat of any invasion threatening American citizens) the British in appreciation magnanimously permits a United States mother to see the records of her son. Thirdly, Col. Young limits the language of his letter to conform to the British SHAEF records and bypasses any commitment about current records regarding Lt. Loyd. Colonel Young's position is hardly fair in view of the fact that 90 percent of the information contained in the WCC file of Lt. Loyd was furnished directly and indirectly through the efforts of Lt. Loyd's mother and at her expense.

It seems to me that if any responsible official of the WCC possessed a sound understanding of the word "security" he would have long ago removed WCC personnel who are undermining the foreign program of the Congress and those who are consorting with condemned Nazi SS criminals by writing awe-inspiring, grave reverential letters with self-composed quotations on the behalf of these Nazi murderers which Nazi's themselves perhaps are not aware of.

There is no question about it, if the WCC personnel will devote just one tenth the energy in getting the job done as they spend in seeking excuses for not doing their job and by reading into letters of request controversial interpretations for stalling purposes, their job will be much easier and they will qualify for the public esteem that other branches of the Armed Services enjoy.

For reasons he apparently kept to himself, John Virgil Case then, somewhat abruptly, chose to exit the drama he seemed so determined to produce. In one of his final letters, he made a small request which was quickly honored. The full text of that letter is reprinted here.

About a year ago while acting in the behalf of my sister, Hazelle Loyd, 1360 N. Van Ness St., Hollywood, Calif., mother of the above deceased soldier, I requested the War Crimes Commission of Washington, D.C., to deliver the balance of Lt. Loyd's clothing, then held at Dachau, Germany, to his mother.

The War Crimes Commission advised that my request was premature in as much as an appeal was pending before General Clay in the case in which clothing was used as exhibits. Several months ago the appeal was reviewed and decided by General Clay and War Crimes Commission now suggests that your office is the proper one to receive this request.

The clothing includes Lt. Loyd's flying uniform, leather flyers jacket, whistle with strap attached, etc.

Although trial records do not include many requests for information *from* families of American victims, documents do exist that reveal a determination to limit information *to* families. The obnoxious behavior of Case was countered by a turf-protection attitude by the Army.

While John Case and the shadowy mother who grieved in the background carried on their agonies—or conceits—in the form of high-level correspondence, Kirschner and Wolf were fighting for their lives. Wolf, the actual executioner, would win his battle; Kirschner, the prosecutor, judge, and sole juror, would not. Their battle with each other was as fierce as it would be with those who held power over their lives. The mother of Wolf suffered no less. The following is her petition for the mercy of the Court.

I, the undersigned widow Maria Wolf, nee Perktold, living at Tarrenze No. 8, received only today by my daughter-in-law Ele Wolf the information which is utmostly said for me as mother, that my son, Hugo Wolf, has been sentenced to death by the American Military Court in Dachau.

I, as mother, cannot imagine that my son Hugo could perpetrate such a punishable act from his own initiative and which should be atoned for by death. If he did a wrong thing, this can have happened only upon instigation and orders of a superior authority. I know my son Hugo as a decent, good, and obedient man, as good father of his family, who lived only for his children and his wife, and he has never seen his youngest child.

As neither my son nor his wife have any property or other income available, the children and his wife would forever be a victim of trouble and misery. There I make the petition together with my daughter-in-law Ele Wolf and the three small children to change the passed death sentence into a prison term.

I am over eighty years old, gave birth to eighteen children, of which twelve children are still alive. It would be my only and last wish that my son Hugo Wolf would partake of a pardoning for which I as well as my children, my daughter-in-law Ele Wolf with her three unsupported children would be thankful all their lives.

For reasons unrelated to the pleas of his mother, Wolf's death sentence was commuted and he was eventually paroled to return to family life.

Soon after the pronouncement of his sentence, Karl Kirschner was defiant in a letter to the president of the International Red Cross in Geneva.

> I am addressing this letter to you, Mr. President, because you are the only impartial authority who could scrutinize war events under the provisions of the Geneva Convention without any bias and without referring to that law which retroactively declares certain actions to be unlawful. I don't ask you to consider that that new law is applicable to the vanquished only, that that International Law is not applicable to all persons, and that there are allegedly persons amongst the victorious nations who have committed similar crimes.
>
> I don't want to burden you, Mr. President, with any unnecessary details; all I want is to give you a general picture of the case. I don't want to discuss the question of "fair play" in regard to subject trial. This would be a chapter in itself.
>
> An American Military Tribunal at Dachau has sentenced to death two combat soldiers, one officer and one NCO, for the murder of an American flier.
>
> On 10 June 1944, four days after the beginning of the invasion of Northern France this flier had set afire a German ambulance by his bullets flying at the height of about 100 meters. The ambulance was clearly marked with the sign of the Red Cross in accordance with the International Convention. Two wounded German officers who were on their way to a hospital were killed by the attack. The flier was shot down at the place of his attack and an ordinary Summary Military Court sentenced him to death by shooting. The two men killed by the flier as well as the flier himself had a military funeral and the three graves were marked with crosses. A report was submitted through channels to the Superior Command. All this has been proved by testimony of witnesses. In spite of all this, the death penalty has been imposed upon me due to the fact that the law applied favors only the victors and that only such evidence is admitted which is necessary to obtain a death sentence. Everything else is disregarded even if the truth has been established.
>
> I beg you to take into consideration particularly that the above mentioned event occurred in the front line during the days of the invasion. It was definitely a clear violation of the Geneva Convention and a typical war crime under International Law to (1) kill wounded soldiers, and (2) to disregard regulations pertaining to the International Red Cross. In a war the perpetrator of such a crime must stand trial; in this specific case he had to be tried by a Summary Court. After the beginning of the invasion, ambulances and first aid stations were continuously attacked and destroyed by American fighters flying at low altitude. Thousands of combat soldiers can testify that this is correct.

In his letter to the Red Cross, Kirschner seems not to deny that he convened the Court or that he ordered the shooting of Lt. Loyd. As his execution date closed in, he developed a new story about the death of the airman. In a letter to a lawyer in July of 1948, Kirschner said that now that his death sentence was final, he hoped the end would come soon so that he would at last find peace, but that, facing death, he would like to "clarify" a few facts.

> My death sentence was probably based upon the fact of giving the order. As you well know, I stated during my first interrogation that I did not give Wolf any order but handed the flier over to Wolf with a movement of my hand which meant that he was responsible for guarding the flier. I was already approximately eight paces away from the group when I heard four to six shots out of an automatic pistol. On account of that I immediately returned to the scene and found out that Wolf had shot the flier upon a sign of Hildebrand [a soldier who was not charged]. I was completely surprised about this incident as I was entirely unconscious of the happenings. It was my intention to transfer the flier together with the records of the Summary Court Martial as I did not want to take the responsibility. If I had had in mind to shoot the flier then it never would have happened about three meters off the main road and right in front of the castle [the headquarters]. Such an action carried out by me as a senior officer simply would have been impossible. It was Hildebrand's idea of having the execution carried out without my knowledge; nobody can lay the blame for this on me.

Kirschner is left with a problem, however, as his explanation is in conflict with his letter to the International Red Cross, and it does not cover other aspects of the record. At this point he claimed that the uncharged Hildebrand was responsible for the shooting. Kirschner had exhibited great confidence in his decisions, and, as always, he continued to have confidence in his ability to explain away the obvious.

> Although I had admitted during the trial of having given the order, this was due to my troubles and the awkward position of Wolf and because I was good-natured and did not feel guilty but wanted to help a comrade without thinking of myself. At Dachau in the bunker I was persuaded by Wolf and his acquaintances to take the responsibility of having given the order for shooting as on account of the Summary Court Martial directives nothing could be held against me anyhow. I even let myself be influenced so far to give the court a description of the exact procedure of the shooting which was a pure fiction for the purpose of exonerating Wolf. I did all that only for Wolf's advantage and now my false statements turned out as very heavy incriminations against myself.
>
> I understand quite well that you naturally will get the idea that I am now trying to excuse myself by means of such an exoneration now that my death sentence is approved. Already last year I informed the lawyer, Dr.

Lafontaine, in my letter dated 8 July 1947, one and one half months after the sentence was announced that I had not given any orders and that I only took the blame on me in the delusion of a sacrifice in Wolf's favor. I also informed the reviewing authority in Munich about these facts in my statement of 19 December 1947. Thus you can see that I did not get this idea only recently.

Kirschner also believed that since Wolf's death sentence had been commuted and Wolf had nothing to lose, Wolf's memory might be more in line with his own. Unfortunately, the best Wolf could say was that he no longer knew for sure whether Kirschner or Hildebrand had given the order to shoot Loyd, this according to Kirschner's letter. Unfortunately, the paragraph that offered this information contradicted the earlier paragraph in the letter, which said that Wolf had misunderstood the waving of his hand as an indication to execute the prisoner. On September 29, Kirschner wrote a letter to his chief defender, providing him with yet another version of the events.

> The truth is that it was Wolf, whom I met in front of the shelter in Rugles, where the aviator was and who told me that he will shoot the aviator there, on the meadow — showing this with his hand — which has been prevented by my intervention. It is Wolf who made this declaration with a certain intention, without I ever thinking of it, never having seen or spoken to the aviator.
>
> Of the indictment of robbing I'm completely free as something not admitted to by my education and my honor. Being a German officer I never stole or robbed a man. The truth is that I saw the portfolio of the aviator at [with?] Wolf, he himself showed me a photo of the aviator. Watch and ring I didn't see. Till now I kept silent; I can't do it any longer.
>
> The truth is that I didn't give Wolf any order of shooting; that Wolf and Hildebrand acted without my knowledge on their own initiative. In Dachau Wolf and others influenced me to take the issue of order on me, as on court martial basis nothing could happen to me and Wolf would be herewith freed of responsibility. I did it for Wolf and let him appear as agent executing an order without pondering the damage I inflict herewith on me.

Kirschner continued through the long letter to say that Wolf was not the innocent he played. Wolf, he said, had been a member of the Nazi Party and had connived to hide participation in other war activities. He also accused Wolf of feigning illness and having his tonsils removed just before the trial. He was brought into the courtroom on a litter and didn't testify because he said he could not talk. "This intention was as he told me later on in Dachau, to avoid these questions," wrote Kirschner. "On the day following the verdict, Wolf tried an escape from the hospital whereby he was caught again outside the camp. He who tries to evade is conscious of a fault." Kirschner ended by saying he was alone and destitute, could not afford an attorney, and was begging for help based upon an appeal to the lawyer's kindness.

It's unlikely any lawyer could have helped Kirschner given his ever-changing stories. The stories, however, are only the smallest part of what humans tried to do in an attempt to escape death. Kirschner begged for his life. It was the same, most likely, for Lt. Loyd. In Kirschner's letter is a glimpse of the desperation and fear millions of victims experienced. Following the guilty to the gallows has something in common with following the concentration camp inmate to the trough of water where he stands in line behind other inmates to be drowned, even though the former is justice and the latter is murder.

Karl Kirschner was hanged at Landsberg Prison.

11

The Atrocity:
The Story of Paul Wolfram

In civilian life Paul Wolfram was a "technical merchant" in his late forties. In December of 1940, he was named manager of the stone quarry in Gusen I, an out-camp of Mauthausen and one of the most brutal satellites associated with this most brutal parent camp. The quarry was owned and operated by the German Earth and Stone Works Company, which was a firm controlled by the SS. Leaders of the SS apparently had substantial personal interests in the enterprise also.

Wolfram was born September 13, 1900, in Geilsdorf. Affidavits claimed that he was hardworking and determined to make every endeavor he attempted work as efficiently as he possibly could. He was one of those men who are driven to secure a good education in a profession for his children. During the early years with the company, Wolfram was technically a civilian employee. He controlled and directed all the work in the stone quarry with most of the labor being forced from concentration camp prisoners of many nations. He had administrative responsibility for discipline, work assignments, and personal resources, such as clothes and shelter. His office was near the stone quarry and he was in the stone quarry every day. Witnesses would claim that far beyond his administrative responsibilities he was extremely demanding and brutal, and everyone feared this powerful man.

Although witnesses would say that Wolfram was directly and indirectly responsible for hundreds—or more likely, thousands—of deaths, he was specifically charged with three crimes: two murders and participation in the Mauthausen "Common Design" Atrocity. He received a life sentence.

The "Common Design" particulars of the charges of Violations of the Laws and Usages of War sprang from precedents set by previous cases and held that camps like Mauthausen with their particular aura of evil were in and of themselves criminal enterprises and that the atrocities perpetrated there were "criminal in nature and that the participants therein, acting in pursuance of a common design, subjected persons to killings, beatings, tortures, etc.," and the Court "was warranted in inferring that those shown to have participated knew of the criminal nature thereof." Although the Court took note of the extent to which each defendant participated, any charge of murder or brutality in any degree could engender the "Common Design" aspects of the greater crime — sometimes called the Mass Atrocity.

The words of the charge against Wolfram are the same as those used to charge others with the same crime.

> Particulars: In that Paul Wolfram, a German national or person acting with German nationals, acting in pursuance of a common design to subject the persons hereinafter described to killings, beatings, tortures, starvation, abuse, and indignities, did, at or in the vicinity of the Mauthausen Concentration Camp, at Castle Hartheim, and at or in the vicinity of the Mauthausen Sub-camps, including but not limited to Ebensee, Gross-Raming, Gunskirchen, Gusen, Hinterbruehl, Lamback, Linz, Loiblpass, Melk, Schwechat, St. Georgen, St. Lambrecht, St. Valentin, Steyr, Vienna, Wiener-Neudorf, all in Austria, at various and sundry times between January 1, 1942, and May 5, 1945, wrongfully encourage, aid, abet, and participate in the subjection of Poles, Frenchmen, Greeks, Yugoslavs, Citizens of the Soviet Union, Norwegians, Danes, Belgians, Citizens of the Netherlands, Citizens of the Grand Duchy of Luxombourg [sic], Turks, British Subjects, stateless persons, Czechs, Chinese, Citizens of the United States of America, and other non–German nationals who were then and there in the custody of the then German Reich, and members of the armed forces of nations then at war with the then German Reich who were then and there surrendered and unarmed prisoners of war in the custody of the then German Reich, to killings, beatings, tortures, starvation, abuses and indignities, the exact names and numbers of such persons being unknown, but aggregating thousands.

For decades, scholars, journalists, and even humanity at large have found it difficult to understand why Nazi atrocities happened. It was the nature of the trials to try to learn the answer to this. Witnesses tried diligently to answer the question, but they could not actually describe it. Another question that plagued inquisitors and still haunts historians was, "How did it happen?" Publishers regularly issue books addressing the topic, but each new effort still seems incomplete and new books continue to pour forth. "Why?" the world begs to know, but more than half a century later, no one can explain it. The trials were only minorly successful in answering "Who?" Even "When?" was elusive.

Dissecting the corpse to discover the cause of an atrocity was beyond the tasks required of pathologists who examined bodies that were tossed into roadside weeds several weeks prior to discovery. Natural curiosity about the dead was not enough incentive to encourage the average investigator into a detailed study. The investigators and prosecutors associated with the trials were, at the least, forced to try to enumerate the crimes, but enumeration and dissection are not the same. What seems obvious is that the Mauthausen Atrocity could not have existed without single atrocities. Chains of events, interwoven, formed the web, but every starting point was a single event, and any attempt to understand must begin with the single events.

Apparently, an assignment to a concentration camp as guard or administrator, or as supervisor for an industrial project for which the SS would provide labor as happened to Paul Wolfram, was not necessarily a desirable assignment for a German. It was somewhat less dangerous than the front, but many knew in advance that they were going to work in a hellish situation. Letters and other documents of the time indicate that Germans seemed to know they would be doing things they would not ordinarily do and that they would certainly prefer not to do. They also seemed to feel that these actions were inevitable and that they would have no choice but to participate. It was also hard duty. However, choice did exist. The choice might have been life or death — not a lesser or greater degree of choice than serving on the eastern front — but choice did exist. Some even managed by luck or force of personality to avoid crossing the lines into criminality. Some actually thought that beating prisoners, the "twenty-five," was compassionate — a more humane punishment than the alternative.

It is impossible to enumerate all the events that constructed the web of the Common Design Atrocity or find much in common among them except their senseless cruelty, but consider the commandant who hanged escaped prisoners in the roll call square after they had been recaptured. It is reasonable to deduct that men were not appointed commandants who did not want to be commandants. The pay was higher and the advantages of rank were obvious. He had access to benefits and could skim off resources if he chose. Although Commandant Karl Otto Koch was convicted for fraud at the Buchenwald concentration camp, a commandant did not excite the displeasure of his superiors if he was discreet and modest in his needs. Greed, like lust, was understood as was evidenced by the profit SS men like Himmler were allowed to take from such endeavors as the Gusen quarry. For purposes of understanding and analysis, the actions that brought the prisoners to the camp might not actually be blamed on the commandant. For purposes of analysis, historians might not blame the commandant for the terrible conditions of the prisoners that arrived or for the work they would be forced to do. Moreover, the commandant was charged with keeping order and preventing escapes, and what better way to discourage escapes than to hang the culprit in the roll call square. It is a deterrent. The argument is given in the United States in support of the death penalty. An argument is still offered in modern societies that it is as acceptable to take the life of a person to frighten other would-be murderers as to punish the person for the crime he has committed, if the penalty would be enacted otherwise. In no developed country is the death penalty allowed for prison escape, however. To carry out such a penalty is at the least excessive and, at even a modest level of reason, criminal. However, illegal acts ordered by a commandant and carried out by those of lower rank did not the Atrocity make. That required much more.

Discipline was the second function of the administration and its assistants. Physical punishment, being both cruel and unusual in the eyes of developed societies, is out of bounds. However, given the chaotic conditions, the angry prisoners, and the compromised mental ability, age, and physical condition of the guards, and given that such traditional solutions to unruly behavior as isolation and solitary confinement were impossible, and considering that a war was raging, one can stretch the imagination to find reason in physical punishment. Physical punishments are primitive and criminal, but they did not the Atrocity make.

On the other hand, it's possible that hangings for escape (and other crimes such as murder) might not have constituted a Mass Atrocity if they had been enacted according to some German law and had been assigned by a German court. The same can be said of physical punishments, but the Atrocity went beyond stretching the law — or even breaking the law. It went beyond pilfering Red Cross packages and isolated brutal acts by unfit guards. It went beyond multiple acts of common-law murder and beyond any system of laws that exists in the world, however brutal that system may be.

A reading of testimony from various trials allows the persuasive argument that many activities by guards falling into the category of an atrocity were not ordered. These activities were sometimes expected. They were excused. They were permitted. Many single instances that made up the Mauthausen Atrocity happened as direct decisions made by day laborers and were tolerated by superiors. Many acts making up the Atrocity did not go from top to bottom; they went from bottom to top. A madman and his minions did not accomplish atrocities by themselves, no matter how much determination their obsessions generated. Perhaps the best way to examine the Atrocity is to examine such daily decisions as illustrated by trial records.

A prisoner took off his hat and that was against the rule. A capo grabbed the hat from his hand and threw it beyond the ring of guards. Anyone who crossed the ring of guards was automatically shot. The capo ordered the prisoner to retrieve the hat by breaching the ring of guards. This series of events happened over and over. Sometimes the hat excuse was not even used; the prisoner was merely chased beyond the ring of guards in a sort of gleeful game.

Guards, capos, and block leaders drowned prisoners in barrels, in tubs, in buckets of urine, and in specially designed baths.

A prisoner used a piece of yellow wire from the scraps left in the tunnels to tie the pieces of his shoe onto his foot. A guard stood on his throat until he perished. Picking up a piece of any property of the quarry company was stealing.

A prisoner removed his shoe and a guard spied a bit of blanket wrapped around his foot in lieu of a sock. German rules did not allow such things. He was murdered on the spot.

Sick, exhausted, frightened prisoners were made to stand naked in the roll call square for days on end, or until they died, while being periodically sprayed with cold water. When the infirmary became crowded, anything handy from gasoline to the odd pesticide was injected into them. All body orifices were violated in never-ending strings of inventions. Prisoners were shot, beaten, stabbed, bludgeoned, hanged, thrown on an electric fence, bathed, worked, and run to their deaths. A German doctor stated that many hundreds starved to death every day at Ebensee, one of the out-camps of Mauthausen.

Prisoners were exposed to oppressive heat and killing cold, to contagious diseases, to dangerous and unsafe working conditions, to dusts, fumes, poisons, and every industrial pollutant imaginable.

On at least one occasion, prisoners were thrown into a ditch of caustic (quick lime), and they returned to camp bearing chemical burns.

A camp administrator called out all the homosexuals in the camp and made them beat each other brutally while he stood by and "masturbated widely."

During March of 1945, less than two months before the capitulation, at Gusen II, an out-camp of Mauthausen that served the Messerschmitt tunnels, all sick inmates, numbering between eight hundred and a thousand, were striped naked and ordered to walk to or were carried to Block 16 where they stood totally exposed to the cold. Then they were murdered in an hours-long orgy of slaughter that left them dead almost to a man. The

The living lay among the dead in unspeakable conditions. This photograph was taken at the liberation of Nordhausen.

resident SS men, block leaders, and capos beat them with sticks, clubs, guns, and axes. The dead included Yugoslavs, French, Russians, Italians, and Poles. The whole massacre had required the efforts of fewer than a dozen men. The camp commandant could not say it didn't happen; he could only say that it happened at night when he wasn't there and he hadn't approved it. He did not say he punished the murderers in any way.

Efforts to prevent disease sometimes resulted in more deaths than would have happened had the prisoners been left to let nature take its course. The Germans were almost pathologically disgusted by lice. At Gusen II, a couple of months before the slaughter of the sick, a massive delousing procedure took the lives of about 800 men. Thousands of men in several blocks were ordered to disrobe entirely and were sent, naked, to live among inmates of other blocks. For days, they had to live in unheated shelters and stand outdoors for three-hour roll calls, still naked, in the deep winter cold. In addition to the hundreds who died of exposure, several died from being returned to the deloused barracks while the poisonous gas still hung in the air. As always, some were also beaten to death for not being quick of foot or for otherwise distressing the guards and capos. Again the commandant could only offer the explanation when questioned about the thousands of naked men running around in the winter cold that he "didn't notice."

Even the most minor infraction of their peculiar rules could result in punishment severe enough to bring on death. Faces had to be clean shaven, hats and caps worn, no additions to the "uniform" for purposes of avoiding exposure were allowed, and salutes had to be just so.

So many died in some of the camps — especially Mauthausen — that the infamous death books contained strings of entries only minutes apart. It would have required a full-time clerk around the clock to ascertain the information — date of birth, nationality, inmate number, date and hour of death, and cause of death — and to record the facts in the careful script that made up the books. Almost always, the cause of death was a disease or condition. Almost always, that was, at the moment and in the history of the dead, a lie.

Exhumed bodies (or bodies left lying around on top of the ground behind buildings or along walkways) would give up the real reasons for their death. Doctors from the camps testified to the real reasons their patients' names were put into the neat rows of the death books.

The camps were rife with sadists. A Rumanian named Andreas Schilling who had been drafted into the Waffen SS was a case in point. (Rumania, for purposes of trial, was considered a co-belligerent of Germany.) Of him, it was said, "The name Schilling is the bloodiest name in all the concentration camp careers there." Schilling had served at Mauthausen early in the war and by 1943 was a corporal at Ebensee, another notorious out-camp of Mauthausen.

During the winter months of 1945, several transports arrived at Ebensee where Schilling played a major role as medic. Many inmates were forced to stand all night in the roll call square without food or water, waiting to be processed. Then they were literally beaten into the bathhouse where their hair was cut, and they were given both hot and cold showers and forced back out into the winter day. About three hundred inmates died during this part of the process. Many simply collapsed in the bathroom. When a capo in charge of the bathroom complained to Schilling about too many men being on the floor of the bathroom, he ordered that they be put on stretchers and dumped behind the disinfecting building. Of the approximately 30 who were dumped, about 20 still showed signs of life. They lay on the ground and froze.

Always, the transports arrived at this last station for the living with many sick, and some of the transports arrived with several dead among the prisoners. Sometimes the sick and the dead were not separated but were placed into a common pile where they awaited their final destination: the crematory.

It was not uncommon for a guard to kick and beat unconscious or nearly unconscious prisoners. Schilling kicked a man's ulcerated leg for 15 minutes. On one occasion, according to a witness, he simply trampled across sick inmates who were tightly packed on the hospital floor. Schilling beat a Polish inmate doctor to death with the leg of a stool and hit a Hungarian inmate doctor with his fist for accepting a patient Schilling did not believe was ill. He tied other inmates to a bunk in such a way that they had to stand on tiptoes to avoid strangulation. He would come by at intervals and hit them with a stick or kick them in the abdomen. After two days of abuse and no food or water, the inmates died. He killed inmates with injections of gasoline. He cut the rations of tubercular patients in half. Doctors would testify that he, not the doctors, made decisions about who would or would not receive hospitalization. Even one of the defense said that he was a "bad SS man." The instances of his brutality were almost too many to number.

The SS operated efficient death camps at several places to rid themselves of those whose race or infirmity disgusted them. Why generate, tolerate, and support such a self-defeating "common design" as a mass atrocity in a camp that existed primarily to supply labor? Could the Nazis have had a need beyond a hunger for power and wealth grabbing? Did their social order *need* atrocities in the same way serial killers need victims? Although the trials managed to begin an enumeration of the single atrocities and confirmed the Atrocity, they did not answer these questions.

Adolescents suffered the same tortures and indignities as adults. This young man was well enough to use the bucket; others with dysentery were not so fortunate and had to defecate on the floor. Photograph taken at the liberation of Zwieberge, an outcamp of Mauthausen and Dachau concentration camps.

Men who had worked as grocers, blacksmiths, construction workers, and office clerks and had never acted in a criminal way before the Atrocity, who, if they escaped the gallows, did not commit a criminal act after the Atrocity, and who were terribly upset to learn they were being assigned to a camp seemed to adjust to the system of brutality without missing a beat. Is this a universal human trait? This worrisome question is still debated among scholars.

Filling in the gaps in the Atrocity were persons who were not patriots with a cause, or the hungry with an ambition, or sadists with an opportunity. Looking for a special kind of degenerate personality is a lost cause. For the most part it is not there — at least it is not there in the conclusions of the trials.

Paul Wolfram had neither orders nor the need to personally dirty his hands with day-to-day interaction with prison laborers. At his trial, he was not convicted of all that was said about him, but the testimony painted a picture of what the life of an atrocity-maker was like.

Wolfram was responsible for workers' clothes, food, work assignments, and discipline, but any direct activity was from his own choice. He had assistants at several levels of the organization whom he could have held responsible for the goals of the organization — goals designed to maximize production in the quarry.

It is hard to imagine that chances of meeting production goals were enhanced by the management style of Wolfram (if prisoners' recollections were reliable). Instead, it seems that achieving a level of brutality which would qualify as atrocity received as much attention as production goals. Almost constantly disabling or killing workers that had to be replaced could not possibly have contributed to production goals. Subjecting workers to lack of sleep and unnecessary exertion could not have contributed to production goals. Siphoning off workers for endless burial details and wasting time with frenetic record keeping could not have been to the advantage of the German Earth and Stone Works Company.

Yet we know that Wolfram did not act without the approval of those who, except for the unfortunate prisoners, had most to lose by the inefficiency generated by brutality: his superiors in the SS such as Himmler.

Witnesses said that Wolfram was always trying to make the capos get more work out of the inmates. They were as fearful of him as were the ordinary inmates. He would walk around looking for weak inmates. He sent sick inmates back to the camp to be exterminated.

Wolfram had nothing against doing his own dirty work and he managed to find someone to abuse almost every day. When he saw a Russian cutting stone that did not meet his standards, he ordered the man to bend over and he hit him twenty-five times with a board. The man crawled to avoid the terrible blows and Wolfram started beating him over the head. The man was sent to the dispensary where he died.

On another occasion Wolfram was the moving force that caused 150 weak inmates to be locked in a building for about a month where they were given only one-eighth of their normal rations. All but 15 died. As he wrote down the numbers, he said, "All cripples will have to die." He repeated this technique on another occasion. He was accused of shooting three Russians who had come out of the tunnels too soon after an air raid. He also beat three French Jews with a pickaxe handle and kicked them over a ledge; they fell 50 meters to their deaths. He was accused by witnesses of standing on the neck of a Yugoslav inmate until he died when he learned a beating by a capo had not killed him. After the man expired, he kicked the dead body several times.

However, Wolfram need not have done any of this to subject himself to the "Common Design" particulars of participating in the Atrocity for which he was found guilty. Having merely been present among murderers without making an effort to protect inmates would have subjected him to this charge.

Wolfram was convicted of murdering two individuals with his bare hands or, more properly stated, with his feet. He hit a Spanish inmate several times with his fist and kicked him. The man fell a distance of about one meter to the next level of the quarry where he landed on another man. Both men then fell 15 more meters to die on sharp stones at the bottom. Later, Wolfram beat another inmate and kicked him off a ledge to die "30 to 50" meters below. The Court found him guilty of both these incidents. The other charges, supported by testimony, whether true in all or in part, fell under the Common Design for which he was also convicted.

Wolfram was sentenced to life imprisonment, which, for most defendants, meant less than ten years. One recalls Wilhelm Grill's argument that administrators and officers with greater guilt were given much lighter sentences than those of lower rank. The transcript of the trial does not explain why Wolfram was not given a death sentence, but a partial explanation might be that he was privileged to put on a more sophisticated defense than was Grill and his peers. It also could have been that the Court simply did not believe all the witnesses.

On the other hand, Wolfram might have had another factor working in his favor that could not be easily disputed. He revealed it in his own words:

About the beginning of April, 1945, I was called to SS Col. Ziereiss in SS Captain Seidler's room. Ziereiss, Seidler, SS 1st Lt. Schuettauf, and I were present. Ziereiss informed us of a secret order which had been issued by Reich Leader Himmler via Kaltenbrunner and Gauleiter Eigruber. It said that all the inmates of Concentration Camp Mauthausen, including the out-camps, were to be exterminated. The following reasons were quoted:
1. That the enemy would not be able to commit the prisoners [100,000 men altogether] against our troops, and

2. That all the witnesses of conditions and incidents in camp were to be eliminated.

We were ordered to keep that order secret and to carry it out strictly. We and our families were threatened with instant death penalty in case of violation. The greater part of the prisoners from Mauthausen as well as Gusen I and II were to be taken into the tunnels and underground factory work shops of the Gusen and St. Georgen plants with the pretense of an air raid warning. The entrances to the tunnels were to be blocked by blowing them up causing thereby death from suffocation. This action was to be carried out upon the code word "cigarette lighter," or such like. The individual duties were allocated as follows:

1. SS Captain Seidler was to take care of getting the air raid warning sounded and have all the prisoners come into the tunnel including the dispensary.

2. SS 1st Lt. Schuettauf had to safeguard the entries with machine guns in order to prevent the prisoners from breaking out.

3. I was to carry out the blasting.

I decided immediately not to carry out this order and started to make objections in order to gain time which resulted in approximately the following conversation:

I: "The prisoners will not carry the explosives in there or else they will not go into tunnels any more during an air raid warning."

Ziereiss: "Then we shall load three trains with explosives, have them ignited and driven into the tunnel. For this purpose you will establish the amount of your explosives and work out an exact calculation so that the matter will come off at all events. You will send me the calculation and the technical drawings."

Ziereiss went away and there I was, unable to do anything about it. I checked the supplies and calculated that a fantastic quantity of explosives would be needed so that we would need approximately three times as much to carry out the blasting. I was able to risk making such calculations since there was no other specialist to doubt my calculations or accuse me of sabotage. I was assigned to this task since I am an expert in blasting. Ziereiss came to me at once and gave me the order to close up two of the three tunnel entrances; that is to say, each tunnel with two walls each. I carried out that order but used up the greater part of the existing explosives in procurement of rocks for the walls. Thus the blasting was again out of the question. Ziereiss inspected the walls and told me that everything was going to be all right now. I replied that I had hardly any explosives left since I had to use them for getting rocks. Ziereiss accused me then of having sabotaged his explicit instructions to keep a reserve of explosives. I defended myself by saying that the second order [of closing up the tunnels] had to be carried out first according to military regulations. However, Ziereiss did not give in and had 20 or 24 bombs brought along from somewhere in order to carry out the blasting. These bombs arrived at Gusen in the evening and were placed in an underground ammunition dump of the plant by SS non-coms only. That room had been assigned for it by Ziereiss. I was the last one to leave the storeroom and quickly hid the detonating agent which had been sent separately in a small box. Ziereiss came for inspection the following day or the day after and I reported that the bombs were useless since there was no detonating agent. Ziereiss accused and abused me again and declared that he was going to find a way out.

Ziereiss ordered 120 sea mines which arrived in two trucks and two trailers. They were placed in the same storeroom again which has been mentioned already by SS non-coms. These mines were without igniters, however, so that they could not be used either. During the inspection I reported that to Ziereiss. He gave me the order to have one of these mines taken to his office. He inspected it minutely and told me to open up the mines and use the explosives contained inside for the blasting. I refused to do it since I knew that these mines often contained friction igniters which would blow up in such a process. Ziereiss went away fuming and sent his artificer, a young Austrian, to me. After I had told him my doubts, he went to Linz and returned with the information that the detonating agents had actually been sent to a different place, but that the mines could be taken apart without any danger. I refused to do that so he proposed to use prisoners for it. I refused that too and referred to the regulations that for the past few days the territory, with its important production, was under the jurisdiction of the special commissioner for jet planes and that under no circumstances he would give his permission for that.

From that time onwards I did not hear any more from Ziereiss. It may have been about the 27th or 28th of April. I only heard that ever since Ziereiss drank from morning till night and again from night till morning and was never sober. Then I made my wife and one son escape — two days later my second son and my daughter; in the afternoon I vanished in somebody else's vehicle and went into the Alps. I threw the key of the underground ammunition dump into the Danube.

Wolfram was taken prisoner by the Austrians in June 1945 and was sent to a POW camp in Germany in October of that same year. His family was held at a camp in Schwanenstadt, Austria, before being expelled to Germany in October 1945, with only "a few pieces of portable luggage." His daughter, in one of her continuing pleas for clemency, said that they had been forced to leave behind their seven rooms of furniture, money, clothes, linens, and all other possessions. They were forced to live under destitute conditions as refugees in Germany. One of Wolfram's greatest concerns was that his sons had not been able to continue their education during his imprisonment. Toward the end as he petitioned for parole, he said that one son had not been able to go to college at all and the other had only recently been able to go to school on his own initiative.

After a year, Wolfram was released from the POW camp, and he started a quarry business. After about another year, he was arrested again, this time by the Americans in September 1947, based on affidavits accusing him of murder and other grievous misconduct at Gusen and Mauthausen. This last arrest would lead to his trial. He had enjoyed a year of freedom before his trial and had been able to acquire the assets that would enable him to move back into business after his imprisonment.

Wolfram's family, in spite of being "destitute," managed to wage a sophisticated battle to obtain his freedom. His files are filled with extensive, intense appeals over the years put together by obviously expensive attorneys. (The family was not forced or did not choose to liquidate their father's quarry equipment; it still remained in sufficient quantities and in sufficient good shape to allow him to eventually open a significant business.) His daughter, who was in her late twenties and early thirties during her father's imprisonment, was the real fighter in the family. She appealed to the U.S. High Commission for Legal Aid in 1952, saying that the family could no longer afford the fees for the legal fight; however, the battle went on.

The volume of affidavits collected by the daughter and Wolfram's legal staff included many from prisoners who said that Wolfram had not been a brutal man. Rarely did this tactic work. The review boards wanted humility, repentance, and reform.

Wolfram's sentence clearly indicated that the Court had weighed evidence and had made a judgment that looked beyond what was recorded on paper. The witnesses would be accused of being professionals and former inmates who had suffered to such an extent that they felt all Germans should pay the ultimate price. The Court might have taken some of the testimony with a grain of salt. Had they believed everything in the record, they would surely have sentenced Wolfram to death. Other than his claim that he had saved the lives of up to 100,000 men by his moral conniving during the last days of the war, he had a few other things going for him. He stated that he did not know in the early years that the SS ran the quarry at Gusen, he had never belonged to the Nazi Party or any of its affiliates; he was forced into the Waffen SS during the final days of the war; and he was able to produce some witnesses who, without obvious bias, were able to say that they had observed decent behavior from him. However, the Court would have found it impossible to believe that anyone could have been present at the infamous quarry, and especially to manage the quarry, and not have realized that it was a hellish, criminal place. As the case moved through appeals and reviews and Wolfram's daughter kept fighting, this attitude remained intact.

Wolfram was an excellent prisoner. He never caused a bit of bother to anyone. During most of the years of his confinement, he remained bitter and believed he had been wrongly convicted. Only with his request for clemency and parole in 1954 could prison administrators say he had lost his bitterness and accepted his punishment. A small measure of clemency (beyond the usual reduction of sentence that all prisoners eventually received) was given Wolfram so that he could be eligible for the parole he received in 1955. He needed this bit of consideration because he had begun his sentence later than most other prisoners because of his "free" year between the end of the war and his trial.

Under parole, Wolfram was to be employed by the owner of a quarry. It appears that the owner abused him by not giving him overtime pay for the long hours he demanded. Further, Wolfram, a devoted family man, was restricted to an area that did not permit him to visit his family. He broke parole by quitting his job and going to see his family. His parole was officially revoked and he lost ninety days' good conduct time, but Wolfram had an ace up his sleeve. He had the equipment, the skills, and the management ability to open a quarry that had been closed after the war in a region where the citizens desperately needed employment. Again the Court system was pragmatic. He was allowed to open his quarry and move on with his life.

12

The Nazi Brother of Distinguished Americans: The Story of Christian Mohr

A letter was sent to Harry S Truman, president of the United States of America, by the Rev. John Mohr, pastor, Campbellsport Reformed Church, Campbellsport, Wisconsin, on August 12, 1947. The Rev. Mohr wrote:

> I am writing to you concerning a brother of mine who has been under arrest by the American Military War Crimes Commission in occupied Germany since the close of the war and is now under sentence of death as the enclosed document will show. For your information I wish to state that I have been an American citizen since 1915; that I never was connected with any organization that fostered Nazi ideologies; that one of my sons served during the war and that I have been a pastor for many years.
>
> My brother Christian Mohr was a German SS man, and during the war assigned as guard to a concentration camp. I am informed that crimes were committed there, that my brother is one of the accused, and that my brother with others has been sentenced to death. My sentenced brother maintains that he carried out execution orders under command of his superior officer; that disobeying would have meant death for him; that he did not commit any crimes on individuals; that he was assigned to an execution squad.
>
> I do not know to what degree he is guilty neither to what extent Nazi indoctrination blunted his conscience but, Mr. President, with the rest of my brothers, two of whom are citizens of our country, one an influential pastor of a large Baptist church, the other in a responsible position, employed by the Federal Government, [I appeal to you].
>
> The German pastor who has been visiting my brother's family and who

129

informed me about my brother's condition has assured me that as far as he knew my brother could not be classified with either hardened Nazi war criminals; that all attempts to have him break with the Christian Church and renounce his faith failed. For that, he wrote, he was glad! I know, Mr. President, the penalties for war crimes are severe and that even my pleas will not change them. My brother no doubt belonged to the little Nazis because he wrote that he was just a corporal and as such carried out orders of his superiors.

Mr. President, you are the Commander in Chief and since all our attempts to have his sentence changed have failed thus far, I plead with you for the life of my brother. In his case let justice be tempered with mercy for the sake of his good wife, his only daughter, and his three American brothers, all good citizens, spare us at least the stigma of having a brother, who, before he became involved in this terrible Nazism, was a good man, use your power not to have him hanged. Remove this dark cloud hanging over three American citizens who ask for mercy for a brother.

It was not at all unusual for the families of defendants to petition the president for pardons. The letters were acknowledged by the President's office, but concerns expressed within the letters were not addressed. A typical response was that given from the office of Colonel Young to the Reverend John Mohr in reference to his brother:

Your letter of August 12, 1947, addressed to the Honorable Harry S. Truman, President of the United States, concerning your brother, Christian Mohr, has been referred to this office for consideration and acknowledgement.

The President has delegated to the Commanding General, European Command, the authority for the final review of all findings by the United States military commissions. Therefore, the President will not intercede with any findings of the Commanding General. A copy of your letter for clemency on behalf of your brother is being forwarded to the Judge Advocate, European Command, for his information and consideration.

Christian Mohr was born in September 1890 in Ersrode, Germany. He was a painter in civilian life. He was a combat veteran of World War I and had been held as a POW for a prolonged period of time by the French. He was a "nervous wreck" after the war and never recovered from the trauma he had suffered. He joined the Nazi Party in 1930 and the Waffen SS in 1939. He was almost immediately sent to Flossenburg concentration camp as a relatively low-level guard. He tells the story of his problems as follows:

During March, 1943, I came to the arrest barracks [at Flossenburg] together with Nies, and I relieved Bendskow. At that time there were only approximately seven prisoners in the Arrest, and consequently I together with six Bible-Investigators [it is possible he is referring to Jehovah's Witnesses] was sent out to do gardening work and in connection with that to the berry-picking detail in the forest. This lasted until the end of August. During the beginning of September, I went on furlough until the 10th or 12th of September. When I came back I became ill. From the hospital, I was sent to a hospital in Namburg and returned to the Arrest a few days before Christmas, 1943. I remained there until the 2nd or 4th of January and then went on a recuperation furlough.

Approximately during the middle of January, I returned to the Arrest in Flossenburg and remained there until the end of May. During that time I executed approximately seven men by shooting them. The prisoners were standing with their face to the wall, their hands tied together on their backs, and I shot at them with a small caliber rifle from a distance of approximately 10 centimeters. At hangings, I brought the prisoners out while the actual hanging was done by Hauptführer [SS officer] Fritsch together with a prisoner most of the time. I saw the prisoner Dietrich there several times. Once I saw Nies shooting at executions. The sentences were read to most prisoners through the interpreter. I assume they were Russian or Polish. Amongst the prisoners in the arrest there was Greenwich, Raffertz, one Canadian Major, Anglett, Nichelsen, Motte, and others.

Mohr had served at Flossenburg as work detail leader (water construction detail and Messerschmitt factory) and as a guard of the prison building (the Arrest). He was 55 when he went to trial. He was accused of allowing, and actually inciting, the capos under him to beat prisoners of many nationalities with sticks. Some persons he had beaten himself. He had participated in executions in numbers larger than those he admitted to in his statement. He actually put the noose around the necks of some prisoners and forced female prisoners to undress themselves prior to hanging. He was accused of shooting numerous individuals working on the coal pile in the prison yard, and one witness said that, "he must have executed two hundred" Russians. He had received cigarettes and liquor for volunteering to participate in the executions. Even an unusually talented lawyer would have had trouble dealing with the onslaught of witnesses brought against Mohr in *U.S. vs. Becker et al.*

Mohr's wife Anna learned about her husband's trial through a newspaper article and, at least for a time, seemed not to know what he had been charged with. The couple had one daughter who was married by the time her father faced the tribunal. He was considered by his acquaintances to be lacking in strong intellect, and the pastor of his church assumed that his association with the SS had "changed his character" and had had "an influence that, by means of suggestion, led his simple and elementary mind onto the wrong path." This places him apart from his brothers who appeared to be well educated and accomplished men. Mohr is said to have grown up in a Christian home, but it seems that he had abandoned his connection with the church. This would be in opposition to his brother's claim that the Nazis were unable to persuade him from his faith. His pastor asked, "Where should an uneducated man like Christian Mohr secure the moral support? The Christian religion could have given him this support, but he did not have it. Today he has this faith!" The pastor further claims that the Nazis preyed deliberately upon uneducated persons and seemed to have the ability to hypnotize them. The untutored did not "recognize the devilish sense of this idea."

George Mohr, another of Christian's brothers, lived in Plymouth, Wisconsin, and hardly knew his German brother. He had left Germany as a boy in 1911 when his brother Christian was twenty-one. George became an American citizen in 1919. By the time of his brother's difficulties he had been employed more than twenty years by the U.S. government as a dairy inspector. He had never met his brother's wife and daughter but corresponded with them after the war ended.

The Reverend A. D. Mohr, the third brother after George and John to be living in America, was pastor of the Grandview Park Baptist Church on East 32nd Street in Des Moines, Iowa. He had stopped corresponding with Christian before the war because of his own opposition to the "Nazi ideology of life." Although his brother had written him pleading for his help, the minister seemed to stop short of a heartfelt effort to seek mercy. He believed the American courts would render just and fair judgment, but, on the other hand he said, "It is only the natural thing for me to make this plea in behalf of my brother. ... I am writing this letter only because it is the last and only thing I can do for my brother, asking that every possible consideration might be given to see if justice might be carried out without the necessity of taking his life." The minister cited the agonies of his brother's wife and daughter, and, in particular, he pleaded to be relieved of the "shame" his brother's execution would bring on himself and his other American brothers who had, after all, "given our sons willingly to serve in the last war." Although the Baptist minister's petition for a clemency that would not come was lukewarm, he, like John, did write a letter to President Truman representing himself and his American brothers and pleading for a pardon, which, like the clemency, was not forthcoming.

The three American brothers could only give as their reasons for clemency that in addition to being easily influenced, Christian was essentially a good man and had acted under orders. Clemency was not given for personal reasons; the only hope the brothers would have had to gain consideration for their brother would have been new, effective evidence. They did not have this.

Under review, Christian Mohr's case was further complicated by the fact that he had shot numerous individuals and had placed ropes around the necks of many who were hanged — also he had volunteered for this duty and had received special rations and other consideration for doing such things. An argument that his case was identical to the "Commando 99" defendants from Buchenwald (who received reductions in their sentences based on their claim that they were acting legally) did not persuade the reviewers.

During the middle of July 1948, Lt. Colonel Earl Smith, a liaison officer, wrote a memorandum summarizing the Mohr case relative to the campaign waged by Mohr's brothers. The memorandum was intended to be used as advice in addressing the matter of informing the brothers that Mohr would be executed.

> It appears that the Mohr family is a highly respectable family which includes two clergymen, one an American citizen and the other a German, and two additional brothers in the United States who are citizens. All of these brothers have already written several letters to Congressmen and various Military Government officials, which letters were given due and proper consideration. Moreover, inasmuch as the letter of the brother John Mohr makes an appeal purely on personal grounds, and since there appears to be no defect in the proceedings or other circumstances which would warrant mitigation of the sentence of Christian Mohr, it is recommended that no further reconsideration be given this case on the basis of the receipt of the letter.
>
> Attached are two letters for the signature of General [Lucius D.] Clay for reply to the Reverend Mohr. The shorter one is as originally prepared for you. The longer one is a revision suggested by you and incorporates certain statements in explanation. However, it is still my recommendation that General Clay sign the shorter letter since it is believed the added statements in the longer letter may only serve to offend or incense the Reverend Mohr and open the door to further controversy and his seeking popular and political support or intervention. It is well founded knowledge and experience in War Crimes matters that to reveal to an interested layman facts or controversial legal considerations which are the sole province of a court to decide frequently serves merely to create new issues and controversy, and invite criticism of a highly biased nature together with a new flood of correspondence. The recital of facts established is seldom accepted as satisfying. This is believed particularly true where the layman has a deep filial interest and possesses unusual sensibilities such as the writer in the instant case.

General Clay (or his assistant) did indeed choose the shorter letter to the Reverend John Mohr.

I have your letter of 26 June 1948 in which you request reconsideration of the case of your brother Christian Mohr now under sentence of death for the murder of inmates at Flossenburg Concentration Camp.

Your brother's case was recently given another very thorough review by the Board of Review in the Office of the Judge Advocate of this Command, and it was determined again that there were no mitigating circumstances which would warrant changing the original sentence of the court. This review resulted from the fact that one of the several witnesses against your brother was tried and found guilty of perjury. However, it was determined that the elimination of the perjured testimony from the record would not detract from the conclusiveness of the remainder of the evidence upon which the conviction was based.

While I can well understand your compassion and recognize the sorrow caused your family, I regret that, owing to the nature of your brother's offenses and the conclusive nature of the evidence against him, I am unable to find justification to alter his sentence.

I assure you that your brother has been given every consideration consistent with the high standards we have endeavored to maintain in the impartial administration of justice in the prosecution for War Crimes.

Offices of the War Crimes Commission had learned the value of minimalism from their dealings with Virgil Case and others like him. They did not make that mistake again. Nonetheless, these efforts would eventually fail them. The effort to fully punish war criminals fell apart due to public opinion and political maneuverings, much of which was possibly tied to a general weariness and a desire to move on into the new, exciting, rock 'n' roll world of the 1950s and an audience that had been little more than children during the war, or to real and propaganda needs associated with the Cold War and the Korean conflict.

Mohr was awarded one stay of execution (alluded to in the memorandum above) by General Lucius D. Clay. The nephew of codefendant Bruno Skierka filed perjury charges against two witnesses in the case. The witnesses had also appeared against Mohr and two other defendants. One of the witnesses was convicted of perjury and was sentenced to six years' imprisonment, but he was not the prosecutor's chief witness. After the case was reviewed, it was determined that more than sufficient evidence existed to uphold the conviction and sentence. Mohr went to the gallows on October 10, 1948.

Mohr's case file also contains one other peculiarity. It seems nearly a half dozen defendants had the last name Mohr, and on occasion a clear distinction with identifying information had to be placed in files to make sure that sentences and individuals were not confused especially since others of the same name received short sentences or were acquitted altogether.

In September 1953, Mohr's widow, Anna Mohr, petitioned to have her husband's body removed from the cemetery at Landsberg Prison. "I take the liberty to approach with the question whether or not I may transfer the corpse of my deceased husband to the home cemetery. If it should be permitted, I ask for information regarding the month in which a transfer is authorized."

The prison administration answered her inquiry promptly.

> It is hereby verified that the Prison Administration has no objections to an exhumation of the corpse and to a transfer to the home cemetery. Such exhumation, however, is subject to the following conditions:
>
> a. The exhumation will be performed by a legally authorized undertaker.
>
> b. The undertaker will contact the Prison Administration at least three days prior to the exhumation.
>
> c. The undertaker will present a Power of Attorney bearing your signature certified by a Notary Public.
>
> d. Upon presentation of the Power of Attorney and upon agreement regarding the exact time of the exhumation, the undertaker will be furnished a certificate, indication that the Prison Administration has no objections to a transfer of the corpse.
>
> e. All costs incident to the exhumation and the transfer of the corpse will be borne by the dependents of the deceased.
>
> f. The exhumation will be performed in accordance with appropriate German laws and directives.
>
> I hope that this information serves your purpose and also inform you that the exhumation may take place at any time.

Anna Mohr had her husband's body removed from the prison cemetery and reburied in the city cemetery in Landsberg.

13

An Innocent in the Grinding Mill: The Story of Lauriano Navas

> …[Y]ou ought not to pardon any of them [the books set to be chastised] seeing they have all been offenders: it is better you throw all into the base-court, and there make a pile of them, and then set them a-fire; if not they may be carried into the yard, and there make a bonfire of them, and the smoke will offend nobody.
>
> [Representing the rhetoric of the niece from "The Burning of … Books," *Don Quixote of the Mancha*, by Miguel de Cervantes.]

Human resources arrived at the camps by many routes. As previously noted, in the beginning the camps held criminals and "enemies of the state." Later they were the sites of concentrations of certain undesirables the Germans believed were unfit to mix with German society. The camps' populations were also made up of conscripted labor from many nations and with POWs of several nations. Still others arrived at the camps by sadly convoluted routes. They were almost lost in the sorting-out effort that took place at the end of the war. The Spaniard Lauriano Navas, tried as a defendant in case # 000-50-5-25 (*U.S. vs. Lauriano Navas et al.*) for participation in the Mauthausen Atrocity, is one of those who arrived at the camp by a most peculiar route.

Navas was 28 when he was tried, and little was known of his background except his nationality. He was not known to have any military, civilian, or party status. Navas, through an interpreter, testified that he arrived at Mauthausen as a prisoner in January 1941 and was then sent to Gusen in June of that same year. He was 22 at that time. He was there until Mauthausen was liberated in May 1945. At Gusen he worked for half a year in the infamous washroom and was later put in charge of a detail of Spanish inmates who were used to repair railroad tracks. Although sixty to seventy Spaniards were assigned to this work, Navas was usually in charge of about a six men, give or take a few according to who was available. Witnesses would say that he was in charge of a much larger detail, up to 150 Russians, Ital-

Lauriano Navas

ians, Spaniards, and other nationalities. He was accused of beating inmates every day, one in particular so badly that he died. He was "commonly known as a killer." There would also be testimony that Navas was so crippled in his right hand that he could not have beaten anyone and that he had to do everything with his left hand. Testimony by some fellow inmates would also support Navas's claim that he never killed anyone and that he was never in charge of more than a few inmates. Navas and his codefendants were actually not accused of particular murders in the charge against them; they were accused of acting in the Common Design. Navas was sentenced to life imprisonment. Guilty as he was judged to be, no evidence was presented that could classify him with those who murdered directly and boldly.

At the time of his trial, the general understanding was that Navas was a common criminal who had evolved into a war criminal. It would take years to determine who he really was, and by that time errors, misjudgments, special cruelties, and neglect had consumed most of his youth and young adulthood.

Lauriano Navas was born in February of 1920 to religious parents from "esteemed" families. He was a very bright boy and at 16 he was a college student in Oviedo, Spain, well on the road to becoming a chemist. He had blue eyes and brown hair, was barely five feet five inches tall and was slight of build. His town was then in the hands of the Republican government and the communists represented a very small minority. Most commissioned officers supported Franco, and his government desperately needed soldiers. Students were given the choice of going directly into the army or volunteering for a military school. Navas chose military school and graduated after twelve months as a lieutenant. By the time he was eighteen, he had received a crippling combat wound in his right hand.

When Franco occupied Catalonia in 1939, Navas and others of his unit were evacuated over the border into France. He was with a group of about 10,000 members of the Spanish Republican Army who were sent to an interment camp in France.

Soon World War II broke out in Europe, and the French asked for volunteers from among the Spanish. Spanish communists would not sign up because in those early stages Russia and Germany were still allies. Because Navas was not a communist, he volunteered and was appointed a lieutenant to the 31st Spanish work company of the 5th Brigade Group in the French Army engineering units. He wore the uniform of a lieutenant of the French Army with all the privileges. In other words, he was not considered a member of the Foreign Legion. He was nineteen at the time.

His company was assigned to Sector 106 of the Maginot Line. For a while they did only engineering work, but later they were issued weapons. In June 1940, he was taken prisoner by the Germans. At first he was held at POW camps and was even once placed on a train and informed that he was being returned to France. It was not so; he ended his journey at Gusen. By that time, through German conniving, he had lost his status as a POW officer. He said that most of his responsibility at both Mauthausen and Gusen was as translator, although he did some office work. He was supervised alternately by two German criminals who were appointed as capos over the Spaniards. He was 25 when Gusen was liberated.

He was arrested on the 13th of May and accused of a wide variety of criminal activities. At first, he was accused of taking part in the cold water experiments of the camp, but he was cleared of this before going to trial. He was taken to Dachau and put in the "line-up." Again no one identified him as having participated in criminal activity. He was held in captivity by the Americans until June 1947, when he was brought into the courtroom three separate times. He would be told that he was to be tried with ten SS men, but after a while he was taken out of the courtroom. In July, he got a second indictment stating that he would be tried along other defendants. Again "it was taken away." On the ninth, he and three other Spaniards were handed indictments and this time he went to trial. He would say he did not get to talk to his lawyer before the trial. He testified, as best he could, in his own behalf, and his lawyer produced a couple of defense witnesses from among men who were already convicted of war crimes. It appears that some defense lawyers, desperate for help and without consulting their clients, would simply ask those that had been convicted or were awaiting trial, "Does anybody here have anything good to say about _____?" In many instances this was the only defense that could be offered. It was not precisely the fault of the military court system; most favored witnesses had left Germany and could not be located easily.

Help came for Navas when a lawyer noticed in 1951 that his case was "interesting." The first thing the lawyer noted during his investigation was that most observers had believed Navas was in charge of the Spaniards as an interpreter — not as a capo as had been believed by the Court. The second point was that the review document said four witnesses had testified against Navas. In actuality, the trial record would reveal that only two had testified against him and the other two had been inserted into the review record *by accident.* Additionally, one of the other two witnesses had been reported by Navas for embezzling from the inmates and had a grudge against Navas for costing him his job. The second of the two witnesses had said he went to the dispensary to make sure the man Navas had beaten was really dead, but it was doubtful he could have checked on the inmate because he didn't know the man either by name or number. The lawyer further pointed out a section of the record the review board had missed. It was a group of statements by the prosecution's own witness. When he was asked what Navas's reputation was among the prisoners, the witness answered, "I don't know anything about his reputation because I saw him only once or twice in the camp." The witness also testified that he had never heard anyone else speak of Navas or his activities in the camp. At Gusen I, it would have been very unlikely that someone who was "a killer" and who beat prisoners daily for years would not have been notorious.

Another prosecution witness when asked if he had seen Navas beat a prisoner except on the one occasion answered, "No." This prisoner had lived in the same barracks with Navas for three years. Not only had two witnesses evaluated by the review board *not* testified against Navas, but two additional inmates, both prosecution witnesses, had testified that they knew nothing of crimes committed by Navas. All that was left was a simple assault charge — or more likely a fistfight between equals. Because Navas was never a capo and had only the responsibility of passing on, in Spanish, orders from the camp guards, he could not have been guilty of abusing someone in his charge.

The lawyer summed up by writing, "I beg you to look into this record with criticism, and I support my request with the story I told you about this man's life, which in my opinion is a deadly struggle to get out of the political grinding mill which this man came into in 1936 [at age 16] and which he has been unable to get out of up to now."

After the intervention by the lawyer, the review board decided to take another look at the Navas case. The review stated that although the Court had been required to take into account the case that established the Common Design precedent, it was now considered significant to note that Navas was "neither an SS man nor a civilian nor an official at the camp and [was not] within the class of persons presumed to be guilty by mere presence at the camp." The Common Design precedent did not apply to Navas.

In addressing the quality of the evidence, the board had another piece of information it decided to enter into its review as a note:

> A memorandum from the Chief of War Crimes Branch, European Command, dated 2 April 1951 states that Pedro Gomez [one of the two men who actually appeared against Navas], although never officially declared unreliable, definitely falls into the class of "professional witness" and that testimony from him should be considered with caution and given little weight unless corroborated.

The board determined that since the Gomez testimony was actually uncorroborated in the record it would not be reliable. They said, "In this particular case, even if his testimony *were* considered, the event would be nothing more than a minor assault as there was no indication of anybody being seriously injured." The Russian, too, was discredited because in reality he had never served under Navas as he had claimed, and this error in statements made his testimony unreliable.

The board also noted the error in the review that incorrectly stated that four witnesses had testified against Navas when actual testimony had included only the two discredited witnesses. Testimony accusing Navas of beating a French citizen to death was actually lodged against another defendant by the witnesses.

The board entered as reasoning for their new decision the following statement:

> We thus find that we have an accused who has been sentenced to life imprisonment on the testimony of one witness, whose testimony, though strong in reference to an actual incident of beating, appears shaky as to the actual identity of the person doing the beating.... In comparing the sentence of this accused with those of war criminals who were guilty of

offenses of a similar nature, it is felt that this sentence is excessive and that executive clemency is warranted to reduce the sentence to time served.

The "Yuletide Clemency of 12 December 1951" stated that, "having considered the cases of the following named war criminals, the following action is directed: The unserved portion of the sentences of each of the following war criminals is remitted as of 18 January 1952." Lauriano Navas's name was fourth on the list of eleven. He was given DM20 and a railroad ticket to Essen in the British Zone where he was given 72 hours to report to the local police as a freed war criminal.

Through all his trials and tribulations, he was never discharged from the French Army or from war captivity as a POW. In 1951, he was still officially an officer of the French Army.

* * *

Among the other defendants in *U.S. vs. Navas et al.* was the Spaniard Moises Fernandez, born July 30, 1912. He was married to Natividad Fernandez of Bilbao, Spain.

In 1937 he was drafted into the Spanish Army and fought against Franco. After Franco's victory he fled to France and then, like Navas, volunteered for the French Army (one account states that the French drafted him). He was never to see his wife and child again. He was taken prisoner by the Germans in 1940 and sent to a POW camp. The Gestapo then took him from the camp, changed his status from POW to regular inmate, and sent him to Mauthausen. He was made a capo at the notorious out-camp Steyr in 1943. He would claim that he did not beat inmates, but as always it was very hard for a capo to defend himself against such a charge. Generally speaking, beating was in the unwritten job description of a capo. Fernandez was given twenty years at Landsberg which was reduced to fifteen years in 1951. Testimony against him was at best muddled if not totally unreliable. He would also claim that he was unable to communicate with his German-speaking inquisitors and lawyers.

Fernandez was ill through it all and in terrible pain. Not long after his conviction, he was put into the hospital and was never well enough to function in the general prison population again. He had rheumatic diseases, including heart troubles, and tuberculosis. He suffered from Brodie's abscess of the left femur and it was believed that this was the primary site of the infection that caused his myocardial disease. Four operations gave him some relief. He was hospitalized again in 1951 with "open TB of the lungs." He was also afflicted with "chronic rheumatism of the muscles." In 1951, tuberculosis was treatable. He had responded to a certain extent to streptomycin, but he would have to be moved to the university hospital at Munich for the several years of treatment he would need to have a chance to survive. It was expected that he would have surgical procedures to remove the diseased part of his lung.

Such plans were in vain. Fernandez could fight no longer and his heart failed him. He died of toxic cardiovascular failure in the hours before midnight on June 25, 1952. He wife was notified by telegraph and he was buried in the cemetery at Landsberg Prison.

14

Physician, Heal Thyself: The Story of Dr. Erika Flocken

> Roth is a Jew and the former inmates of Muehldorf were all Jews.
>
> [From Dr. Erika Flocken's explanation for why
> witnesses might have testified against her
> in case #000-50-136: *U.S. vs. Auer et al.*]

If Dr. Erika Flocken had held her tongue on three small words, she might have saved herself decades of grief. Dr. Flocken purchased her death sentence with a short statement she made to an inmate, which translates roughly as: "You are lucky." With those words she lost for herself the iron-clad cloak of deniability that concentration camp workers needed to escape conviction as a conspirator in the Common Design. The inmate had recently had his name removed from the list of sick who would be sent to Auschwitz for treatment. Her statement revealed that she knew those going to Auschwitz were not going to be treated; they were going to Auschwitz to be murdered.

Dr. Flocken was a war widow and a physician in her early thirties who was assigned to the Muehldorf Ring, a string of work camps. Her father and his brother were both doctors, and she would be supported and defended by their friends and colleagues. Her father was proud of her, and she had been one of those superior students whom teachers remember well. She had a history of service to the needy and possessed an attitude of charity. She was brilliant and fortunate.

Flocken's case is interesting because she was a woman and a doctor. That was unusual then and perhaps would still be so. Her case offers history something else, however, because she was one of those defendants who chose to write at length.

Flocken was not a Nazi and had never belonged to the Party. Many of her friends when she was younger were Jews. She believed in generosity and charity. She was "merry" and sweet and beloved by family and friends and professors. She held fast to her Catholic religion even to the point of having a showy wedding in a glorious thirteenth-century cathedral in spite of the disapproval she would receive from Nazis. Something about her personality, however, led her to believe that she was in possession of greater wit and had rights to greater expectations than "others." She fought in every way she could to prove her own righteousness and purity, but she never seemed to grieve the first moment for those she would not (or could not, as she would say) protect. Like many Germans, Flocken was dumbfounded that anyone could consider that inactivity was just as merciless as activity. Her writing is a window into the world of those who had education, sophistication, and intellectual capacity but yet could not understand the horror of what they were doing.

Late in the war, Adolf Hitler decided that a new effort should be made to manufacture airplanes, and two important German subcultures, industry and the concentration camp system — immediately brought Hitler's desire to fruition.

A businessman named Fritz Todt headed a government agency that specialized in planning and implementation. After the death of Todt, the organization was taken over by Albert Speer, Hitler's architect and urban planner. The "Organization Todt" (OT) had usually functioned in areas occupied by the Germans and had worked on such projects as the so-called Atlantic Wall and certain military highways. The OT was also a supervisory and enforcement agency, but actual construction was done by a variety of subcontractors including the firm of Polensky and Zollner (PZ). PZ was — and still is — one of the largest construction companies in Germany. The OT would have the responsibility for supplying materials to the subcontractors and the SS would have the responsibility for supplying labor from the Muehldorf concentration camp in connection with their operation of Dachau. The contract called for the OT to provide housing, food, medical supplies, and medical treatment for both civilian and inmate laborers.

Although it was technically associated with the main camp at Dachau, Muehldorf itself was the center of a variety of smaller camps, which taken together made up the Muehldorf Ring. The Ring held more than 8,000 souls as prisoners including 750 females. More than 40 percent of the inmates died during the months of the OT project.

The prisoners were housed in extremely overcrowded, filthy, unheated hovels. They were forced to sleep on the floor on wet, mildewed straw. They had no heat and no ventilation except for small holes in the roof. Prisoners were issued one set of clothes: thin jacket, striped shirt and trousers, one pair of socks or foot rags, a cap, and wooden shoes. In late November 1944, they were issued heavier coats. The wooden shoes offered next to no protection and toes were often amputated due to frostbite. The shoes caused blisters, which became infected and abscessed. For some, even wooden shoes were not available and many had to go to work barefoot.

The OT had the responsibility for supplying food, but they would only supply food for workers on the job. Since large numbers of workers were unable to stand up if not be downright unconscious, the food provided, already low in volume and caloric content, was not nearly sufficient to meet the needs of the camps. Breakfast generally consisted of bread and coffee, lunch of two or three cups of very watery soup, supper of less soup made from "cabbage or weeds" and three or four "uncleaned, usually unedible potatoes." Workers needing 3,000–5,000 calories were given only about 1,000 calories. Sick inmates received considerably less, somewhere in the range of four to five hundred calories. Inmates rummaged through garbage cans, stole, bartered, and did everything they could to get food. Water was insufficient and in some cases nonexistent except for puddles and streams.

The trial review revealed what it was like to be an inmate:

> In the beginning of 1945 the condition of all the inmates was disastrous. Inmates often broke down. The legs of most of them were swollen. In many instances inmates lost weight and looked like skeletons. In other instances, their bodies became swollen. Fifteen-year-old boys looked like 50-year-old men or pregnant women. Their bellies and sex organs were swollen and distended.
>
> At the main construction site, inmates ranging in age from 14 to 60 were required to carry 50-kilogram sacks of cement from a railroad siding to the mixing machines. During a routine day each man carried 100 to 120 sacks of cement up a 30 to 40 percent incline for distances varying from 40 to 300 steps.

Inmates worked twelve-hour days with little rest and were beaten "continually." Roving OT guards beat adolescent children to hurry them along when they were unable to carry the loads or because they sat down from exhaustion. They had no washing or toilet facilities. Scaffolding was poorly constructed and ladders were not strong enough to hold inmates' weight, causing them to fall to their deaths when the structures collapsed. Cement covered everything and hung in the air. Construction accidents took a heavy toll on the inmates. Girls as young as 14 had to work wet concrete and carry cement. At one point 400 healthy French and Italian inmates came to Muehldorf. The camp commander called the capos in and told them that the men were to carry cement until they died. Within three months, almost all were indeed dead. Physicians were made to carry cement. Two Antwerp diamond dealers (recorded in the death book as being laborers) died in the endeavor. The working inmates were covered with sores and suffered from combinations of diarrhea, tuberculosis, pneumonia, pleurisy, ulcers, and other diseases. The list barely touches the revelations of the trial.

In addition to deaths from overwork and starvation, inmates were beaten to death with anything at hand, and many of the bodies examined in preparation for the trial revealed that inmates had been shot.

Every day was a drive by the OT administration, the PZ company, and the SS to deliver the most labor possible with no consideration for human life at all. Some medical facilities, personnel, and rations were available, but these resources were present only for those with remaining labor potential to get back on the job. Most who were past work conveniently died or were killed by the beatings and shootings. Others who were past work but were still alive were sent to Auschwitz to be dealt with in the gas chambers. Hitler had to have more airplanes and the Muehldorf cabal was determined to see that he got them. No part of the Muehldorf Ring would allow resources to be distributed to those who couldn't contribute to the goals.

In 1944, Dr. Erika Flocken secured a position with the OT as chief physician for the Muehldorf Ring.

Flocken was born on November 12, 1912, in Hesse-Nassau, Germany. She was the daughter of physician Julius Hosenberg and his wife Johanna Krass Hosenberg. Dr. Hosenberg was a prominent physician and was president of a physicians' organization several times over.

Between 1918 and 1932, Flocken attended a Catholic girls' school and municipal girls' secondary schools. Between 1933 and 1938, she attended the universities of Koenigsberg, Cologne, and Marburg, and in August 1938, she passed the state medical exam. In the late 1930s, she married Erich Flocken, a physician born in the Rhineland.

In 1938, she went to work as a physician at the Goddelau Asylum for the insane. In 1939 and 1940 she worked for a miners' relief organization hospital, held a general practice contract with the RADWJ (Girls' Labor Service), and worked at the municipal hospital in Dueren/Rhineland. From 1941–1944 she held a service contract with the Berlin Union of Panel Doctors. In June 1944, she went to work for the OT subcontractor for the

Muehldorf Ring at a handsome salary. Additional benefits included a driver and a personal maid paid for by the company.

Sometime between her marriage and receiving the job at the concentration camp complex, her husband died. One suspects he might have died in the war, but her personal papers do not address the exact circumstances of his death.

It was reported by her acquaintances that she hated the Nazis. After reading her history and her letters, one is inclined to suspect that she felt their grubbiness was beneath her.

According to her driver, Flocken followed a busy schedule in the first months after she came to the camp. She was already at the hospital in Schwindegg (where the central medical depot was located) when he picked her up at seven each morning. From there they drove to Ampfing to pick up her mail at her office. Then she visited the main construction office. Then he drove the doctor to the Ecksberg camp for consultation with the OT personnel. Those chores would be finished between 10:30 and 11:00. Then they went to the district hospital at Muehldorf. She had taken over as deputy to the local doctor and had "taken over the consultation hours" there. She normally then inspected the "medical stations." They would arrive back at Schwindegg at four or five in the afternoon. Then she usually went back to some of the OT camps and the main OT office. Sometimes she went back to the district hospital at Muehldorf and assisted in operations there. Flocken only rarely visited camps other than the OT camps (the OT did not consider their camps concentration camps), but her driver said that "in her kindness" she took some medications to the Mettenheim camp from the depot at Schwindegg. She did not see patients, but left the medicines with the camp leader. The camps not under Flocken's jurisdiction were the so-called "wood camps," primitive hovels in outlying areas that received little humanitarian attention of any kind. Workers in these camps (the Waldlager) lived in structures of medieval design that were built partially underground. Except for a slightly peaked roof instead of a shed roof, these building were roughly akin to the "soddies" built by immigrants as they moved into the American West. Her driver would say that to her credit, she was a good doctor for the OT camps, and that she should not have been held responsible for the other camps.

In the fall of 1944, a German Air Force doctor arrived at Muehldorf and relieved Flocken of many of her duties. This seems to have been because of the enormous job she had to do and not because she wasn't pleasing the OT. After the arrival of the new doctor, she didn't need a driver so often because her main responsibility was the administration of the hospital at Schwindegg. She did have to be driven to the main construction office and to the hospital in the city of Muehldorf where she was still assisting the resident physician. At the trial, her driver was concerned that the prosecutors did not separate the wood camp problems from the OT situation. Other than to say that she took some medicines to the wood camps from the depot (which would be found to be fully stocked with no particular shortages when the Americans arrived), he did not recite instances when she wept for the horrors she had viewed daily as she went about the camps. He did not volunteer any stories about her holding the hand of a feces-encrusted adolescent as he died from abuse, preventable disease, and starvation. Although Flocken believed that she was gravely wronged by the trial and its consequences and tried to get General Clay and the Pope to understand her sufferings, she never recalled any particular discomfort concerning memories of the nearly 4,000 people who died in the Muehldorf Ring while she was a physician for the Organization Todt.

When Americans arrested a suspected war criminal, that person sometimes seemed to disappear completely from the historical record. The following is a letter from Charles Fahy, legal adviser to the military governor, to Brigadier General E. C. Betts, theater Judge Advocate, concerning Flocken and the general situation involving suspects in the spring of 1946:

> I am inclosing a file of papers beginning with a letter dated 5 November 1945 from a German father stating that he had heard rumors that his daughter was in a war criminal enclosure and begging for information as to whether the daughter is alive. The file concludes with an internal route slip from the War Crimes Branch of your office, dated 9 April 1946, declining, in effect, to permit the German father to learn whether his daughter is alive.
>
> Military Government legal officers in the field tell me that the policy of holding prisoners and internees completely incommunicado, as expressed in the rough slip from your office, is not confined to persons in war criminal enclosures but extends to all CIC arrestees. They say that this policy has been a handicap in the administration of justice since it is impossible to secure the testimony of such persons, in person or by deposition.
>
> The policy was, no doubt, necessary during combat and for a time thereafter. It probably saves work now, an important consideration to agencies suffering from shortage of personnel. However that may be, I do not consider the cruelty and inhumanity of such a policy warranted in the present stage of occupation. I appreciate the necessity of severe restrictions upon communications with the interned persons, imposed by security considerations, lack of personnel and the need of keeping witnesses and accused persons from outside influence, but I think that you and I, as the principal legal adviser of the Theater Commander, should make some attempt to mitigate the harshness of the present policy. As the policy

appears to be one imposed by the Army rather than by the Military Government, I wonder if you would be willing to initiate a recommendation for modification.

The policy was indeed changed and Flocken's father soon learned that she was an internee facing a death penalty charge which was supported by strong evidence.

In addition to affidavits collected by the investigating team, the evidence included exhibits and expansive testimony that demonstrated the sorts of things a physician would surely have seen at the camps if she had only looked about herself with any degree of curiosity.

One adolescent who testified, fifteen-year-old Erwin Steiner, born in Budapest, Hungary, told of the abuse he endured. The prosecutor asked him to tell the Court the date when he had come to the primitive out-camp associated with Muehldorf.

"20 August 1944."

He would have been only fourteen at the time. The prosecutor wondered why someone would do that to him.

"Because I was Jewish," he answered.

He was asked to describe the kind of work he did at the camp.

"The first five months I carried [boxes of] cement ... and after that I peeled potatoes." He testified that he weighed 46 kilos (100 pounds) and the cement he carried weighed 30 kilos (66 pounds).

He explained that he worked from eight to twelve hours each day and was beaten. "Many times," he said, "I don't know how many."

Was he ever seriously injured?

"Yes, on the right hip.... In February I was taken to the hospital for consultation and I was not admitted. My hip then became infected and swollen up and I was finally admitted to the hospital in the middle of April and I stayed there until the Americans arrived [about two weeks later]."

The Americans had operated on him and saved his life, he said.

Jonina Krawozak, at age 17, was an example of "conscripted" labor. She was forced by the Gestapo to go from her hometown to work on the farms of the Muehldorf Ring at the rate of DM5 per week, not enough to purchase decent food. While working in the Muehldorf system she became pregnant and delivered, without medication and with only the assistance of a nurse and a midwife, a son in January 1945, about four months before the liberation of the camps. The nursery had a delivery room, but it was so cold during January the nurses and midwives delivered the babies on the ward. "The sheets were dirty and were not even changed when a new expectant mother came into the nursery." After her recuperation, she was forced to go back to work and leave her healthy baby at the nursery. While she was there she saw that after mothers were forced to leave, their babies were given only water and skimmed milk with some sugar in it. They received about 100cc four times a day. Very sick babies were fed black coffee to hasten their death. The babies were always wet, dirty, and crying, and their sheets had excreta on them. Jonina visited her baby on two occasions. When she came back to visit two weeks after she had to leave the baby, he was "sickly." Three weeks later when she saw him just before they buried him, "the whole body was very thin, the eyes were sunken in on the head, the body was very dark and open wounds were on the heels of both feet penetrating deeply and exposing the bones of the feet." She said that while she was at the nursery about 80 children were born, and she saw about 40 to 50 of the sickly babies die. In fact, most babies born in the nursery failed to survive after their mothers were forced back to work.

Whether Flocken did or did not see the misery of suffering children and adolescents the charge she was never able to shake even with years of maneuvering was based on her failure to provide supplies and on her failure to improve the unsanitary conditions at Muehldorf.

In the invalid section of the hospital where the most ill were kept, many patients lay on plain boards without any clothing except ragged shirts. The toilet was so far away that patients who were unable to walk had to relieve themselves in their "beds." Some patients lay for days without food and frequently the dead lay among the living for extended periods of time. In the convalescent section two inmates had to share a single bed. The odor was unbearable. In one of the camp hospitals for periods of up to ten days, patients were bandaged with paper from the cement bags because (the patients were told) there was no gauze. There were never enough blankets, so two or three patients had to share and those that were available were passed from patient to patient, frequently after a previous patient had died of a contagious disease. The presence of these conditions was established by testimony and other evidence.

All suffering caused by a supposed supply shortage was unnecessary. In October 1944, the supply depot actually "contained supplies of medicines, surgical instruments, etc., enough to supply many camps for a year." Even plentiful typhus serum was not given while an epidemic raged. Other medicines requisitioned for the Ring were stolen by the SS when they arrived. When the wards became congested with patients who would likely be unable to go back to work, they were simply loaded on transports and sent to Auschwitz and disposed of permanently.

In one of the camps, naked invalids were ordered out of bed, and a clerk wrote their numbers down. A doctor told the clerk of the diarrhea cases, "Mark down all of them." The sick were forced to walk, or, if they were too sick to walk, were moved by oxcart to the central site of Muehldorf to join invalids from other camps being collected for Auschwitz. There was no argument about whether this actually happened; the defense would concur with this fact. The prisoners were placed in box-cars for a ride of several days with no water and a small piece of bread. Many died on their way. "Evidence of cannibalism was found," observers testified. Unfortunately, these were only examples of the cruelties that took place on the journeys. At least one of these transports was liberated and the witnesses were almost unable to describe what they saw.

Witness after witness said that Flocken on many occasions selected inmates to be sent on the transports. Flocken would not deny that she had participated in the selection process. She explained that she did not know they were going to Auschwitz to be killed. Someone had heard otherwise, however. Flocken was having an affair with the camp commander, and, one day while the two of them were riding, the commandant told her that he had removed his chauffeur from the transport because he was a good driver. Flocken told the chauffeur he was "very lucky." She said, "You can thank the Camp Commandant that he saved your life." By these words, Flocken revealed that she knew very well what would happen to those sent to Auschwitz.

Although many accusations were made against Flocken, two facts could simply not be disputed: (1) She contributed to the deaths of many inmates by failing to enforce hygiene standards and attending to proper medical treatments when resources were available, and (2) she selected inmates who went to die at Auschwitz.

Flocken was sentenced to death at Dachau on May 13, 1947. Almost immediately she sent a letter directly to General Lucius Clay in which she stated she was not necessarily asking for clemency but was asking for an opportunity to "disprove the charges brought against me and to rehabilitate myself." She complained of not having the time, staff, and means to defend herself properly.

Flocken, in her letter, made accusations that incensed the various groups and individuals who held her life in their hands; she made a long list of accusations of criminal or near-criminal activities by the Court, the prosecution, and the investigators. She said important witnesses had been "systematically" eliminated by the War Crimes Branch. The prosecutor had unduly influenced witnesses. The Court had refused her the time to prepare her defense. She said Americans had refused to prosecute witnesses who committed perjury because they served the Americans' needs.

The authorities claimed falsely not to be able to procure defense witnesses, they had refused to procure witnesses, they had threatened to later charge defense witnesses if they testified, they threatened private individuals with investigations if they testified ("for who is there in Germany today who does not have some vulnerable point? Who does not engage in some black market activity?"), they threatened to stop relief of former concentration camp inmates if they testified for the defense; and they had allowed the prosecution to yell at defense witnesses.

Flocken had not even learned to keep her mouth shut about the prejudices she claimed never to have had. In her letter she said the "Jew Adolf Eisler of Vienna" had to admit on the stand that he had given conflicting statements concerning her case.

She wrote that a German lawyer and his secretary had been sentenced to a prison term for influencing witnesses. "What about [the prosecutor] Roth?" she asked. "What explanation other than influencing can be found be it by means of threats or promises in the case of German witnesses or by means of appealing to the common interest of his Jewish friends—for Roth is a Jew and the former inmates of Muehldorf were all Jews—for the sudden vagueness of those people who would have been able to testify for the defense or uncover the mass production of perjury?"

The attacks went on for many handwritten pages.

Roth did not find the attacks amusing. He wrote a point-by-point defense, which, if it wasn't convincing in every instance, was convincing in the overwhelming majority of instances. To Roth, she was first, last, and always a Nazi:

> It is noteworthy that while there are at least four references in defendant's petition to the fact that your deponent [Roth] is Jewish, there is not one word contained therein regarding the innocence of the defendant. The Latin quotations—which by the way are incorrectly quoted—are used to describe poor misused war criminals as "gladiators" who "served as head tribute to the Jewish war financiers of the U.S.A." In true Nazi fashion, an apology follows the defendant's scurrilous remarks. However, defamation has been the keynote of this defendant's defense from the very inception of the trial.
>
> During the trial, the defendant Flocken wrote a letter which was intended for secret passage outside the cage. This letter was intercepted by the security officer who passed it on to the prosecution. The letter, instead of containing a suggestion of penitence, criticized the prosecution staff, your deponent included, by reason of their racial heredity. Not one word was uttered by this defendant in her own defense during the entire trial. Flocken has relied upon slander, libel, and upon the line which the Nazis so well taught her during her long and effective period of inculcation.

In July, about two months after Flocken's conviction, her father, Dr. Hosenberg, petitioned for clemency. His petition is full of panic and desperation. Neither he nor any of his friends or acquaintances could imagine that his daughter had done anything wrong. (Dr. Hosenberg and his wife, by this time, were living with a friend and fellow doctor; their own home had been destroyed during the bombing near the end of the war. Their son, Erika's brother, had been killed during the war.) He attempted some concrete defense, but that route was hopeless. He said that she liked Jews and had Jewish friends growing up. She and all their family were opposed to the Nazis. His own brother, a doctor, was sent to a concentration camp by the Gestapo because of remarks he had made about the Nazis. He did not return after the war and the family believed he had died at the camp. In his petition he did not accuse the Court of being prejudiced as his daughter did; he preferred to say that the Court was the victim of untruthful witnesses. Finally, he regretted his daughter's "love affairs" with Camp Commandant Walter Langleist. That had done her no good in the eyes of anyone. (Langleist was convicted of ruthlessness at the several camps he had commanded and had already been hanged by the time of Flocken's trial.)

Flocken and her father were in luck in spite of themselves. Almost by the time the sentence was passed, personnel in the war crimes offices were trying to find a way out of executing her. What they needed was a reason, and they hit upon a couple of important details. She had never been in the SS, and she had only been at the concentration camp site for a short period of time. In spite of the testimony of Langleist's chauffeur, they did not believe that hard and fast evidence existed to prove that she knew positively that those she was separating away as too weak to work were actually going to be murdered. Most believed persons of her rank had deducted what was happening, but suspicion of deduction was not evidence. The review board had some wiggle room in their desire to commute her death sentence to life. The need to find the wiggle room was frankly written:

> Women war criminals have been executed in the past, not by the United States but by the British government. In the Belsen Concentration Camp trial, Juana Borman, Irma Grese, and Elizabeth Bolkenrath were executed for their participation in the atrocities committed at the Belsen and Auschwitz Concentration Camps. These women, in addition to selecting inmates for extermination also indulged in personal atrocities against inmates. There is no evidence that Flocken, the accused in this case, personally beat or killed any inmate. After careful consideration of all the factors in this case I am of the opinion that the ends of justice will be satisfied by the commutation of the sentence to life imprisonment. In arriving at

this conclusion I must concede that I have been influenced to a certain extent by the fact that the accused is a woman.

In June 1948, a little more than a year after her conviction, her death sentence was commuted to life. While the review board was looking for a way out for her, Flocken was scheming. She had managed to get a letter to the Pope in Rome via the International Red Cross in Geneva. The letter ran to more than a dozen pages and restated the harsh accusations she had sent to General Clay. Her letter to "Your Sanctity" expressed confidence that her word would inspire him to action and his action would solve her problems. The Red Cross sent copies to the Counsel for War Crimes. The letter was also sent by the Pope to the Bishop of Wurm who sent a copy to the War Crimes Group. Her letter and letters from two other defendants contained statements that inquiries should be sent to particular lawyers, leading the reader to believe at that early time that the letters might have originated from lawyers. The "lawyer" named in the Flocken letter was Dr. Julius Hosenberg. The legal consultant to the trials had mistaken her father's name for that of a lawyer, most likely because Germans addressed their lawyers as "doctors" and their physicians as "doctors of medicine." Nevertheless, the consultant informed his clients that "if the extremely grave accusations contained in them prove to be true and if the extremely grave accusations contained in them prove to be slanderous, appropriate action by the U.S. and British occupation authorities, respectively, and/or by German authorities in Bavaria and the Rhineland, respectively, may be indicated." Whether or not lawyers, or Flocken's father, participated in the letters seems not to be known, but the letters originated with the defendant. There were those in the community of the WCC who expressed some dismay that her sentence had been commuted just at the time she was continuing her blistering attack on their office. Her charges were again investigated and no such irregularities were discovered. Flocken settled into Landsberg Prison as a "lifer."

Dr. Hosenberg lived just long enough to see his daughter's life saved. In April 1949, the city physician of Dueren, most likely a friend of the family, sent a telegram to the Judge Advocate along with DM350, requesting that Flocken be allowed to visit her dying father. To that point, "no requests for compassionate leaves of absence have been granted to any war criminal serving a sentence of imprisonment imposed by the Dachau Tribunal," and it was determined that Flocken had no right to be the exception. They further put forth some practical considerations:

A. The trip to Dueren (near Cologne in the British Sector) will require at least three experienced guards in order to provide continuous safeguarding of the prisoner. Inasmuch as the prisoner is a woman, it will be necessary for her to be accompanied by an enlisted member of the WAC. At least one of the custodial group, preferably the WAC, will be required to speak fluent German.

B. The trip would require a minimum of five days to permit Dr. Flocken to remain at her father's side for any part of one day.

C. During layovers between trains, etc., British facilities may have to be used and clearance for this use will have to be made in advance.

D. The guards will have to be quartered and fed while in Dueren and this may entail utilization of the German economy. Experienced enlisted men, preferably those from War Criminal Prison No. 1, should be used for this task. If this is done, the already limited strength of the enlisted personnel at the prison will be reduced.

E. Although no decision has been reached as yet concerning the reimbursement of the cost of this trip from the DM350 which have been forwarded to the prison, it is doubtful that, even if reimbursement could be accomplished legally, this amount would cover the cost of the trip.

F. Even if the problems and difficulties referred to (above) were overcome with respect to the case of Erika Flocken, this division is still of the opinion that the request contained should not be favorably considered. Among the principal reasons which can be advanced to support this objection is the fact that the granting of this particular request will result in a flood of similar requests from other prisoners confined at Landsberg, which if granted only in part would in turn place an unforeseen and unwarranted demand upon this Headquarters in general and upon the Provost Marshal, EUCOM, in particular.

In the end, Flocken did not see her father before he died.

During her years in prison, Flocken kept up with her professional field. She also studied several languages, increasing her fluency in English, Spanish, and French. Flocken could play the piano and practiced diligently; she was described as being "accomplished." When a group of new female inmates came to the prison, she facilitated their adjustment and supervised them.

Never during all the next ten years would she stop fighting her conviction. She was rigid in maintaining her innocence and maintained an attitude of "bitterness." She refused even to consider a capitulation even though it meant she would remain in prison long after those who had actively killed inmates, airmen, and POWs were home with their families and getting on with their lives.

Flocken also suffered physically while in prison. She had terrible gall bladder attacks with accompanying jaundice. Eventually her gall bladder was removed, but she had to be put on such a strict diet that she developed pellagra as a result of a vitamin deficiency. She suffered other complications as well.

Although the official file does not provide much information, Flocken was probably sued for malpractice while she was in prison. An attorney representing the widow of a man who had died in the Schwindegg Hospital wrote the Judge Advocate to seek information about Flocken's trial. His client did not believe that her husband died of the "cancer of the stomach and hemorrhage of the stomach" that Flocken had said was the cause of his death. There had been no operation, diagnostic procedures, or history of symptoms by which Flocken could have made the diagnosis. The records were made available to the attorney.

In August 1956, the Mixed Board reduced her sentence from "life" to 38 years. In 1957, Flocken's family, her lawyer, and the prison administration had a heart-to-heart talk with her. Hardly anyone was left in prison. She was 44 years old with a substantial chronic illness, and she had long been eligible to apply for parole. All she had to do was drop her petulant attitude and her bitterness, to at least make an appearance of coming to grips with her part in the Muehldorf affair, and to apply for parole. If she could do those things, without a doubt she could leave prison.

Flocken wanted to go into a field that was related to her training interests. It was noted that she had no other practical skills, and a job as a laboratory assistant was found for her. It paid only DM350 per month. This was a big change compared with the days when she had been supervising doctors at the concentration camp, with her own driver and personal maid. The DM350, on the other hand, looked quite substantial compared with the DM80 per month paid to Johann Vican when he went on parole or the DM20 per month paid to young Jonina while she worked the farms at the concentration camp and lost her baby to starvation and maltreatment.

Flocken didn't want to live with her mother so a room was found for her in the apartment of an 80-year-old woman. She was even free to travel to visit her mother across distances that would have been strictly forbidden when most prisoners were being paroled in the early fifties. Flocken was entering into a modern world she would hardly be able to fathom. In 1957, young people who could hardly remember the war were going to college.

Flocken was unhappy with the laboratory assistant job, and she left within weeks. Her parole supervisors didn't seem to mind much. A physician in general practice offered her a job at DM1,500 a month as his assistant. She accepted and life moved on. She was practicing medicine again.

In 1958, the German government petitioned the Mixed Board to release Flocken from her parole and any other conditions. The Board agreed and she was free to go into private practice if she so chose.

15

They Were Good Boys: The Story of Julius Straub and Peter Goldmann

Julius Straub was the victim of incredibly bad luck and almost historic irony, and he was the author of both. While Erika Flocken condemned herself with a few words, Straub became a war criminal by a distance of three or four meters and within only minutes.

At about the same time the inmates of out-camp Sonnenberg, with Heinrich Buuck trailing the column, began to move toward Czechoslovakia, the main camp at Flossenburg began to drive inmates west and south for a similar journey. It was, according to witnesses, a "special Jewish transport," which would attempt to take prisoners by the thousands from Flossenburg and its out-camps to an overflowing Dachau. As a longtime inmate of Flossenburg, Straub was a familiar figure who was not known for having problems with fellow inmates or with the SS. He was older and, at 38, perhaps more mature and resigned than the teenagers who were his fellow prisoners.

Jakob Silbermann was sixteen when he came to Flossenburg in August 1944. He worked as a turner, a semiskilled laborer who uses a lathe, and he wore a red triangle marked with a "P" to show that he was from Poland and the numbers "16089" to show that he was an inmate; he was Jewish. He knew Straub by sight but they were not really acquainted. They didn't live on the same block and they did not work together. Straub wore a green triangle; he was a criminal.

When Silbermann saw Straub on Monday, April 16, 1945, he was not dressed in his usual prisoner's garb. He wore a gray-green uniform and carried a carbine. "He wore a pointed field cap with a death-head insignia on it and also wore the SS insignia on the collar." Straub set his cap at an angle. This was a cobbled-together uniform. Silbermann knew that some of the guards wore Italian uniforms and he thought that might have been what Straub was wearing. They were made of better material than regulation German uniforms. Silbermann saw other prisoners, who were mostly volunteers, similarly dressed and armed.

Silbermann was questioned as to whether he knew if Straub was a volunteer.

His reply was, "I can't tell you, but most of them were, and I also tell you ... they were given double rations and were also given tobacco and cigarettes and didn't have to go to work."

On April 16, 1945, almost 3,000 prisoners set off on the forced move from Flossenburg. By Friday, after a week of tribulation on the journey, part of it by train, and a forced layover in Swarzenfeld, the men were told that "all those who were healthy or believed themselves to be healthy should line up to march off and that the others should remain behind." Silbermann and two of his friends considered themselves healthy, and they marched off with about two hundred other men who were divided into about ten groups. Silbermann's group was "rather towards the end, but there were other groups behind."

David Tannenbaum, a shoemaker, was in his mid-teens and Josef Steinlauf had just turned eighteen when they were transported to Flossenburg during August 1944. Like Silbermann, they were Polish Jews. They had seen Straub only two or three times at the prison. Steinlauf had noticed that during the last days all capos and Germans wore the new gray-green "Italian" uniforms. Also, on the night before the transport left the main camp, they had been issued weapons.

As they began the march, Straub didn't seem to be assigned

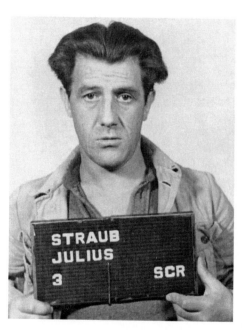

Julius Straub

to any group in particular, and for three days thereafter Silbermann, Tannenbaum, and Steinlauf did not see Straub. After three days—at ten o'clock in the morning of April 23—the group arrived in Stamsried where they stayed overnight in a barn. In the morning, they lined up to get their rations of potatoes. An inmate who was too weak to go outside relieved himself in the barn. Straub hit him with a piece of firewood, and during the beating Tannenbaum noticed that he had a swastika on his lapel. Straub had not yet bought himself a place in infamy, however.

The number of men had decreased considerably over the three days. They had "perished," according to testimony. Their group had become so small they were combined with another group, which brought their numbers back to three or four hundred. This newly formed group walked out of Stamsried and marched up a hill into a forest. Silbermann and his friends were in the next-to-the-last row. The hill was a problem and three inmates in the row behind Silbermann, Steinlauf, and Tannenbaum became very weak and started leaning on each other. Someone behind the column shouted, "If you can't go on you will be taken out!"

The three sick, weak, exhausted inmates "left the row and sat down on the road side." Straub placed the butt of his carbine under the pit of his arm and "fired several volleys at the inmates." One of the inmates fell backward and the other two fell to the side. Their heads were mangled and they bled profusely. The column proceeded forward about three or four meters when they heard an order for all SS men to come to the head of the column. The inmates heard firing ahead and were aware that "the liberators, the Americans," were probably in the distance. The inmates marched on a few meters and began to realize that they were alone. The SS men had disappeared. For them, suddenly, the war was over.

The inmates didn't know where they were and knew they couldn't make their way through the woods. They decided to go back into town. On their way, they examined the fallen and determined that they were dead. When they got back into town, they told a column of Germans who had been gathering dead inmates for burial for several days to "bring in the three dead who were lying up on the hill."

Silbermann, Tannenbaum, and Steinlauf settled in displaced persons facilities in the town of Cham. Later that summer, while they were out walking, they saw Straub on the street. They performed a citizen's arrest and took Straub to the authorities. The next time they would see Straub would be at his trial in the old administration building at Dachau during the first week of October 1947.

Straub's lawyer could offer very little defense at his trial. One Paul Toermer, a political prisoner who had once been acquitted of high treason but had nevertheless been sent to the concentration camp for being "politically unreliable," was called to the stand by the defense. He had been made a "camp policeman" at Flossenburg a day or two before the transport left; he did not go with the transport. After the witness gave his name and before he could state his age, the prosecution objected that they had not been "informed that this man would act as a witness here in accordance with standard operating procedure."

Straub's lawyer responded by saying, "May it please the court, I withdraw this witness. May it please the court the defense rests." The defense lawyer further stated that a possible witness existed in France but that he could not get in touch with him. The president of the Court decided that they should hear what Toermer had to say despite irregularities.

Toermer could only say that he had seen the defendant on the morning of April 16 and that he had no insignia or swastika on his makeshift uniform but that he did carry a rifle. He had not gone on the transport and could not know what happened on the road. He did explain that the guards carried a variety of weapons, some of them inoperable. He, for example, had been issued a "Danish rifle with Czechoslovakian ammunition which did not function at all."

Just before Christmas in 1947, Julius Straub submitted a sworn statement in his own behalf during the appeals process. He claimed that he had been sent to Flossenburg in 1940 for political reasons, suffered more at the camp for that reason, and that prisoners who were called upon to be guards could not be compared with the SS men and should not be sentenced to death. He claimed the testimony of the former inmates was false and was made out of hate and vengeance. In his large, even, manuscript style he suggested that the witnesses had testified against him because he was a German, and, as was well known at that time, everyone hated Germans. He wanted them to know that he was an unskilled laborer and had been forced to work in the Flossenburg quarry for over two years. It appears that very few fellow humans were interested in fighting for his life.

Straub was hanged at Landsberg Prison on November 17, 1948.

Like Julius Straub, Peter Goldmann was on the transport from Flossenburg that never arrived at Dachau. Unlike Straub, when he found himself charged with war crimes, his wife, his many personal friends, members of his church, and even the Bishop of Rottenburg flew to his aid. They wanted the world to know that Goldmann was a good Catholic boy who had met secretly with the Catholic Young Man's Organization in opposition to national socialism. They said he could not possibly have been a vicious war criminal.

Goldmann, who was from Schoenwald near Gleiwitz in eastern Germany, was a machinist in civilian life and a Pfc. (drafted) in the Waffen SS. As a guard at Flossenburg, he was assigned to the transport that left on April 16, 1945. An order had been passed around the camp that all Jews were to report to the roll call area and prepare to be moved to another location. Between 2,000 and 3,000 prisoners were rounded up and marched to the camp railroad station. Once there, they were loaded on about forty cars, or "wagons" as they were sometimes called, at about fifty to sixty prisoners per car. Some were placed in closed cars to endure the suffocating stench and lack of fresh air. Others were placed in open-topped cars to endure the

Peter Goldmann

elements: the most difficult being a blazing spring sun. One engine pulled and a second engine pushed from the back of the train.

Almost immediately, the transport was spotted by American fliers. The planes began to buzz the transport. The train moved from the Flossenburg station to the town of Floss, a distance of about eight kilometers, which took about half an hour or so. There, the Americans destroyed both engines with machine-gun fire. SS men abandoned the train and headed for ditches or for the nearby villages and woods. Those prisoners who could get out of the cars attempted to run for cover. Most hid under the cars. The Americans seemed not to be interested in the cars and only about a dozen prisoners were injured. Ludwig Drattler was from Czechoslovakia, but he was reported as being from Hungary. He and most others who would testify against Goldmann had entered concentration camps when they were fifteen; at the time of the trial in October 1947, they were just entering the youngest years of their manhood. "After the war broke out, one part of Czechoslovakia was taken by the Germans. The other part was taken by the Hungarians. That is how I came to the Hungarians." He was one of the prisoners who fled the cars during the shooting and returned back into one of the cars when the planes left the area.

When the attack was over, the SS men returned and began shooting men who were not in the cars. The men scurried back into the cars, but apparently some prisoners escaped altogether. The SS men, "like wild dogs," began looking for their kit bags only to find that some had been trampled and others had been looted. Peter Goldmann was furious and began to go from car to car looking for his resources. Ludwig Drattler said he acted like he was king of the transport. When he found his bag looted and destroyed, he immediately named a suspect and beat him to death on the spot.

When Goldmann left the car, he saw a prisoner wearing light, rubber shoes similar to those worn by the SS. Although the prisoner protested that he had been issued those shoes for the trip, Goldmann insisted that he had stolen them during the crisis; he shot the prisoner four times in the stomach. The man, a Polish Jew, fell over the rails "where the train was standing" where he lay for about fifteen minutes before Goldmann brought back a prison detail of three inmates who carried the corpse by its arms and legs and threw it on top on a pile of bodies the SS had killed at the station. Only about a dozen men had been wounded by the American attack.

David Gruenblatt, a forty-two-year-old locksmith from Nuremberg, gave the shortest possible answers at Goldmann's trial and had to be reminded on more than one occasion to speak louder.

Who was on the transport?

"Jews."

How long did he stay with the transport?

"Until the liberation."

Did he see the accused after Schwarzenfeld?

"No."

What kind of Jew got shot?

"From Krakow."

What did he do at his first concentration camp?

"We dug."

Gruenblatt saw Goldmann shoot one of the men at Floss and "he was dead."

The new engines arrived after about two hours and the train moved on — through Neustadt, Weiden, and Luewildenau arriving in Schwarzenfeld on Friday, April 23. Along the way the Americans persisted in their attacks. Stopping the transport seemed to be their goal. When the train paused, the attacks ceased. "Every time they saw us in motion they attacked the engines." The planes were flying very low and at one point the inmates were told to wave their prison clothes in an attempt to show the Americans that it was a prisoner transport and not a troop movement. The demonstration did not work, and at Schwarzenfeld, the train was finally put out of commission. Some of the prisoners stayed in Schwazenfeld for two days before they could be moved out on foot. At liberation, the empty train was still sitting on the tracks where the Americans had stopped it.

During the attack at Schwarzenfeld, some prisoners were injured. In Ludwig Drattler's car a man with a reddish face and sparse yellow hair was hit in the mouth. Drattler helped the man to the area where doctors (Jewish prisoners) and medics were bandaging the injured. "He [Goldmann] came and approached us because that man was crying. He made him sit down. Then he shot him."

Was he sure the man was dead?

"After he received the shot he fell over and began to bleed heavily. Then I saw how all the dead people were loaded on a car and he was loaded on the car also." Drattler also saw many other prisoners shot by SS men other than Goldmann at Schwarzenfeld.

Lajos Krauss, also a Hungarian Jew and a carpenter before the war, acted as a medic at Schwarzenfeld. He saw Goldmann's handiwork before Drattler brought the man with yellow hair in for treatment. "One prisoner had a shot in his arm. Then he [Goldmann] said we should not bandage that prisoner's wounds any more, and he shot him. I was about three steps away from him, the accused." Then he saw Goldmann shoot the man with yellow hair. "Then he [Goldmann] went away and I can say with certainty that he shot at least ten or fifteen prisoners because I heard other shots." Krauss could not say precisely that he had actually seen Goldmann kill more than the two men at the medics' station. Later, Krauss had to help load dead prisoners onto a cart and pull the cart before the transport moved out, on foot, at six o'clock in the morning. They were in the last hours of their ordeal.

About two weeks after Goldmann and the other SS men deserted the transport train outside Schwarzenfeld and the men on foot in the woods near Stamsried where Julius Straub had became a wartime criminal, Germany officially capitulated. Most SS men tried to blend as quickly as possible back into society while others fled toward the American lines. Anything seemed more appealing than being captured by the Russians. Still others attempted to carry the fight as long as possible, even to the point of dragging people from their homes and murdering them after the formal surrender. The prisoners suddenly left alone were also in a precarious position. Although some braved the towns where townspeople could see the handwriting on the wall and were willing to give of their small resources, other prisoners hid out in barns or woods and lived off handouts from farmers. After the formal surrender, large numbers huddled for extended periods of time in displaced persons camps or, if they had a useful skill, found work. Many foreign Jews simply became a part of the new German culture because there was no other place to go. Some would make their way to other countries including the United States and Palestine.

When a final tally was made, Goldmann was convicted by corroborating testimony of killing six prisoners—most of whom had simply annoyed him in some way. Because of confusion and the inability of prisoners to see what was going on, the murderers of hundreds of men on the transport were never identified. Goldmann, for his part, was sentenced to death by hanging.

The quickest to fly to the aid of Goldmann was the Catholic Church. About six weeks after Goldmann's conviction, the Bishop of Rottenburg (on official Church letterhead) recommended that a petition for "benevolent consideration" by Frau Goldmann be considered by the 7708 War Crimes Group. Although he didn't know Goldmann personally, he was requesting an official parish reference, which he expected would be forwarded soon. He signed the letter and added the official stamp of his appointment.

For his part, Georg Garius, the former "Pastor in the Catholic Diocese" in the community of Schoenwald, Gleiwitz District, Goldmann's home community, apologized for being late in answering the request. He cited "sickness, lack of electricity, and a mountain of unfinished business. By day I am usually on the road. In the evening I come home tired and exhausted and when I try to take care of the mail and my household duties there is no light. Today I am writing to you in the light of my last half a candle."

Chaplain Garius remembered Goldmann as a convinced and active Catholic who sang in the Church choir. He had been "well behaved, decent, and politically disinterested" and he was "astonished to hear that he was in an internment camp." He had equal respect for Goldmann's wife and begged that Goldmann's case be expedited as quickly as possible. He wished them to "listen to our request and the testimony" they would offer in this post-trial period. By May, the Pastor for the Homeless, "Pastor of his [Goldmann's] family," was asking for a pardon for the sentenced man. He believed the struggles and agonies of the family coupled with the relief the pardon would bring should move the reviewing committee. He said, "I do not know if the Western Powers still consider the word or the request of a pastor."

The wife of Goldmann seemed shocked to learn that the word of the Church as written by the Bishop of Rottenburg could not override a legal verdict. She opened her letter above the Bishop's and her salutation with "Praise be the Lord!"

Her salutation was "Petition to the Right Honorable Eminence, The Bishop John Baptist, Venerable Eminence." She asked him "respectfully to submit a petition for clemency in favor of my husband because it might be heard by an ecclesiastical office before it is too late. Where else is a Christian supposed to address himself if not to the Highest of the Church?" The wife did not tell the Bishop that her husband was convicted of killing six humans, only that he was wrongly accused of killing "two Jews."

She believed it might help if the Bishop told them she had been sick for a year and a half of typhoid fever and was having trouble taking care of her child (born 1943). She sent the Bishop "10m." for expenses. She told the Bishop, "God Bless You a thousand times."

The Bishop honored the wife's request to "submit a petition for clemency," but the petition consisted of a request for benevolent consideration for her and a statement that, even though he didn't know Goldmann, he would get his former pastor to write a letter. Letters from both churchmen contained so few words that together they would not fill a page.

Goldmann's neighbors had no doubt about his character and they flooded the review committee with statements of reference. He was decent and did not fight. He was a definite opponent of the Nazis and so was all his family, especially his older brothers. He was conservative and "consecrated to his religion." He had a noble character. He belonged to the Catholic Young Man's Organization. "This organization consisted of the young men and youths from the best families of the community and stood under the care of the Church." This was an anti–Nazi group, which met secretly until it was "violently deactivated."

It was also stated that Goldmann cried when he was drafted into the SS because he didn't want to do the kinds of things those people did. The plus of the statement is that many drafted into the SS were against their activities; the unintended minus is that it is a confirmation that Germans were aware of the nature of the SS. According to the letters, none of the neighbors had ever held sympathy for the Nazis.

Goldmann's lawyer made some effort to present an alibi for the review committee. Goldmann claimed he had been in town during the Schwarzenfeld incident and that witnesses at Floss had mistaken him for someone else. The Burgermeister of the village investigated and could only offer that some SS men did indeed ask locals for food. "Mistaken identity" was a frequently used defense among the defendants and it was not taken seriously. Julius Straub wrote a letter to the committee stating that Goldmann was not with the train when the murders happened.

Goldmann was hanged on the same day as Straub. They were posed on the gallows just before their hanging and a photograph was taken for the record. After the hanging, they were stripped naked and put into coffins made of rough sawn boards that had shavings (or perhaps dirt) placed in the bottom to soak up leaking body fluids. The coffins were of an old-fashioned design — wider at the end to accommodate the shoulders; narrower at the other end. Their naked bodies were photographed in the boxes, and they were buried in the Landsberg Prison cemetery.

*   *   *

An interesting aside to the Goldmann-Straub episode was the trial of Friedrich Lutz, a schoolteacher nearing his sixtieth birthday who looked every inch his age and profession. Appearing against Lutz as the only prosecution witnesses were two squabbling brothers named Isaac and Leo Seiden. (The Seiden brothers were from Flossenburg proper; Lutz was from Hersbruck, an out-camp of Flossenburg.) In company with the other Polish Jews, the Seiden brothers endured the misbegotten train ride that stopped in Schwarzenfeld. They continued on in one of the columns that headed toward Stamsried on foot. Although they were not walking together, both of them testified that they saw Lutz shoot three men who were too weak to go on.

Lutz would have none of the Seiden brothers' accusations; he had explanations and witnesses. His first explanation defended his membership in the Nazi Party since 1933.

> I had never been interested in politics according to the education I had in the house of my parents, in the elementary school, and the seminary. For instance, it was forbidden by the seminary to have any dealings with politics, or to be interested in any way in politics. I intended to carry out that basic idea of mine after 1933, but because we were involved in a dispute over two colleagues against other colleagues we were called to the magistrate's office and ordered to justify ourselves. As a result of two conferences we had we were asked as to whether both of us were members of the Party. When we said, "No," we were told that nothing could be done against that third person because he was a member of the Party. Therefore in order to get our justice we both joined the Party.

He also had an explanation for why he wore a death's-head insignia on his Waffen SS uniform.

> I was just about to explain that. In the middle of January I was detailed to Buchenwald with some other thirty non-commissioned officers. There I had an opportunity to exchange my worn cap for another one. It was a cap somewhat like a ski cap and on this cap was a little space of field gray

and on this triangle there was embroidered or sewn a death-head. Otherwise I didn't wear any insignia.

He had witnesses to explain for him the reason he could not have been on the road at Stamsreid killing prisoners. On the fifth of April, the older guards had been sent out with a trainload of nearly 2,000 sick prisoners, headed for Dachau. Given the facilities at Dachau, one wonders how the camp could have housed these and the other several thousands being sent there. Nevertheless, the Hersbruck transport set out with the older guards. It was determined that they should ride the train because they would have had difficulty on a march. On April 7, the train arrived at Dachau. The camp accepted the prisoners but sent the guards back. When the guards arrived back at Hersbruck on Saturday, April 14, they found the camp deserted. They could not return to the main camp at Flossenburg because it had been overrun by Russians just after the "retreat" of the Germans and their prisoners. They knew the bridge across the Danube River would soon be destroyed, and, aged or not, they headed back to Dachau on foot. The prosecution contended that the aging guards overtook the main Flossenburg transport and had been assigned to accompany the column wherein the Seiden brothers marched. Lutz contended that they walked eleven and a half days and reached Dachau on the 25th or 26th. They never made contact with the Flossenburg transport or any other transport. However, Lutz could not remember the name of a single other guard on the trek to the Danube.

A Protestant minister who had been a chaplain with the Air Corps had known Lutz well. He testified that the Kreisleiter of his district "saw to it that I was transferred to the Waffen SS." He was assigned to Hersbruck.

The prosecutor asked him if he had been a clergyman at Hersbruck.

"No. There was no such thing." Actually, he did clerical and telephone duties. He knew the large transport had left for Dachau and the aging guards had returned — although he couldn't remember if that second leaving was before or after he set off on April 14. He didn't belong to any particular column, he said, and he had no particular duties. He left after the "fifth" transport and all those transports left on foot — headed for Dachau.

The prosecutor asked how he had traveled.

"I was sitting in a passenger car which was without gas and therefore was hitched to a truck and I was sitting in that passenger car."

Did he catch up with any of the columns?

Actually, he did. And he did have a responsibility. He was in charge of the officers' luggage. "I had to see to it that there was [sic] horses and wagons or any other means that that luggage was being transported." He made it to Dachau and did not pass through or in the vicinity of Schwarzenfeld or Nuremberg and he had never heard of Stamsried. He had not seen Lutz during any of this time. On the other hand, he couldn't guarantee that Lutz hadn't been part of a transport.

Josef Gossner, 56, who had been a businessman before he became caught up in the Nazi cause, could do better by Lutz. He had been on the round trip to Dachau and he left with the small group of men who were the final occupants of Hersbruck. He had trouble remembering the route they took or the name of any single person of the twenty or so men who went with them on the eleven-day walk, but he assured the court that Lutz was on the trip. They had run out of food and had had to beg from civilians along the way, but they indeed had arrived in Dachau. They did not run into any transports on their way.

At some point during the last days of the war, Lutz had removed the death's-head patch from his hat. He had made a decision to seek out the Americans and surrender to them. He had a feisty lawyer who growled at all the right places. He put on a smarter defense than many of the less well educated had received, and Lutz was acquitted.

No one knows how many died on the chaotic transports, but for every guard convicted, hundreds, or perhaps thousands, of prisoners were murdered or died from maltreatment.

16

Profiles in Darkness: *The Stories of the Bitch of Buchenwald, Prince zu Waldeck, Otto Skorzeny, the Hadamar Murder Factory, and the Malmedy Massacre*

Of the nearly 500 cases and 1,700 defendants at Dachau, only a very few received any appreciable amount of press coverage at the time. The "Malmedy Massacre" case, the "Hadamar Murder Factory" case, and the trials of Otto Skorzeny and Josias, Prince zu Waldeck were exceptions. The case of Ilse Koch, the "Bitch of Buchenwald," probably fascinated the public most. It still remains one of the most unsettling and inconclusive cases in the series.

According to a "history" prepared for the report on Koch's case, Buchenwald was established after Dachau exhausted its boundaries.

> By summer, 1937, it was necessary to found a new camp. A huge, centralized murder-factory…. On a wooded hill six miles from Weimar the site was selected. Near the source of German culture and freedom, the greatest dungeon of democracy was created. Thus began the infamous career of Buchenwald.
>
> Prisoners representing over 30 nations, including Americans, lived, suffered, and died in its confines.

For almost eight years every type of horror known to man was practiced with sadistic pleasure. Whether simple extermination, as in the earlier years, or extermination by "working to death," as later on, the pattern followed was always the same. Break the body; break the spirit; break the heart.

Inmates were given typhus injections in spotted fever experiments; burned alive with phosphorus to try medical remedies; given yellow fever in senseless guinea-pig tests. Thousands were shot to death in "Commando 99" murders in the horse stable. Driven mad, many inmates rushed through the guard chain in the quarry or in the garden and were gleefully shot by the mighty SS. Tattooed inmates disappeared suddenly and reappeared as lampshades, book covers or gloves. Prisoners were crushed with rocks, drowned in manure, whipped, castrated, starved, and mutilated. Life was torture and torture was life.

The history goes on to report that the camp was overrun by General George Patton on April 11, 1945, and that a day later Army General Dwight D. Eisenhower visited. "White with horror, he summoned his staff and gave the order to call in the press." He also invited members of both houses of the American Congress, their British counterparts, and a United Nations committee to view the carnage. Although many nations were interested in prosecuting the culprits, it was decided that America should do the job because they had overrun the camp.

The history reports that more than 6,000 suspects were investigated and that, for this main case, 31 "arch criminals" would be prosecuted as "representative of the horror that was Buchenwald." Lesser criminals and those associated with the large string of out-camps would be tried separately. Case #000-50-9 would be known as *The United States of America vs. Josias, Prince zu Waldeck, et al.*

Ilse Koch was the wife of Buchenwald Camp Commander Karl Otto Koch. He had been commander of several camps but was executed for trying to intimidate other officers and civilians, profiteering, and producing fake papers. His wife was sometimes called the "Commandeuse of Buchenwald," and it was alleged that she and her husband together commanded Buchenwald from 1939 until December 1941, when her husband was transferred elsewhere. After her husband's transfer, she remained at the camp until August 24, 1943. The prosecution expected to prove that

1. As Commandeuse of Buchenwald Concentration Camp, [she] indulged in personal sadism against inmates.

2. By virtue of her position [she] caused the deaths of many hundreds of inmates.

3. [She] indulged in the sadistic practice of using human skin of inmates for such personal items as gloves, book covers, and lampshades.

At the time of her trial, Koch was 40 years old. A witness testified that her husband had given a directive that her orders were to be obeyed just the same as if he had given them himself. A witness testified that she had reported him for drinking a glass of wine and for that he was beaten, forced to run across a pile of rocks several times, and hanged by his arms for three hours. Koch had complained to her husband about "dirty Jews" looking at her and he had had them beaten. He also had punished those he saw looking at her. She observed an inmate with diarrhea relieving himself and ordered an SS lieutenant to put a stop to it. The lieutenant overworked the man for an hour, and a death report showed that he died the next day. She had inmates punished for picking berries near her house and personally hit Jews with a stick. In one of the more infamous incidents, Koch, dressed in a short skirt and no underwear, was supposed to have stood over men working in a ditch and then hit them with her riding crop for looking at her. She gave an order to have rocks carried from the quarry to her house and hit those who could not walk fast enough. A witness testified that he had seen lampshades in the lounge of her home made of human skin — one with tattoos on it. She was reported to have had a photo album, a briefcase, and a pair of gloves made from tattooed skin. A witness stated that he had seen Koch admire a tattoo on a worker, that six months later he saw the skin with the same tattoo in the pathology department, and that still later he saw the tattooed skin covering an album belonging to Koch. Witnesses claimed that it was common knowledge around the camp that Koch ordered inmates with tattoos killed in order to obtain their skin.

Koch denied all, and her defense produced a few witnesses who supported her. She said she had reported inmates who had illegally entered her house. She said she was an innocent housewife with three children to care for and that during the times of some of the beatings she was accused of, she was away from camp. She said that she never had anything to do with human skin.

The Court found her guilty of reporting inmates who then received unwarranted punishment and of striking inmates. She was also found guilty of participation in the execution of the Common Design. They did not find her guilty of dealing in human parts. They sentenced her to life imprisonment, but the sentence, under review, was found to be excessive. On review, her sentence was reduced to four years, commencing on October 18, 1945, and by the time of the trial and the review, she was already eligible to apply for relief.

Were human remains ever a real factor in the Buchenwald case? The answers are "yes" and "no." The Court did at one time have in its possession a human head shrunken after the fashion of those "done in Ecuador."

The Court also possessed some sheets of tattooed skin including some that were cut into a shape that might have fit a lampshade and were perforated around the edges as if they might have been sewn to other pieces. Gloves made of human skin were also possibly in its possession. The items were "found" in the commandant's office when the Americans arrived. A chain of possession was never established. These items were photographed and the pictures were printed in the press. A strange thing happened, however. All the items disappeared while in the possession of the Americans and have never resurfaced. One guess is that an American soldier (or soldiers) took the items as souvenirs. Absolute proof does not exist that Koch had inmates killed for their tattooed skin or that she ever possessed human skin. There seems to be no doubt, however, that she was cruel and sadistic.

While she was in the custody of the Americans, Koch became pregnant. The Americans would claim that an old lover dug a tunnel into her cell. Others would say that the most likely culprit was an American serviceman. It was rumored that the pregnancy had saved her from a death sentence during the trial.

Righteous members of Congress, in large numbers, accompanied by some religious leaders, took General Clay and Colonel Straight to severe task for allowing her sentence to be reduced so dramatically, thereby permitting her to be released following the short sentence. They understood that she could not be put back into prison, but they pleaded for the WCC to find new charges or for the German people to find other grounds on which to try her. She was recharged by the new German government and sentenced to prison. She committed suicide in prison in 1967.

Although few can actually put a name to the "Bitch of Buchenwald," to this day the public has yet to let go of the case of Ilse Koch. Her life was to inspire a continuing interest and a cause for years to come. From the time she first surfaced until she disappeared behind prison walls for good, the press spilled a considerable amount of ink on her behalf. At least one film has taken advantage of her notoriety and writers have given their attention to her situation on several occasions. She has become an icon for those revisionists called "Holocaust deniers" who would like to claim that the maelstrom never happened.

*   *   *

For centuries, Germany was made up of hundreds of small states that enjoyed considerable autonomy. Rules of succession allowed the states to be divided among heirs, which tended to further increase the number of states. Some of the states were small, rural scraps of land that became the background for modern fairy tales. There were so many stories about the poor village girl who married a prince because there were so many poor village girls and so many princes. Never mind that the prince might have enjoyed no more wealth or privilege than the son of a county judge. More likely, the prince would marry a cousin from a nearby state, and some states became larger and stronger by these strategic matrimonial alliances.

Because of the extraordinary numbers of persons in Germanic countries who could claim aristocratic heritage, "royalty" was sometimes a bit difficult to identify after World War I — and even more so after World War II. By the time of the Dachau trials, the lines of aristocracy had become so muddled it had become possible for average Germans to fake claims to significant ancestry. It's probable that more than one American fell for the trick, but, once aware the Americans became mistrustful of such claims.

On November 13, 1950, "Princess Elizabeth of Isenberg," at her own initiative, had lunch with members of the U.S. High Commission for Germany and requested consideration for a schoolteacher and a cement worker who had been sentenced to death. The office of the commissioner identified the cases and learned that she was appealing to the wrong office; the cases were under the jurisdiction of other officials. The second office wrote to the first office, suggesting they "run a check on this gal." The official to whom the information had been sent replied that, "It wouldn't surprise me if she was as phony as the Prince and Princess Christian of Hesse." The Dachau records don't report whether the Princess Elizabeth turned out to be real or as fake as others who had tried the same stunt. On the whole, the ubiquitous princes and princesses seemed to have had no effect on war crimes trials.

Some who claimed royal blood were authentic, however. An example would be the princes and princesses of Saxe-Coberg or Waldeck-Pyrmont. The Waldeck family dates its family beginnings to the fourteenth century. Waldeck-Pyrmont was a typical backwater county in Hesse and became a principality in 1712.

After World War I and the end of the German monarchy, the princes lived an uncertain political existence. Some were allied with current or former royal families in Europe and enjoyed considerable prestige and the support of their "people." Their political and private statuses were becoming exceedingly more fragile as the Nazis took over Germany and most were put into the position of having to support or at least tolerate the Nazis if they wished to continue to use their newly worthless titles.

Josias, Prince zu Waldeck (Josias, Erbprinz von Waldeck-Pyrmont) wholeheartedly supported the Nazi cause. He became an SS lieutenant general and set up a "Bureau for the Germanization of Eastern Peoples." He was, at the end of the war, "Higher SS and Police Leader for [the] area including Buchenwald Concentration Camp and sub-camps." He prose-cuted Karl Otto Koch and ordered his execution just before the Ameri-cans arrived in 1945. He had personally intervened with Himmler to let the case against Koch go forward. The business about Koch didn't inter-est the Americans in particular, but accusations that he abused inmates resulted in war crimes charges being placed against the prince.

In 1944, an order was issued that, in case of emergency, the higher SS and police leaders (like Waldeck) would assume authority over the con-centration camps in their respective areas. After German failures in the Battle of the Bulge, no one could claim that an emergency didn't exist. Waldeck moved his office to the administration building at Buchenwald early in the spring of 1945. Before that, he frequently visited the camp in connection with legal cases and during the corruption scandal of Koch. He would say that he learned of unlawful killings at Buchenwald, but he did not know of the "Commando 99" affair during which Russian POWs were killed by the hundreds. He admitted having seen bodies that looked as if they had died from "over-exertion." The camp commander be-came his subordinate during the last days of the war. Waldeck was in charge of ordering the evacuation of Buchenwald, but the camp commander attended to the actual details. Testimony would indicate that he dis-cussed public hygiene with the camp physician, but that he did not know of the med-ical experiments carried out by the camp physician. It was his job to investigate any unnatural deaths of inmates reported to him, but appar-ently almost all deaths were entered into records, one after the other within min-utes of each other sometimes, as "natural." He would state that he saw about ten bodies

Otto Skorzeny testifies at his own trial in the courtroom at Dachau.

along the evacuation route. It would seem from his statements that he believed himself to be among gentlemen and that gentlemen might understand his situation.

The prince, who was already fifty at the time of the trial, was sentenced to life imprisonment, but he was released after a relatively short time because of severe illness.

*   *   *

If Otto Skorzeny had not actually lived, someone would have invented him. To this day, he has a small cult following which studies and admires his supposed bravado and derring-do. He was a tall, imposing young man with the requisite scar across his cheek. Hitler admired his daring, believed in his unusual abilities, and supported his elevation to the status of German hero. Among Skorzeny's exploits was the rescue of Mussolini from a mountaintop where he was being held prisoner by his political opposition. The immediate rescue succeeded, and the news was flashed around the world. (Mussolini's freedom was to be short-lived, and he would be taken again by his countrymen who killed him and his mistress and hung them head down in a public street.) Although Skorzeny became one of the legends of WWII, when his ability to permanently affect history is measured, his accomplishments take second place to his flamboyance.

Skorzeny and several of his associates were tried in the Dachau series for activities during the Battle of the Bulge: the Ardennes Forest Offensive. Early in the planning stage of the Ardennes Forest Offensive, Hitler had personally asked Skorzeny to work behind enemy (American) lines to confuse troop activities and to carry out certain acts of sabotage, the most effective of which was to be the removal of explosives from bridges the Germans hoped to use during their offensive.

Skorzeny and his men secured uniforms, Red Cross rations, weapons and ammunition, ribbons and medals, and other bits of Americana from POWs in camps, by pilfering Red Cross packages, and from depots of supplies the Germans had collected over time. The unit Skorzeny was to command observed American mannerisms and tried to pick up slang by taking advantage of the opportunity offered by the presence of the POWs.

It is not against the law to spy. If the spy manages to return to his own lines, he has not committed an international crime. Woe be to the spy who gets caught by the enemy while in the enemy's uniform during war. Skorzeny and his men carried poison capsules for just that circumstance. It is definitely against the laws of war to wear the uniforms of the opposing nation while in battle.

The Skorzeny mission was a failure. They were able to cause some

The Court sits in the matter of *U.S. vs. Otto Skorzeny et al.* in the courtroom at Dachau.

confusion, but they had to abandon their bridge plans. Many of the young Germans lost their lives in the adventure. The remnants of the special unit were acquitted at the trial primarily because of their ineffectiveness and because of the doubts raised that the unit was actually fighting.

Skorzeny was able to parlay his investments into a comfortable living, and he spent his mature years in Spain. He died there in 1975.

* * *

Outside the town of Hadamar, not far from Limburg, an insane asylum sat on a hill overlooking the village below. The asylum was described as beyond anything Hollywood had ever imagined as a set; it included underground passages with dripping water and bats that took to the air upon being disturbed. Three hundred "babbling" inmates were held as permanent residents in its "underground labyrinth" and in the far reaches of the upstairs floor. Their constant commotion was used to cover events far more sinister than holding unfortunate persons in deplorable conditions without treatment.

The head warden seemed to be from central casting. He was tall and projected a menacing look created in part by an old dueling scar across his cheek that was the result of living the romance of student life at the University of Heidelberg. The asylum also harbored huge assistants (sometimes referred to as the "Amazons") who could manhandle those who resisted, diabolical trusties from among the population of the insane, and a gravedigger who was generally taken to be an idiot.

In 1941, Hitler had issued an order to kill incurables by euthanasia. At Hadamar, the staff was free to identify all who were delivered to their door in trucks, up to tens of thousands, without medical examinations, as fitting the profile of being incurable. Average German citizens—those who were not criminals or classified as enemies of the state — were not sent to extermination or concentration camps (with the exception of Jews or certain other undesirables). Hadamar made no such distinction. An undesirable German of any stripe could end up at the insane asylum. Certainly most of the inconvenient insane who were not needed to continue the cover-up were murdered. Others included Jewish women and their half–Jewish children, slave laborers who were beyond work, those with tuberculosis or other diseases, and even victims of air raids who had become a liability. One of the defendants would explain that these were not "cruel murders." They were only helping the people die, he said. "Healthy, valuable lives were not sacrificed." This was also the explanation given by Franz Stangl, commandant of Treblinka, the largest of the five Nazi extermination camps, who had cut his teeth, so to speak, on those souls at Hadamar who could not live "healthy, valuable" lives. (After the war, Stangl escaped to Syria with the help of the Church in Rome, and from there he went to South America where he lived until he was finally apprehended in late middle age and sent to Düsseldorf Prison to spend the last few years of his life.)

One of the nurses at Hadamar said that she took the opportunity to leave work in a home missionary society hospital to go into concentration camp work because she wanted to earn more than just "pocket money." Generally speaking, the staff thought they were doing the right thing for the right reasons. Some claimed to understand what the true nature of the institution was, but, they testified, they were too frightened of being sent to concentration camps to make a fuss.

Injections became the most viable and useful method of killing at the "Hadamar Murder Factory" although another frequently used option was the administration of oral poisons. The latter worked fairly well with the men, but the women would spit out the pills because they were bitter. For unexplained reasons, many were starved almost to death before they were finally killed.

The anniversary of the 10,000th killing at the asylum was said to have been celebrated with a drunken orgy, this news furnished by a local magistrate who came to the investigators as soon as he saw them at the site. Visitors from Berlin came to evaluate the program and seemed to go away satisfied. Daily staff meetings were held to determine which patients were starved enough to kill. Incoming patients were told that if they would be quiet, everything would be all right the next day.

Graves were dug by the idiot gravedigger and the caretaker saw that up to 30 bodies were placed in each grave. He, too, was methodical. His graves were laid out in a nearly perfect grid and continued on in his perfect pattern over acres. The doctor insisted that he keep three graves ahead for expected deaths, and he supplied the soon-to-die to help dig the graves. The factory had continued to operate until just eight days before investigators arrived. The gravedigger gave his statement, apparently leaving out nothing, and then escaped from the insane asylum where he had been placed while the trial was readied. His deposition was accepted at the trial because all parts of it were corroborated by forensic reports and testimony.

The Judge Advocate and head of prosecutor at the trial was Colonel Leon Jawarski who would see much media attention almost thirty years later as a "special prosecutor" in the Watergate case. In both situations he would find himself plowing new ground. The Hadamar trial was one of the ground floor war crimes cases, without precedents or even a recognized authority. Previous cases had dealt only with attacks upon American airmen. Clearly, America had an interest in those cases. If the Hadamar case had not gone forward, the entire series that became known as the Dachau trials would not have happened. Captain Melvin R. Wintman, for the defense, read an editorial statement from *The New Yorker* at the trial: "The chief thing to remember about international law is that it is not law and has never worked."

Jawarski's citing of unwritten international law and the Hague Convention of 1907 as protecting citizens of occupied territory might not have succeeded if it had not fallen on friendly ears. The Americans would not be trying the Hadamar defendants for murdering thousands of Germans anyway (because they indeed did not have jurisdiction here); they would be trying them for killing 400 Poles and Russians. He said that a ruling by the United States Judge Advocate General stating that American jurisdiction is concurrent for offenses against United Nations citizens was precedent. He further cited a directive by Eisenhower that the case should be brought to trial and added, "I don't think it is necessary to go much beyond that." The trial against six men and one woman continued in the city of Wiesbaden and precedent built upon precedent until the calendar was full of prosecutable cases.

Seven Germans were convicted in the deaths of Poles and Russians at Hadamar. Three of the men, the administrative head and two attendants who admitted giving death injections, received the death penalty. The chief medical officer, the chief nurse, the camp undertaker, and a clerk who knowingly falsified death certificates received sentences ranging from 20 years to life imprisonment.

*   *   *

Toward the late fall and winter of 1944, Germany had been driven back almost to its original borders. Africa and Italy were lost and the eastern front had been breached. Much of France was liberated and

Irmgard Huber: A defendant in the "Hadamar Murder Factory" case.

Belgium and the Netherlands were giving way to the Western Allies. Hitler and his men planned a fast, secret, violent attack on the Western Allies in several places. He believed that if Germany could retake significant territory, including Antwerp in Belgium, it would cause enough confusion and disgruntlement among the Allies to buy time for another move. He even imagined that he could force the Allies to sue for a separate peace, and that he could then turn his armies to the East. Hitler called his initiative "The Watch on the Rhine," later changed to "Autumn Mist," but this war-within-a-war would become known as the Battle of the Bulge because of its pushing battle plan relating to geographical goals. The "bulge" was to have enabled the Germans to break through and then surround the Allies. The battle was engaged December 16, 1944, and was to cost nearly 200,000 casualties before it ended. The German plan worked for the short term, but the Allies managed to hold on until reinforcements, including General George Patton and his Third Army, arrived. At the end of the battle on January 28, 1945, the German Army had only about 100 days left before its final gasp. This is the battle that brought such American military divisions as the "Golden Lions," the "Bloody Bucket," the "Ivy," the "Phantom," and the "Old Hickory" to new or reinforced fame.

An important part of the plan of Autumn Mist was to move with lightning speed and to avoid all encumbering elements. Prisoners of war would have been encumbering in the worst way; they would have demanded precious manpower and supplies. It was clearly understood among the Germans that an order existed from a high-ranking authority to take no prisoners, and men in the field could see the advantage of dispensing with such burdens as quickly as possible. Additionally, "daily orders" were given, bolstered with pep talks that were designed to incite the battle-weary veterans and the teenagers newly plucked from the Hitler Youth to proceed with whatever savagery was needed to get the job done.

At a crossroads near the town of Malmedy, Belgium, and in its immediate region more than a hundred captured Americans were fired upon by German tank guns and other weapons. The Americans tried first to fall down and minimize the carnage, but the Germans began to walk among the fallen men and shoot them at close range. They desecrated some of the bodies. Several Americans broke and ran and were able to live to tell the story.

Because of these stories, the world knew about the massacre before the bodies were recovered. When Americans returned to the scene, a deep snow covered a horror that has gone down in infamy.

Strangely enough, the story of the massacre received two kinds of media attention. During the contemporary coverage, the perpetrators were written of as being beyond the bounds of humanity. The military boiled with anger. They would run these animals to ground, they said, and dispose of them as the curs they were.

A latter-day debate seeks to argue the reasons why most cases in the Dachau series received little or no coverage in the newspapers. It's said that some Jewish-owned papers did not wish to appear vindictive or "pushy." Others claimed that political pressure forced the military to keep a low profile because of the suspicion the United States had for Russia from the first day of peace and the need to save Germany from the kinds of mistakes made after World War I. Indeed, the public was willing and even anxious to move on; everyone was sick of war and anything to do with war. The Malmedy Massacre was one of the few exceptions.

The trial brought to justice a long list of individuals who had participated in the massacre and several other acts of atrocity including the murder of hundreds of civilians. Germans killed as many as 500 Belgium civilians in or near the town of Stavelot, for example. Part of Autumn Mist could be classified under no other heading than "murder spree," and the trial was covered as such by newspapers and magazines.

In fact, the Malmedy Massacre would not disappear. The trial and its follow-up maneuvering turned out to be a cumbersome affair. With many defendants, many lawyers, and many avenues of appeal, it dragged on. The Supreme Court of the United States had decided in a previous case that it did not have jurisdiction over the Dachau series, but that didn't stop the principals from trying. Claims of sloppiness and downright misconduct by investigators and the Military Court began to surface. Prestigious magazines and newspapers began to ask questions about how the investigation of the massacre was managed and to editorialize on the disturbing answers they received.

Were witnesses and defendants intimidated, threatened, beaten? Was it a kangaroo court? Did the investigators use mock trials? Colonel A. H. Rosenfeld was quoted in *Stars and Stripes*, October 13, 1948, on techniques that had been used on suspects in various cases:

> It was tough breaking those birds down or getting them to admit anything. So interrogators hit upon the following plan which worked like a charm. A prisoner was brought in with a hood over his head. It was a German hood — one of their very own. When the hood was removed he found himself in a room with six American Army officers sitting around a table....
>
> Then one of the officers would begin questioning him. If he appeared to answer truthfully an officer at one end of the table would mark down a plus sign with white chalk on the black cloth in plain view of the prisoner. If he appeared to answer falsely, an officer at the other end of the table would mark down a minus sign.
>
> The prisoner was not told he was on trial. He was just questioned, but as the questioning continued and the plusses and minuses increased, he would become nervous. Usually then he told all. If he did not, another prisoner, one who had squealed on him, would be brought in to confront him. Gradually, through many such interrogations, the prosecution was able to find out which prisoners were responsible for ... atrocities.

In the late summer of 1949, a subcommittee of the Senate Armed Services Committee went to Germany to investigate ongoing claims by the Malmedy defendants and their champions that the Americans had used threats, intimidation, and physical abuse, including beatings, to get the Germans to make false statements incriminating individuals in the massacre. The senators would be accompanied by several medical experts. Evidence of maltreatment or uncorrected, corrupted evidence could not be found, and the committee could not find fault sufficient to recommend any particular action, but the aura of wrongdoing managed to compromise the efforts to bring criminals from the Battle of the Bulge to justice.

As history sometimes dictates, perpetrators of some of the most vicious acts escaped. After the military trials ceased to function and the problems of Dachau defendants were placed into other hands, the defendants in the Malmedy case were returned to society along with others who were being eased out of the system if they in any way cooperated with the terms of imprisonment and parole. Not a single man who participated in the murder spree was hanged.

The Malmedy case is still of interest and television and print journalism still occasionally revisits the subject.

17

Will We Ever Learn?
An Analysis

The Nazi insult was supported by many spindles but it stood upon three legs: the war, the Common Design Atrocity, and the extermination of Jews and other "undesirables." The war grew out of unfettered ambition, the Atrocity out of unfettered criminality, and the extermination out of unfettered racism. The trials seem to support this construction at every turn and at no turn do they seem to contradict it. This identification does not contradict claims that the insults overlap or that they were a single massive insult.

In many ways, Hitler admired the United States, at least according to historians. He thought that, like the States, Germany had a Manifest Destiny. John Toland says:

> Hitler's concept of concentration camps as well as the practicality of genocide owed much, so he claimed, to his studies of English and United States history. He admired the camps for Boer prisoners in South Africa and for the Indians in the Wild West; and often praised to his inner circle the efficiency of America's extermination — by starvation and uneven combat — of the red savages who could not be tamed by captivity.

America the beautiful had been accomplished by the near extermination of American Indians and upon the backs of African slaves. It had also exploited Asians, subjugated women, and taken unfair advantage of other groups it found vulnerable or unworthy. As America needed land, it rolled over everything in its way as it expanded to the Pacific Ocean. Germany, to be equally great, had to do likewise. It is not surprising that many who were brought to trial were guilty of abusing or murdering airmen; the practice was just one more aspect of an aggressive war. The war interrupted the fragile stability of Europe and in so doing eventually cost the lives of tens of millions, but, to Hitler, war was a simple necessity.

From the very beginning, Hitler attracted and tolerated criminals, and criminals shared Hitler's power to the very end. Instead of protecting society from criminals, Hitler's enforcement officers protected criminals from society. In Germany, criminals reigned in society at large and they reigned in the concentration camps. The trials suggest that a strong majority of those who died in the work camps (as opposed to the "death camps" where extermination was the central task) did so because of overt criminal activity or criminal neglect that was outside or in addition to the war. Much of the Atrocity was not directly associated with the doctrine that became the Final Solution. It was instead a separate criminal, sadistic indulgence on the part of criminals.

The Atrocity was not limited to the concentration camps, but the camps represented the epicenter of the endeavor. Technically, it was unlawful to kill or abuse inmates of the camps. Technically, the camps were for the detainment and concentration of "enemies of the state." In fact, most inmates were not criminals, spies, saboteurs, or traitors. They were mostly Jews, POWs, "resettled persons," "dangerous" elements such as Quakers, and the offensive, such as homosexuals, gypsys, foreigners, and a wide variety of those who were different in any way. For the state and for the criminal, inmates became a natural resource—like coal or timber. They provided free labor, a handy target for relieving stress or anger, an excuse for fraternal association among men infected with a particular, deadly personality flaw; and the inmates were entirely expendable. The trials revealed the ease with which "normal" humans can become criminals when they keep the company of other criminals and are given opportunity and motive, real or imagined. Trial evidence revealed that many among the civilian population in Germany were aware of the terrible things happening in the camps, and they knew that it was wrong. Almost to a person they denied or excused their actions, however. During a time when almost everyone was willing to die for the Reich, almost no one was willing to become a martyr for the cause of right.

Evidence presented at the trials also contradicts "Holocaust deniers:" when the war ended, enough bodies were found lying around on top of the ground and enough walking skeletons were found living in concentration camps to amply justify charges of a Mass Atrocity and a criminal society.

The third leg of the Nazi horror, the nearly successful attempt to eliminate Jews from the face of Europe, was the result of unfettered racism. The trials showed that in the concentration camps, the extermination of Jews was almost a diversion. It was the Germans' pleasure that the Jews suffer.

As opposed to concentration camps, extermination camps were efficient and deadly earnest. There, it was the Nazi goal to eliminate as many as possible with the least effort, expense, and bother. The trials support a deduction that the Germans had a loathing for Jews which could easily support a diagnosis of mental instability. This is borne out not only by the contempt with which they held other "races" but, more importantly, by the irrational and unsupported pride they held for their own "pure" race, a race, which, when examined at even the shallowest level, has as complex a gene pool as any other people. They could not stand any degree of humiliation or insult even as they were willing to dish it out in enormous measure. The trials support the observation that they chose to act enthusiastically in their special hatred for Jews.

Neither concentration camps nor extermination camps were a secret from the rest of the world. For the two or three years before the end of the war, rather specific descriptions of the camps were being published all over the world. Historians suggest that the Allies chose to ignore the situation from fear that too much attention in that direction would divert attention from the war effort. Undoubtedly racism allowed this and other decisions to be made with more ease than would have been possible had not racism existed in the west.

It is possible that during the years the Nazi Party was growing, racists and racism in America were equal in numbers and intensity to that in Germany. One hesitates to imagine the consequences if Franklin D. Roosevelt had been the German leader and Adolf Hitler the American leader. In Germany, so few stood up and said *no* that, as Wilhelm Grill said, a voice could not be raised. One thinks of the bravery and boldness of an Eleanor Roosevelt and the very few other public leaders who publicly expressed concern about racism. Those leaders gave America the chance to deal with racism without the context of a Hitler-like war and its opportunities to exploit racism.

Analysis must not entice the seeker away from the terrible whole, but it is everyone's goal to try to understand the parts of the Nazi reign in an effort to try to understand the whole. However, this book has attempted to look at the types of persons who have families and go to work every day to an average job. It is very worrisome to discover that these persons, often with as much enthusiasm as the arch criminals, were devoted contributors to the great Nazi insult to humanity.

Hitler was insanely ambitious, was almost surely criminally insane, and he was diabolical in his bigotry and racism. He was also clever enough to use the existing political and cultural systems to realize his goals and ambitions. He remains a focus of interest and research, but the trials did not cast new light into this darkness. They did reveal something about those who would not stand up to him, who tolerated him, or who joined him. Most acts addressed during the prosecutions resulted from a personal decision make by someone whose name was not Hitler. This is the lesson of the Dachau trials.

Appendix

"Cases Tried," 7708 War Crimes Group, from Record Group 549, National Archives and Records Administration, College Park, Maryland.

The 5, 6, and 11 Series

Case Number	*Defendant(s)*	*Case Number*	*Defendant(s)*
5-37	Goetz et al.	6-56	Bruns
5-66	Lienhart	6-100	Skorzeny et al.
5-67/5-71	Hangobl	6-155	Ruester
5-88	Grisl	8-27	Strasser
5-92	Wandrey	11-18	Konrad
5-100	Karolyi et al.	11-23	Hackert
5-113a/b	Taurer et al.	11-52	Koenke
5-114	Rath et al.	11-96	Kirschner et al.
5-150	Thaler et al.	11-511	Pauly et al.
5-173	Stieblaichinger	11-514	Schmid
6-24	Bersin et al.	11-519	Petersdorf et al.
6-55	Engelhard	11-562	Suntz
		11-584	Isenmann et al.

The 12 Series

Case Number	*Defendant(s)*	*Case Number*	*Defendant(s)*
12-25	Baumgartner	12-80	Stern
12-27	Ostenrieder	12-336	Doesch et al.
12-43	Gross et al.	12-348	Starek et al.
12-45	Heim et al.	12-355	Hermann et al.
12-57	Rueger et al.	12-413	Dressler

(The 12 Series, *continued*)

Case Number	Defendant(s)	Case Number	Defendant(s)
12-413-1	Heitkamp	12-1149	Schosser
12-449	Klein et al.	12-1149-1/2	Breitenstein
12-468	Bloch	12-1155	Kobus
12-472	Noack et al.	12-1155-1	Stredele
12-481	Thomas	12-1155-2	Boehm et al.
12-485	Mueller	12-1160	Polus
12-489	Goebel et al.	12-1168	Luethje
12-489-1	Haesiker	12-1182	Endress
12-494	Thile	12-1182-1	Drauz
12-494-1	Schwaben	12-1182-2	Otto
12-524	Rudolph	12-1203	Scholz
12-531	Bohrs et al.	12-1217	Hinkel et al.
12-551	Ehlen	12-1247	Stork et al.
12-551-1	Eggert	12-1290	Hagendorf
12-581	Zierhut et al.	12-1292	Hess et al.
12-643	Dieterman et al.	12-1299	Salzmann et al.
12-658	Behme et al.	12-1307	Hammer et al.
12-714	Brehm et al.	12-1368/1369	Hildebrandt et al.
12-765	Menrath et al.	12-1370	Saur
12-779	Werner et al.	12-1394	Rudmann et al.
12-788	Thoma	12-1395	Grosch et al.
12-793	Flauaus et al.	12-1397	Bury
12-793-1	Deubert et al.	12-1418	Schultheiss
12-793-2	Sturm	12-1422	Heidmann et al.
12-819	Katz	12-1449	Dirnagel et al.
12-926	Weger et al.	12-1457	Loesch
12-926-1	Neuber	12-1497	Hartgen et al.
12-931	Siebold et al.	12-1502	Kluettgen
12-932	Foerster	12-1534	Bruns et al.
12-966	Wippermann	12-1538	Weiss et al.
12-966-1	Hagenbuch	12-1542	Hermann et al.
12-1022	Winter	12-1545	Dietrich et al.
12-1034	Blum et al.	12-1576	Bodenstein et al.
12-1067	Staudinger et al.	12-1576-1	Eck
12-1068	Altena	12-1592	Haferburg
12-1077	Lauterbacher et al.	12-1595	Schickert
12-1086	Heene et al.	12-1622	Kornalewicz
12-1093	Battalo et al.	12-1666	Mack
12-1104	Beck et al.	12-1685	Rieke et al.
12-1104-1	Kanschat	12-1733	Curdts et al.
12-1106	Bock	12-1740	Steig et al.
12-1109	Gross	12-1742	Schauer et al.
12-1115	Firmenich et al.	12-1745	Pohla et al.
12-1119	Hanselmann	12-1752	Englebrecht et al.
12-1140	Rixen	12-1761	Blessman et al.
12-1145	Wiegand	12-1774	Hartman et al.
12-1146	Albishausen et al.		

(The 12 Series, *continued*)

Case Number	Defendant(s)	Case Number	Defendant(s)
12-1776	Hartung	12-2025	Hitzer
12-1783	Schiedhering et al.	12-2034	Doerr et al.
12-1790	Schlarp	12-2036	Rothacker et al.
12-1807	Conzmann	12-2052	Pelizaeus
12-1812	Mette et al.	12-2058	Klaebe
12-1813	Utermark	12-2064	Hollacher et al.
12-1814	Gerstenberg	12-2067	Bracht et al.
12-1821	Melchior	12-2068	Baum et al.
12-1833	Lang et al.	12-2074	Hartmann
12-1836	Metz et al.	12-2114	Scherf
12-1848	Katzenmeier	12-2119	Sonner
12-1851	Sukopp et al.	12-2129	Kahnert
12-1852	Scheilz	12-2150	Kohler et al.
12-1866	Lippmann et al.	12-2157	Schmauder
12-1871	Schardt	12-2162	Ellers
12-1871-1	Lassak	12-2175	Waldmann
12-1880	Pohl	12-2176	Schweitzer
12-1881	Riesberg et al.	12-2185	Feix et al.
12-1885	Weiss	12-2202	Schult
12-1890	Weisshuhn	12-2218	Mayer et al.
12-1894	Koller	12-2261	Zahnen
12-1898	Kremer et al.	12-2270	Schneider et al.
12-1905	Auburger et al.	12-2283	Moeller et al.
12-1911	Brueckner et al.	12-2313	Stoll
12-1915	Rubsamen et al.	12-2337	Reinke
12-1930	Etsch et al.	12-2381	Umstatter
12-1930-1	Geggus	12-2400	Schlickau
12-1934	Rudmann et al.	12-2404	Eckstein et al.
12-1949	Minx	12-2409	Franke
12-1950	Sauter	12-2420	Ningelgen
12-1958	Schwarz	12-2422	Kohn et al.
12-1960	Wolter	12-2422-1	Back
12-1960-1	Kowitzke	12-2581	Montscher et al.
12-1961	Franke	12-2593	Merten et al.
12-1966	Friedrich et al.	12-2595	Hofmann et al.
12-1967	Wegmann	12-2616	Kaiser
12-1968	Otte, at al.	12-2662	Hess et al.
12-1973	Utermark	12-2694	Scherer
12-1989	Kolb et al.	12-2823	Gartmann et al.
12-1993	Peschke et al.	12-2823-1	Adler
12-2000	Stroop et al.	12-2887	Freitag
12-2000-1	Wrede	12-2971	Jaeger et al.
12-2009	Dietzschold	12-3121	Langeloh
12-2011	Sionsel et al.	12-3193-B	Baumann et al.
12-2013	Koch	12-3193-D	Petersdorf et al.
12-2018	Toelle et al.	12-3205	Dreger

The Buchenwald, Dachau, Flossenburg, Mauthausen, and Nordhausen Series

Case Number	Defendant(s)
000-Buchenwald-2	Hinderer et al.
000-Buchenwald-3	Jackobs
000-Buchenwald-4	Hoffmann
000-Buchenwald-5	Mueller
000-Buchenwald-6	Weyrauch
000-Buchenwald-7	Blume
000-Buchenwald-8	Hantscharenko
000-Buchenwald-9	Buuck
000-Buchenwald-11	Seitz et al.
000-Buchenwald-13	Kunikowski
000-Buchenwald-14	Vogel
000-Buchenwald-17	Ankenbrand
000-Buchenwald-20	Demmer
000-Buchenwald-23	Singer
000-Buchenwald-25	Giese
000-Buchenwald-26	Mueller
000-Buchenwald-31	Fischer
000-Buchenwald-36	Heuls
000-Buchenwald-37	Zwickl
000-Buchenwald-40	Wuttke
000-Buchenwald-41	Schramm
000-Buchenwald-42	Krause
000-Buchenwald-49	Lemke
000-Buchenwald-50	Berger et al.
000-Dachau-1	Stinglwagner et al.
000-Dachau-2	Schmid
000-Flossenburg-1	Degner
000-Flossenburg-2	Wodak
000-Flossenburg-3	Vican
000-Flossenburg-4	Fritzsche
000-Flossenburg-7	Schulmeister
000-Flossenburg-8	Brauner
000-Flossenburg-10	Auerswald
000-Flossenburg-11	Goldmann
000-Flossenburg-12	Gottzmann
000-Flossenburg-15	Straub
000-Flossenburg-16	Lutz
000-Flossenburg-18	Ziehmer
000-Mauthausen-1	Erb
000-Mauthausen-2	Bloy
000-Mauthausen-4	Damaschke
000-Mauthausen-5	Otto
000-Mauthausen-6	Curten
000-Mauthausen-7	Brust
000-Mauthausen-10	Kauffeld
000-Mauthausen-12	Kania

(The Buchenwald, Dachau, Flossenburg,
Mauthausen, and Nordhausen Series, *continued*)

Case Number	Defendant(s)
000-Mauthausen-13	Albrecht
000-Mauthausen-15	Schallenberg
000-Mauthausen-16	Lamm
000-Mauthausen-19	Espinosa
000-Mauthausen-20	Noky
000-Mauthausen-21	Tuntke
000-Nordhausen-1	Grebinski
000-Nordhausen-2	Mueller
000-Nordhausen-3	Finkenzeller
000-Nordhausen-4	Schwalm
000-Nordhausen-5	Klein
000-Nordhausen-6	Palko

Cases #000-50-2 to #000-50-136

Case Number	Defendant(s)	Case Number	Defendant(s)
000-50-2	Weiss	000-50-2-28	Fleischer et al.
000-50-2-1	Adami et al.	000-50-2-29	Moeller et al.
000-50-2-2	Barzen et al.	000-50-2-30	Pfaller et al.
000-50-2-3	Arzberger et al.	000-50-2-31	Eberhardt et al.
000-50-2-4	Bruecker et al.	000-50-2-32	Velten et al.
000-50-2-5	Becker et al.	000-50-2-33	Buenger et al.
000-50-2-6	Bablick et al.	000-50-2-34	Burger et al.
000-50-2-7	Dippe et al.	000-50-2-35	Sturm et al.
000-50-2-8	Au et al.	000-50-2-36	Hachenberger et al.
000-50-2-9	Bezak et al.	000-50-2-37	Schmidt et al.
000-50-2-10	Buehler et al.	000-50-2-39	Orend et al.
000-50-2-11	Gombkoto et al.	000-50-2-40	Stefan et al.
000-50-2-12	Mueller et al.	000-50-2-41	Beck et al.
000-50-2-13	Fraenzl et al.	000-50-2-42	Zisch
000-50-2-14	Elgert et al.	000-50-2-43	Palme
000-50-2-15	Heller et al.	000-50-2-44	Broese. et al.
000-50-2-16	Leonhardt et al.	000-50-2-45	Hermer et al.
000-50-2-17	Ulrich et al.	000-50-2-46	Carl et al.
000-50-2-18	Batoha et al.	000-50-2-47	Glashauer et al.
000-50-2-19	Bloesser et al.	000-50-2-48	Kuehner et al.
000-50-2-20	Baumgartner	000-50-2-49	Forster et al.
000-50-2-21	Eisenhardt et al.	000-50-2-50	Boos et al.
000-50-2-22	Angerer et al.	000-50-2-51	Greiner et al.
000-50-2-23	Piorkowski et al.	000-50-2-52	Schloeter et al.
000-50-2-24	Wipplinger	000-50-2-53	Winter
000-50-2-25	Weber et al.	000-50-2-55	Koch et al.
000-50-2-26	Behrens et al.	000-50-2-57	Heske et al.
000-50-2-27	Hennecke et al.	000-50-2-58	Adolf

Appendix

(Cases #000-50-2 to #000-50-136, *continued*)

Case Number	Defendant(s)	Case Number	Defendant(s)
000-50-2-59	Herrloss et al.	000-50-2-108	Ehrenboeck
000-50-2-60	Ernst et al.	000-50-2-109	Berscheid et al.
000-50-2-61	Calenberg et al.	000-50-2-110	Remmele
000-50-2-62	Fischer et al.	000-50-2-111	Frisch
000-50-2-63	Deutsch et al.	000-50-2-112	Vogel et al.
000-50-2-64	Pfeiffer	000-50-2-113	Thorenz
000-50-2-65	Deffner	000-50-2-115	Koenig et al.
000-50-2-66	Beer et al.	000-50-2-116	Sibermann et al.
000-50-2-67	Stiller et al.	000-50-2-117	Beck et al.
000-50-2-68	Hintermayer et al.	000-50-2-118	Wielenz
000-50-2-69	Uelzhoeffer	000-50-2-119	Schmidt
000-50-2-70	Kreber et al.	000-50-2-120	Otter
000-50-2-72	Wuelfert et al.	000-50-2-121	Schallermair
000-50-2-73	Deiner	000-50-5	Altfuldish et al.
000-50-2-74	Haeussler et al.	000-50-5-1	Bergerhoff et al.
000-50-2-75	Ruhnke et al.	000-50-5-2	Dura et al.
000-50-2-76	Schaal et al.	000-50-5-3	Schuettauf et al.
000-50-2-77	Stirnweis	000-50-5-4	Goetz et al.
000-50-2-78	Neuner	000-50-5-5	Werner et al.
000-50-2-79	Soelken	000-50-5-6	Geiger et al.
000-50-2-80	Trixl	000-50-5-8	Auerswald et al.
000-50-2-81	Ohnmacht	000-50-5-9	Lukan et al.
000-50-2-82	Koessel	000-50-5-10	Bach et al.
000-50-2-83	Knocke et al.	000-50-5-11	Battermann et al.
000-50-2-84	Greil et al.	000-50-5-12	Giovanazzi et al.
000-50-2-85	Kuczkierczyk	000-50-5-13	Haider et al.
000-50-2-86	Froeschl et al.	000-50-5-14	Dlouhy et al.
000-50-2-87	Fiedler et al.	000-50-5-15	Fenner et al.
000-50-2-89	Metzler et al.	000-50-5-17	Barner et al.
000-50-2-90	Kahles et al.	000-50-5-18	Bernhardt et al.
000-50-2-91	Meyer	000-50-5-19	Klerner et al.
000-50-2-92	Muth	000-50-5-20	Biersack et al.
000-50-2-93	Schairer	000-50-5-21	Kattner et al.
000-50-2-94	Arz	000-50-5-22	Baerens et al.
000-50-2-95	Bendl	000-50-5-23	Kofler et al.
000-50-2-96	Antkowiak et al.	000-50-5-24	Bartl et al.
000-50-2-97	Muehlbauer et al.	000-50-5-25	Navas et al.
000-50-2-98	Bittruf	000-50-5-26	Moegle et al.
000-50-2-99	Kohn et al.	000-50-5-28	Berg et al.
000-50-2-100	Kemm et al.	000-50-5-29	Bertsch et al.
000-50-2-101	Burkhardt et al.	000-50-5-30	Fernikorn et al.
000-50-2-102	Kastner et al.	000-50-5-31	Glas et al.
000-50-2-103	Brachtel et al.	000-50-5-32	Horcicka et al.
000-50-2-104	Lippmann et al.	000-50-5-33	Schmitz et al.
000-50-2-105	Schluppeck et al.	000-50-5-34	Goennemann et al.
000-50-2-106	Grunk et al.	000-50-5-37	Kurbel et al.
000-50-2-107	Heller, at al.	000-50-2-38	Frisch et al.

(Cases #000-50-2 to #000-50-136, *continued*)

Case Number	Defendant(s)	Case Number	Defendant(s)
000-50-5-39	Schiller	000-50-5-50	Berg et al.
000-50-5-40	Richter et al.	000-50-5-51	Klein
000-50-5-41	Sturm	000-50-9	Waldeck et al.
000-50-5-42	Pirner et al.	000-50-37	Andre et al.
000-50-5-43	Pavela	000-50-46	Becker et al.
000-50-5-44	Tremmel	000-50-46-1	Loh et al.
000-50-5-45	Fleischer	000-50-46-2	Wilhelm et al.
000-50-5-46	Von Posern	000-50-46-3	Heerde et al.
000-50-5-47	Dopierala	000-50-46-4	Fischer et al.
000-50-5-48	Bollhorst	000-50-46-5	Mayer et al.
000-50-5-49	Wolfram	000-50-46-6	Tuma et al.
		000-50-136	Auer et al.

Resources

Arendt, Hannah. *The Origins of Totalitarianism*. New York: Harcourt, 1976.

_____. *Eichmann in Jerusalem*. New York: Penguin Books, 1992.

Astor, Gerald. *A Blood-Dimmed Tide: The Battle of the Bulge by the Men Who Fought It*. New York: Random House, 1992.

Bosworth, R. J. B. *Explaining Auschwitz and Hiroshima: History Writing and the Second World War, 1945–1990*. London: Routledge, 1993.

Browning, Christopher R. *Ordinary Men*. New York: HarperCollins, 1992.

Calleo, David. *The German Problem Reconsidered*. Cambridge: Cambridge University Press, 1978.

Calvocoressi, Peter, with Guy Wint and John Prichard. *Total War: The Causes and Courses of the Second World War, Vol. I*. New York: Pantheon Books, 1989.

Carsten, F. L. *The Rise of Fascism*. Berkeley and Los Angeles: University of California Press, 1967.

"Cases Tried." Record Group 549. 7708 War Crimes Group. College Park, Maryland: National Archives and Records Administration.

Cervantes, Miguel de. *Don Quixote of the Mancha*. New York: Collier & Son, 1909.

Goldhagen, Daniel Jonah. *Hitler's Willing Executioners*. New York: Random House, 1996.

Hilton, Wesley V. "Otto Skorzeny: A Master's Thesis." East Tennessee State University, 1996.

Hitler, Adolf. *Mein Kampf*. Boston: Houghton Mifflin, 1943.

Joint Four-Nation Declaration. The Moscow Conference, October 1943. The Avalon Project at Yale University Law School. http://www.yale.edy/lawweb/avalon/wwii/moscow.htm.

Kershaw, Ian. *The Nazi Dictatorship*. London: Edward Arnold, 1985.

_____. *Hitler 1936–1945: Nemesis*. New York: W.W. Norton, 2000.

Kitchen, Martin. *Europe between the Wars*. New York: Longman, 1988.

Levi, Primo. *Survival in Auschwitz*. New York: Simon & Schuster, 1996.

Lieber, Francis. "Instructions for the Government of Armies of the United States in the Field." *Laws of War: General Orders No. 100*. The Avalon Project at Yale University Law School. http"//www.yale.edu/lawweb/avalon/lieber.htm.

Milward, Alan S. *War, Economy and Society: 1939–1945*. Berkeley and Los Angeles: University of California Press, 1977.

Orlow, Dietrich. *A History of Modern Germany*. Englewood Cliffs, New Jersey: Prentice-Hall, 1945.

Planning Memorandum." *International Conference on Military Trials: London, 1945*. The Avalon Project at Yale University Law School http://www.yale.edu/lawweb/avalon/imt/jackson/jack11.htm.

"Revised Definition of 'Crimes'." (Prepared by British Delegation and Accepted by French Delegation, July 28, 1945). *International Conference on Military Trials: London, 1945*. The Internet: The Avalon Project at Yale University Law School, retrieved 2002.

Sereny, Gitta. *Into that Darkness*. New York: Random House, 1974.

Shirer, William L. *The Rise and Fall of the Third Reich*. New York: Simon & Schuster, 1990.

Straight, C. E. "Report of the 7708 War Crimes Group." Record Group 549. College Park, Maryland: National Archives and Records Administration, 1948.

Toland, John. *Adolf Hitler*. New York: Doubleday, 1976.

Urwin, Derek W. *Western Europe Since 1945: A Political History*. New York: Longman, 1989.

Index